CC

Brigham Young University
Harold B Lee Library

WITHDRAWN

Biodegradable Man

: : : : : : : : : : : : :

AC
8
.M4125
1990

Biodegradable Man

: : : : : : : : : : : : :

Selected Essays by Milton Mayer

EDITED BY LEONE STEIN

Foreword by Stanley W. Lindberg

The University of Georgia Press : *Athens & London*

© 1990 by Jane Mayer
Foreword by Stanley W. Lindberg
© 1990 by the University of Georgia Press
Published by the University of Georgia Press
Athens, Georgia 30602
All rights reserved
Designed by Richard Hendel
Set in Stempel Garamond by
Tseng Information Systems
Printed and bound by Thomson-Shore
The paper in this book meets the guidelines for
permanence and durability of the Committee on
Production Guidelines for Book Longevity of the
Council on Library Resources.

Printed in the United States of America
94 93 92 91 90   5 4 3 2 1

Library of Congress Cataloging in Publication Data

Mayer, Milton Sanford, 1908–
Biodegradable man : selected essays / by Milton
Mayer ; edited by Leone Stein ; foreword by
Stanley W. Lindberg.
p.   cm.
ISBN 0-8203-1244-4 (alk. paper)
I. Stein, Leone.   II. Title.
AC8.M4125   1990
081—dc20   90-30058
CIP

British Library Cataloging in Publication Data available

HAROLD B. LEE LIBRARY
BRIGHAM YOUNG UNIVERSITY
PROVO, UTAH

: : : *Contents* : : :

: : : *Foreword* : : :

Although Milton Mayer (1908–86) delighted in calling himself "an unemployed newspaperman," he was in fact a highly
regarded and honored magazine journalist and commentator,
having published in many of America's leading magazines for
more than forty years. Yet except for the appreciative but relatively small readership of *The Progressive* magazine (in which
he appeared as a "roving reporter" for most of that period),
not many readers got to follow his writings on a regular basis
—and far too many younger readers have never heard of his
work. In my opinion, such a situation begs to be remedied, for
the intrinsic merit of Mayer's best work lifts it well above the
ephemeral journalism of its time and invites serious attention
by subsequent generations. Indeed, as the present gathering of
essays demonstrates, Mayer was a writer who possessed not
only sharp perceptions and a mastery of language but also a
rare sense of commitment, a courageous sense of values that
makes most syndicated columnists and commentators of our
"value-free" time appear shallow and self-serving.

   Great journalism has always been in scarce supply, of
course, and most journalism—including a good deal that
clearly announces its literary pretensions—fails to transcend
its origins sufficiently enough to sustain repeated readings and
literary evaluation. Even though one can point to journalists
of the past now judged to be important essayists, from Samuel
Johnson to George Orwell and E. B. White, the fact remains
that journalism is by nature tied to time-bound specifics. As
Irving Howe has pointed out in *Politics and the Novel* (1957):

There are some writers who live most significantly for their own age;
they are writers who help redeem their time by forcing it to accept the
truth about itself, and therefore saving it, perhaps, from the truth about
itself. Such writers, it is possible, will not survive their time, for what

makes them so valuable and so endearing to their contemporaries—that mixture of desperate topicality and desperate tenderness—is not likely to be a quality conducive to the greatest art. But [this] should not matter to us. . . . We know what they do for us, and we know that no other writers, including the greater ones, can do it.

Although Howe offered these remarks in reference to George Orwell, they seem marvelously appropriate also for Milton Mayer and his particular "mixture of desperate topicality and desperate tenderness." Mayer did indeed live very much in and for his time, and he clearly tried his damnedest to redeem that time by "forcing it to accept the truth about itself." But though he expressly addressed his readers of that moment, not Posterity, much of his writing deserves to survive longer and to reach yet other readers. It speaks just as clearly and as urgently today as it did to its initial audiences.

The exceptional range and depth of Milton Mayer's reading informs most of what he wrote, though it seldom calls attention to itself as erudite allusion or authenticating support. Learning is but one of the tools he employs, and he is far more likely to call on wit, anecdote, memory, ironic juxtaposition, history, speculation, or personal outrage—whatever, in short, he finds most efficacious in seizing and holding his readers' attention. What drives his writing is firm moral conviction, a passion for truth, justice, and the highest human values; and what results is a distinctive, opinionated voice—one not given to equivocating.

Since Mayer has been successful in persuading me to his positions most of the time, I have no trouble at all in personally finding his writing to be remarkably impressive in range and depth of thought, delightfully witty, deceptively well-crafted. Others, I realize, may well take exception, for Mayer's passion often led him into stances that infuriated many readers —particularly when he insisted on offering uncomfortable reassessments of matters on which a public consensus had already been reached. Take, for example, his analysis of one of our time's most famous, and almost immediately hallowed, quotations:

"Ask not what your country can do for you, but what you can do for your country." When Mr. Kennedy spoke these words at his inaugural, I knew that I was at odds with a Society which did not immediately rebel against them. They are the words of totalitarianism pure; no Jefferson could have spoken them, and no Khrushchev could have spoken them better. Could a man say what Mr. Kennedy said and also say that the difference between *us* and *them* is that *they* believe that man exists for the State and *we* believe that the State exists for man? He couldn't, but he did. And in doing so, he read me out of society. ("Rendered unto Caesar," p. 86)

:

Such a jarring judgment—which he offered immediately after the inauguration and then repeated after President Kennedy's assassination—is characteristic of Mayer at his most provocative. It also illustrates why so few readers of his work can remain unengaged—even so many years after Kennedy spoke, the nation applauded, and one feisty commentator answered.

The extended personal essay proved to be an ideal genre for Milton Mayer, as his column space expanded, for it allowed him room to range widely without requiring him to adhere to any prescribed rhetorical structure. Here was congenial space, enough to allow him to explore a major topic in depth and still develop some of the related side issues. As Scott Russell Sanders has noted,

The essay is a haven for the private, idiosyncratic voice in an era of anonymous babble. Like the blandburgers served in their millions along our highways, most language served up in public these days is textureless, tasteless mush. On television, over the phone, in the newspaper, wherever humans bandy words about, we encounter more and more abstractions, more empty formulas. Think of the pablum ladled out by politicians. Think of the fluffy white bread of advertising. Think, Lord help us, of committee reports. In contrast, the essay remains stubbornly concrete amd particular. . . . Following the zigzag motions of an inquisitive mind, the essay renews language and clears trash from the springs of thought.*

*"The Singular First Person," *Essays on the Essay: Redefining the Genre*, ed. Alexander J.Butrym (Athens: University of Georgia Press, 1989), p. 33.

Remaining "stubbornly concrete and particular" does not, of course, keep a good essayist from leading readers toward, and forcing them to recognize, significant conclusions about their culture—as Mayer consistently demonstrates. Even when he begins an essay with a generalized thesis—as in his indispensable "Ivory Tower of Babel" (which continues to stand as one of the most incisive statements ever offered on the value of a liberal education)—it is the telling specifics he cites that clear the trash from our minds. But it is primarily through his quiet portraits of personal heroes that Mayer guides us into examining the most important moral questions. Identifying heroes is not easy, he admits:

You have to find your hero at just the right time and in just the right place. The heroism of Ma and Pa is too close, Pa hustling his paperbox samples on the streetcars until he can't make those streetcar steps anymore, Ma scrubbing the clothes on the scrub board in the basement until her wrists and knuckles give out. The heroism of a public figure is too far, of a big brother too oscillate, of a doctor or a preacher too fearsome, of a candy-store lady or a milkman too busy, of a professor in college too remote, too remote and too late. . . . Your likelihood of finding a hero is circumscribed and scant. ("Teacher's Pet," p. 256)

Yet Mayer finds his heroes—and makes them ours. One of them, not surprisingly, is his long-time colleague/supervisor/associate Robert M. Hutchins, president of the University of Chicago; another is the preeminent socialist Eugene Debs. But most of them are far less public figures—the Quaker Red Schaal, the Catholic Dorothy Day, the journalist/editor Morry Rubin, and Mayer's high-school Latin teacher, Mrs. Florence Ball Manley—and it is his reflections on their lives that enables (and justifies) Mayer's leading us, repeatedly, into asking ourselves such ultimate questions as, "What can a man do in order to be human?"

Milton Mayer was, in his life and words, a Jewish Quaker as well as a pacifist and a would-be socialist. None of these labels, of course, is in itself enough to describe the man or his writings, since no allegiance deflected his intelligent probing or his scorn when he zeroed in on a target. He was a citizen of the world, ready to cast his sharp focus on many different countries (including especially Switzerland, France, Israel, and England), but he saved his special attention for his native America—and any American who reads Milton Mayer will benefit from his willingness to both penetrate and go beyond the surface pieties of our culture. What he wrote was without question timely; there is much to suggest that it is also timeless.

Stanley W. Lindberg

: : : *Preface* : : :

Biodegradable Man is a gathering of articles by Milton Mayer, selected especially from those written during the last decade of his life but also including some of his most memorable earlier works. It is intended to introduce Milton Mayer to a new generation of readers.

Clues to what Milton Mayer considered the main concerns of his lifework are suggested by the essays included, with his approval, in two anthologies published during his lifetime, *What Can A Man Do?* (1964) and *The Nature of the Beast* (1975), both edited by Eric F. Gustafson. In addition to these collections, Milton Mayer was the author of numerous works whose titles evoke the concerns of his long career as a writer. They include *They Thought They Were Free: The Germans, 1935–45* (1955; reprint, 1988), *Young Man in a Hurry: William Rainey Harper* (1957), *Man. v the State* (1969), *The Art of the Impossible: A Study of the Czech Resistance* (1969), and *If Men Were Angels* (1972). With Mortimer J. Adler he published *The Revolution in Education* (1958), and with others, *Humanistic Education and Western Civilization* (1964) and *Anatomy of Anti-Communism* (1969). A year before his death in 1986, he completed the manuscript of *Robert Maynard Hutchins: A Memoir* (edited by Jane Mayer and John Hicks, forthcoming, University of California Press), a study of his longtime friend and associate.

From 1942 to 1986, Milton Mayer was Roving Editor for *The Progressive,* and many of the articles in this collection originally appeared in its pages. Under the editorship of Morris Rubin and his successor Erwin Knoll, Mayer found the freedom to say what he needed to say in the way only he could say it, a way which sometimes outraged readers and cost the magazine subscriptions but did not move him, or his editors, from their clear purpose. Something of the importance of that meeting of true minds is conveyed in "A Long, Long Talk," a tribute to Morris Rubin, which concludes this book.

Much of what Milton Mayer wrote was autobiographical and reveals a life remarkably consistent with his thought. "Sit Down and Shut Up," for example, concerns his reactions to attending a Quaker Meeting for Worship for the first time, especially to the admonition to be silent unless the spirit moved. He later became a member of the Religious Society of Friends and throughout his life heeded that admonition so scrupulously that he rarely if ever spoke during Meetings for Worship, a self-control unexpected in a man whose profession was words. "Rendered unto Caesar," also included in this collection, is one of a number of articles he wrote over the years expressing his moral and rational opposition to war. Beginning with "I Think I'll Sit This One Out" (*The Saturday Evening Post*, 1939), in which he explained why he would not serve in World War II if called, he consistently expressed that opposition in his writings, and for many years refused to pay that portion of his income tax which the government allocated to the military, on conscientious grounds.

That Jane and Milton Mayer had the good fortune to meet is celebrated in these pages, and throughout his other writings. She is at first "Baby Mayer," and then, in response to protests from readers of *The Progressive*, "Ms. Baby Mayer." He relished bestowing upon her these and other preposterous designations, knowing with whom his wit could be trusted. Her encouragement and hospitality enhanced the pleasure of editing *Biodegradable Man*, and I am very grateful to her.

Leone Stein

America the Beautiful

: : : : : : : : : : : : : : : :

: : : *Sore Thumbs* : : :

The desert was dusty then; U.S. 66 (buried beneath Interstate 40 now) was unpaved. And a good thing; the blacktop would have been too hot on the soles of the hitchhiker's shoes. I was the hitchhiker. The sorrows that were poisoning my life had become unbearable and I had run away from home to bum to California and ship out to China and never come back. (I came back.) The desert in western Arizona was dusty and hot, and the occasional car carried a couple of gallon cans of radiator water. The occasional car was a drummer's or a produce farmer's or an emigrant family's Model T; nary a transcontinental tourist, not in July of 1925.

I was the intrepid hitchhiker, age fifteen, striking out for freedom, carrying my poor persecuted belongings in a briefcase on which I'd pasted a University of Chicago paper pennant so that passing motorists would take me for a clean-cut college boy (I was neither); carrying, besides, $9 in my burning shoe and an Ingersoll timepiece with the tiny faces (cut from the group photographs in the Englewood High School yearbook) of Greta Esk, Roselle Moses, Marjorie Gibson, Carolyn Teetzel, and Marcella Einarson pasted on the dial at 12, 3, 6, and 9 and (this was Marjorie) at the pivot on the center of the face.

In my shoe, too, besides my $9, I carried a set (two sets, in two shoes) of bunioned blisters acquired walking maybe a quarter of the way from Chicago, for the hitchhiker walked manfully along and never sat. In this way he stood a better chance of getting a hitch, since his walking, with a slight limp, was a sign to the approaching motorist that here was a clean-cut college boy with true grit who was going to get to

From *The Progressive*, August 1982.

California or bust. (In 1925 hitchhikers were not as tired as they are now.)

The evening was drawing in, somewhere around Seligman, Arizona, with nothing to be seen for miles and miles and miles but mesquite and chaparral, never a shanty, never a fence. (The whole Mojave Desert would be fenced away from I-40 fifty years or so later, the whole desert owned by somebody.) The sun, man, that sun, going down without taking the heat away with it, and a long way to walk to Seligman and nothing there when you got there, and nothing for another 75 miles after that but Kingman, and then the muddy Colorado, low in its banks, and California and then Needles, the Santa Fe section point, and nothing for 150 miles beyond Needles, nothing at all but the Santa Fe's single track (which was the only reason there was any Seligman, Kingman, Needles) and the beautiful adobe Fred Harvey House oases at the town stations, where the passengers lolled and bought Navajo jewelry and blankets and kachina dolls from the Indians while the locomotive was coaled and watered and the crew changed.

:

A night in the desert was a night walking U.S. 66; the desert supported snakes (on what?) and the snakes came slithering out in the belated cool of the evening. So our clean-cut young adventurer went venturing on, with his blistered bunions burning. And then, far behind him, the miragelike murmur of a motor car, audible in the high desert long before its dust was visible. The adventurer went slower, but he kept walking. The slower you walked (but kept walking), the better an opportunity the approaching motorist has to size you up. The car came close, a heavy car (a Hudson Super-Six Sedan, as it turned out) doing a good thirty miles an hour. (Fifty years later cars went too fast to enable the motorist to size up the hitchhiker; so fast that even if the motorist thought of stopping he'd be so far ahead of the hitchhiker by the time he could stop that he'd give up the impulse to.)

The Hudson came up to me and stopped. The driver was a

middle-aged man alone, with his sample cases in the back seat. He opened the door and said howdy, or, likelier, hello, and I said, "Thanks, mister," and got in. He asked me where I was going. I said, "To the Coast." He said nothing. Two or three hours later we came into Needles. It was just getting dark. He pulled up in front of the Harvey House at the station – it was that, along the Santa Fe Trail, or the Chinaman's, and the Chinaman had no ceiling fan.

"Want something to eat?" said the driver. I lied and said, "No, thanks, but I'll wait for you." He said, "Come on in." So we sat at the lunch counter under the ceiling fan – the dining room was closed between trains – and he said, "Do you know how to drive?" Hesitant, and with good reason to be, I said I did. He seemed to catch the hesitation; he said, "It's a straight road all the way. You just stay on the road. You want to drive on through with me?" I said, "Yes, sir," and he said, "You'd better have something to eat. I'll pay, as long as you're helping drive."

So I had pork and beans and watermelon and we drove, taking turns, all night, making the section of San Bernardino ("San Berdoo," the railroaders and the hoboes called it) around noon and Los Angeles before supper. The driver paid for more food at the Harvey Houses in Barstow and San Berdoo, and when he said, in Los Angeles, "This is as far as I go," and I said, "Thank you very much," he said, "Thanks for helping drive," and that was all.

I had (and have) no idea who he was, or who were the dozens of other people, many of them farmers in Fords, who gave me long and short (mostly short) rides that summer through Illinois, Missouri, Oklahoma, Texas, and New Mexico. Years later, too, when I hitchhiked from Chicago to Alabama to see my girl, I never learned the identity of my benefactors. A few years ago I had to get from Modesto to Monterey, and there was no handy transport, and I hitchhiked again, this time a clean-cut old college professor, and a hundred or a thousand cars went whizzing by me and a Chicano farmer picked me up in an old truck. None of those people who gave me a lift over all those years ever said much, if anything, to me. But I owed, and owe, them each a hitch, and how am I to repay them?

Why, by picking up hitchhikers.

But I don't.

Not anymore.

That fellow in the Hudson Super-Six who took me across pretty close to five hundred miles of desert into L.A. – how am I to repay him? I'm not.

:

For years Ms. Baby Mayer and I picked up hitchhikers nearly always, and always if they appeared to be clean-cut college boys, as I'd once appeared. Some of them rode with us enormous distances. Some of them as good as moved in on us. Some of them, like me on U.S. 66, needed to be fed and were short of the ready. One of them rode with us from Linz, in Austria, to Athens, and two weeks later from Athens to Switzerland. In a VW microbus we picked up seven or eight of them at once in Ostrava, in Moravia, and took them to Prague. Oh, we gave a lot of people a lot of rides – but not as many as we'd got. And then, five years or so back, we just stopped doing it.

We told ourselves (or I told myself) that we were tired of having to keep up casual conversation; your grateful rider (less sensitive than I was that afternoon on U.S. 66) seems to figure that the least he can do to repay you is to play you some chin music. I prefer to look out the window – Ms. Baby won't let me drive – or read manuscripts or magazines. We have a tape deck in the car, with tapes of His and Hers music, and sometimes we play them. And many is the time, on the long haul, when we want to talk a little, or a lot; there's so little time to talk at home and so much to talk about. So by and by we quit picking up hitchhikers, especially on long trips when we'd be in danger of being stuck with one all the way from, say, Seligman into L.A.

:

But it isn't because we don't enjoy the chin music that we quit taking them. It's because we're afraid of them. We're afraid of strange men, the way little girls are told by their mothers to be. We're afraid to be secreted with a stranger, afraid of his knife or his gun. At my age Socrates was daring death to come and get him and here am I afraid of the stranger behind me on the sidewalk, in front of me on the road. I'm afraid of the stranger within the gate – him whom my religion told me to receive. So I pass in my car, ashamed and making the usually false gesture to indicate that the car is full or we're turning off soon. I pass them by in my need. I need to give them a ride.

I tell myself, me and my machismo, that I'm afraid for Ms. Baby. But I don't pick them up when I'm alone, except for a kid or two from the local junior college. I tell myself that I haven't the time, that I'm going too fast to stop, that I'm not going far enough to do them any good. In Tennessee a while ago a car was pulled up on the no-parking shoulder of the interstate with two young men outside it, one fooling around in the trunk, the other sitting on a dismounted tire and waving for help. We passed them by, and a little later another car was pulled off on the shoulder, its hood up, and a man and a woman standing outside it, and we passed them by too, and a minute later we passed a car backing up with two big men in it to help the stranded couple. (To help them?)

Stay away from strange men, in the nineteen hundred eighty-second year of the Christian era. There's a fellow named Boyd who does a syndicated column of well-waddaya-know items, and he had one recently that read: "A police check of hitch-hikers revealed 84 out of 100 had criminal records. Twelve others were juvenile runaways" – like me on U.S. 66 in 1925 – "or AWOL servicemen. Only four were what lawmen called clean." I don't believe Brother Boyd (or his police check, which comes to the same thing). But the end result of that little item, like the road sign on I-40, is to frighten more people away from the stranger, especially the young stranger (or the old stranger who has the look on the road of an old con).

The newspapers are full of high crimes committed sometimes by the hikers and sometimes by the people who pick them up. In the midst of the random hostility that overspreads the land the care of the stranger waxes cold. One day in slow traffic, with the car windows down, I passed a clean-cut young man and indicated that I was turning off, and he said, "F—— you."

:

With public transportation worse and increasingly expensive, motorists have been picking up hitchhikers less and less since the late 1960s, for good reasons, bad reasons or none. The roadside uniform of what seemed to be the whole generation of middle-class young whites – jeans, boots, guitar, sometimes a dog, sometimes even a cat – has long since lost enchantment for the elderly. So I speed away from the drummer who picked me up in the Super-Six, from the farmer in the Tin Lizzie going out of Rolla, Missouri, who didn't even ask me where I was going and who moved his wife and kids into a pile to make room for the clean-cut young fellow with the briefcase. The hikers aren't, most of them, that clean-cut anymore, and they sit with a tired thumb aloft. And maybe they're on dope and maybe they don't have any good reason for being on the road instead of in school or at work. (Or moving on, looking for work?)

But a couple of hours after the hot sun goes down in the desert and the light goes from gold to pink to red to purple to night, the desert gets cold, cold at night in 1925, and the cold-blooded snakes move around in the dark. It's dark and it's cold at night in 1982. Keep walking. Keep driving.

: : : *Anyone for Russian Roulette?* : : :

I wouldn't have married her if I'd known it was going to turn out like this. She'd told me she had money. She had it, but it was in her coin purse. She says I'd told her that I had money. What I'd told her was that I *had* had money.

So it's been pretty slim pickings, except for that old Cadillac that Ansley Salz gave us because we couldn't afford a car. But we couldn't afford a free one getting a mile to a gallon or two of gas (and gas up to seventeen cents; this was a while back). So we drove it a mile or two, just to be seen in it, and sold it to Honest John Setchel for $42.50 – $40 for the scrap, $2.50 for the gas in the tank.

If we'd kept it we'd have had a $50,000 Vintage Car now. But we were short of the ready.

This happened in Carmel, California, where people gave other people old Cadillacs. I was born in Chicago, Illinois, and died there, and then moved to Carmel, California, because Ms. Baby ("My name is Jane") Mayer wanted to live in California.

(Her name isn't even Jane. It's Dorothy Jane, but nobody is supposed to know that. I shouldn't have married her.)

Carmel, California, as late as the 1950s had vestiges of the far-out writers-artists-musicians colony it had been (or was supposed to have been). It was pretty much a shanty town, but the shanties were marvelously hidden in the marvelous trees. There were no lights – people carried lanterns – and no sidewalks to roll up at 9 P.M. No street numbers; so the P.O. would not deliver the mail. Everybody went to the P.O. and spent the day there.

It had the world's worst climate outside England – fog all

From *The Progressive*, October 1975.

: 9 :

summer, rain all winter. The fuchsias and the rhododendron had a field day. Nobody gardened; everybody degardened. The State Reserve at Point Lobos south of town – Do Not Disturb Anything Living or Dead – was surer proof of God's existence than St. Thomas's Five Proofs, the Monterey Cypress gnarled by the world's champion gnarler.

The town was quaint. It was the place where old folks went to live with their parents.

But the developers and their camp-followers, the kitsch merchants, were taking over. And the retired generals and admirals. The generals and admirals had all lied to get into the killing at sixteen. Now they were forty-six, with that thirty-year pension, and they volunteered for all the volunteer jobs. We were going to have a meeting on capital punishment at the Parish House of All Saints Church, and the rector canceled us out because the admiral who was chairman of the Parish House Committee objected.

By and by the developers and the merchants and the generals and the admirals took the place over root and branch, uprooting the branches to build wall-to-wall houses with wall-to-wall carpeting. Forty-foot lots. No lots left.

Harry Dickinson came to Carmel around 1912. He, too, had lived and died in Chicago, a lawyer. One day he realized that he wore the same suit, carried the same suitcase, and had the same ideas as all the other lawyers in Chicago. He up and quit and headed for the woods of Carmel Point. Robin Jeffers, the poet fellow, had gone there, like Harry, to get away from it all (or them all). There was a hand-hewn sign on the point: LOTS $50. Harry hadn't left his Chicago chicane behind him. He offered the lot man $25 apiece for all of the lots and became a millionaire. (Robin Jeffers had to sell off his land to pay taxes.)

There were still, in the 1950s, a few artists, writers, and musicians around. But they were getting on, and thinning out, and every time one of them died a retired admiral took his place. They were getting into everywhere. Carmel had always been a Jim Crow town by accident. Now it was a Jim Crow town.

Ed Kennedy was a real newspaperman, and he was now editor of the *Monterey Peninsula Herald,* which wasn't a real newspaper. Ed was the instant-hero-turned-instant-villain who Betrayed His Trust – and saved fifty thousand soldiers' lives – by breaking the German surrender story prematurely in 1945 and was cashiered by the crummy AP at crummy President Truman's suggestion. Ed was a fighting fool, and Carmel was still a livable place.

But just.

Ed died. Everybody died. It was time to get out of Carmel; the place was becoming a tourist trap nonpareil. It had been great for the kids, not so great for the adolescents. (A few years later there were junior junkies in the *junior* high school.)

In 1964 we heard there was money in Amherst, Massachusetts. We sold our shanty – it had cost us $14,500 ten years before – for $53,000 and bought a $14,500 shanty in Amherst for $53,000.

The Connecticut River Valley was bad, bad, bad, for Ms. Baby's asthma. She wilted on the stem, and I was the stem. She wanted to go back to Carmel, and whither she goeth I go. (I have a pleasant personality but a weak will.)

What she wanted to go back to was not Carmel but the 1950s. (She doesn't know that you can't go home again. She has a strong will and an interesting personality.) (I told her that she could be my hearth rug in heaven if she was my footstool on earth. It didn't help.)

So I set up the usual fake assignments to make it a tax-deductible business trip, in case 1975 should be a better year than 1974. (1974 was a slow year.) We got into our poor-man's-Porsche and Motel-Sixed it out to Carmel. We had a good friend who let us have a $1,000-a-month house for $100. (We have many good friends, on account of my pleasant personality.)

Carmel was a goner; the absence of lights and sidewalks was

now the centerpiece of the hard sell. Clip joints everywhere, the main street a parade of motels and restaurants and gift shops and gourmet groceries. (Like Napoleon's army, Californians travel on their bellies.)

Eighty-three art galleries in town, peddling imports; no Carmel artists and writers left in the artists-and-writers colony. The tour buses rolled through the admirals-and-generals colony. "And this, ladies and gentlemen, was the home of Robinson Jeffers." (Who's Robinson Crusoe, Pop?)

The climate was still wonderfully cold and foggy – a good place to work if you brought your work with you.

At least it wasn't *southern* California. But it was California. A wonderful place to get a picture postcard from, but you wouldn't want to visit there.

Ms. Baby wanted to build us a barn-type house cheap. She knows how to do things like that. (Everybody knows a little something.) We figure $65,000 for a building lot and a barn, just like that. Go for broke. You only live once, if that often.

A building lot in or around Carmel costs $25,000–$40,000, depending on whether it's under water. The barn would cost maybe $65,000–$75,000, depending on whether you wanted to water the horse indoors or out. You can get a rat-trap for $65,000–$75,000, a full-blown cracker-box for $100,000–$150,000. Ms. Baby got depresseder and depresseder, and went on looking.

I played it cool, conning Ms. Baby. Ms. Baby is even tighter that I am. I told her that everything she showed me was peachy. She showed me a place she kind of liked: $100,000. (She was crazy, thinking I was crazy talking about $100,000.)

She didn't find anything, but she's going back to go on looking. (As my friend John D. Harms used to say, before Ms. came in, "That's some Baby, that Baby.")

The companion of my sorrows, and the cause of them all.

Our son Rock has an eighty-acre gulch in the back country above Sebastopol (California, not Russia). Rock – that's his name – is the manager of a string quartet called The Grateful

Dead. (His little brother Dicken calls him the Hippie Patri-arch.) Rock wants us to build a barn on his Gentleman's Tobacco Road. Free land. Good boy. Bona fide rural slum. Short of water, dark in the winter, dusty in the dry, and a couple of hundred miles north of Ah! Carmel!

:

I don't want to die in California. I don't even want to live there. "Soft climates," says Herodotus, "make soft men."

(The begonias enter the soul.)

I'm already as soft as a man can be without splattering – living in a *hard* climate. I can't abide beauty, and neither can anyone else. The people who come to California are lovers of beauty. Every time I see a picture of H. R. Haldeman I don't want to die in California.

But that's where I'm going to – mark my words. I can't do without Ms. Baby. I can't do with anybody – or anything – else. Ms. Baby and I have gone up the hill together and down the hill together and it's toboggan all the way. When she's out of the house for more than five minutes I mope. When she's unhappy – confound it, what has *she* got to be unhappy about? – I bawl.

Up and down the hill, and now the Western Slope.

I wouldn't have married her if I'd known it was going to be like this. But I'd have lived in sin with her, loving, honoring, obeying, and grousing until death did us part (or our money ran out, whichever should occur first). To live in California is to live in sin, wedding license or no wedding license.

When the Joads left California to go back where they came from – the Oklahoma dustbowl – they hung a sign on the back of their jalopy: Good-bye, California, You And Your Great Big Geraniums.

Then came the freeways and the developers and the rest of that ruinous rout. What God hath joined together – earth and sea and sky – man with his bulldozer put asunder in California. I'm a crusty old New Englander born and half-bred. Freeze in the winter, broil in the summer, fight the snow and the ice and the mosquitoes. A Chicago boy whose pappy didn't believe them when they told him that John D. had $65,000.

Hello, California, You And Your Great Big Geraniums.

: : : *The Gracious Dead* : : :

Smelling money on Mrs. Huddleston, I began drooling like Pavlov's shameless dog. She said she had just bought a condominium cottage at Hidden Hills. I asked her what Hidden Hills was and she said, "An adult community." I asked her what an Adult Community was and she said, "Come up" – it's always *up* – "and see." So Ms. Baby Mayer and I went up and saw.

Hidden Hills is, or are, well hidden. There's a sign at the bottom of the road reading, *Private – Residents Only,* and, to italicize the point, a gatehouse with a guard with a gun. Clearance at the gatehouse was surprisingly easy; it always is, with my classy Baby along. I said, "Mrs. Huddleston, Cottage 37." The guard took our name and license number and let us in.

The road wound up through the woods to the manicured plateau of Hidden Hills, its hundred or so garden cottages (of the $100,000 to $150,000 variety) nestled here and there along curving walks in the trees.

Mrs. Huddleston showed us the quiet clubhouse with its quiet restaurant and a few quiet people about, all in their obviously robust sixties. And then she took us into a large structure labeled The Pool. The Pool it was, and a large pool at that, with a large jacuzzi at one end – and nobody in either. I began drooling again, audibly.

"I'd be delighted to have you swim here," said Mrs. Huddleston graciously, or richly (it's always hard for me to tell which). "I have to run back to the city for a bit before I settle in here. Day guests are not permitted at Hidden Hills, but I can register you as my Resident Guests for fifteen days. After fifteen days you'd have to go before the Resident Committee and pass the examination."

From *The Progressive*, May 1978.

: *15* :

"The examination?"

"You know – financial, character, that sort of thing, quite rigorous. *And* the physical."

"The physical?"

"Oh, yes. An Adult Community isn't a Retirement Home, or a Rest Home, or whatever those dreadful places are called where people go to die." – A shudder just touched her as it passed. – "There's no infirmary here, no nurse, no doctor, nothing of that sort." – Another touch of shudder. – "You have to be in perfect health – and over forty-five."

No sick and no dying, no children, no poor. No dogs – Mrs. Huddleston said they were allowed on a leash, but I never saw one – and if no dogs no Sheenies or Polacks or Jigaboos. (Maybe no Micks either, but since the Kennedys they've been getting in everywhere.) Only robust rich Wasps in their late prime, the new Early Retirees, out of the rat race with deep pockets and a cream-colored Mercedes to take them to the golf course and the three-martini-lunch in town and a look-in on their purveyors of common stocks and preferred delicacies and then back up the hill for a pre-prandial snooze. Paradise enow. Paradise, too, for a mugger up there at night, with only the subdued soft glow of the widely spaced ornamental gas lamps – if only a mugger could get past the gatehouse guard. (There was no other way in or out.)

Twice a day for fifteen days I leaped, every day livelier, into my shiny old Plymouth and went "up" and went swimming and restored my aching back, my dislocated shoulder, my fallen metatarsal arch in the splendid spacious jacuzzi. Most of the time I was in The Pool alone. Occasionally there was another exertionist or two, never more. At the end of fifteen days I was a rosy new man under the skin and over – but the fifteen days had ended and with them the paradise enow.

But with them, too, a card from Mrs. Huddleston saying she would not be back "for a month or two." There was, however, no extension of the Resident Guest privilege and I knew I'd never get past the Committee. Even if they wanted me (which they wouldn't) they'd want money, and handling money (except to receive it) on or off the Sabbath is against my religion; and my religion would be against me. Besides, I despised them and their hills.

But it was do – in The Pool and the jacuzzi – or die. I thought I might as well try to do.

What wouldn't I give for another month or two of paradise enow? What I would give was what Faust had given – no more, no less. But unlike Faust I'd have no friend at court. I'd have to hack it on my own.

The gatehouse guards were a cinch. By now they knew who I was (or thought they did): Mrs. Huddleston's Resident Guest. I could have come up there with a ten-ton semi and emptied the place and they'd wave as I went past them on my way out (and I'd wave back).

The Administrator was something else. His office overlooked the parking area. He wouldn't pay any attention to my Plymouth, but he would to the rear bumper sticker. With the car backed into a slot, the Administrator wouldn't see the rear bumper, but any Resident strolling down the walk across from the parking area would see it and, reading the sticker, suppose that the car belonged to a low delivery man (until he saw it there every day, or saw me getting in or out of it and recognized me from the pool). The sticker might be my undoing. But I was damned – no, I was already damned – I was saved if I was going to remove that bumper sticker. It read: I SHOP CO-OP.

The occasional Resident I passed between the parking lot and The Pool I passed too haughtily ever to be accosted. Once I was in the water I was safe. The problem was the jacuzzi, jacuzzis being conducive to conversation, and more particularly the gents' dressing room for the same reason. The first few times I had a companion and he introduced himself – "I don't believe we've met" – I found myself at a dangerous disadvantage. *I* had to respond to *him*, explaining, for starters, that "we" were baby-sitting Mrs. Huddleston's cottage – "Huddleston, Huddleston, oh, yes, the new Resident, I haven't met her" – "No, she's away" – "Well, it's nice to have you up"

The Gracious Dead : *17*

– always up – "here. Are you from the East [West, North, South]?" I realized that I could not keep the conversation away from me unless I took the initiative and kept it.

"I'm Professor Mayer." – The "Professor" might psych him out, unless he'd ever been a professor. – "Mrs. Mayer and I are baby-sitting Dora" – no need to tell him that we'd just met "Dora" – "Huddleston's cottage, Number 37, while she's gone back to the City to close her place there. She's just become a Resident. I dare say" – I knew darned well – "you haven't met her. You're from – ?" No matter where he was from, I'd been there often, had cousins there, had lectured there, Jorgensen still president of the college, I suppose, fact is, I can't imagine anybody's ever moving away from there, the climate, of course, that's a consideration, my wife's asthma, we just couldn't take that part of the country any more, devil of a thing, asthma, any asthma in your family?

I had to keep him off center, keep pushing him. . . . We're thinking of moving up here ourselves, Mrs. Mayer and I, and I'd certainly appreciate your telling me how you folks like it, how long have you been here? And on, and on. Let him get a word in edgeways, like "Seattle," and keep pushing him. Seattle? Well, now, fancy that, my wife was brought up in Seattle. The Bartons there? Why, of course she knew them, she's spoken of them often, how are they, wasn't there something about a son of theirs, or was it a daughter, or a niece? Well, Mrs. Mayer will certainly be interested to hear that, we'll have to get together, delighted, delighted, I'd better get into the pool now, delighted. Over and out.

For all my pushing, my companion in the dressing room or the jacuzzi would manage to ask where we were from. "Actually, we're local people, our place is on The Point, so it's no problem to pop up here every day or two and check out the cottage for Dora, not that there's," and so on. Actually we *were* local people, but it was stretching the point, stretching it considerably, to say that our "place" was on The Point, The Point being the most elegant section of town (and sure to be known as such to the Residents of Hidden Hills). The Point almost tripped me up once. I had counted, successfully, on every Resident's having come from far away – . "The Point? Well, now, that *is* a coincidence. Mrs. Arbuthnot and I lived on The Point for eighteen years, just off Scenic on Seventeenth. Where is your place on The Point?" I had to move fast: "Off Scenic on Seventeenth? Why, you must have been neighbors of the McGillicuddys, or, let me see, they came out here in '72, summer of '72, or was it '73? Just when did you folks move up here?" (Mr. Arbuthnot never did find out where our place on The Point was.)

:

Our little boy Dicken came out to see if we were still alive, and I cued him in on my Hidden Hills caper and promised to take him "up" there – though I could not, of course, get him into The Pool until he was forty-five. When I told him about my seizing and holding the initiative, and about the close shave with Mr. Arbuthnot, Dicken (who has been to night school) said, "You're a regular Raskolnikov, that's what you are, playing games with them to see if they are smart enough to catch you, giving them clues they couldn't possibly miss – the bumper sticker, for instance – except for their half-wittedness."

"Why would I want to be caught?"

"To make fools of the idle rich. If they don't catch you, they'll never know they've been made fools of. You want them to know they're fools. But I don't think they'll catch you."

"Why not?"

"Don't you know about the idle rich?" said Dicken.

"Tell me about the idle rich."

"When they hole up in a place like that, they figure it's impenetrable. Impenetrability is the whole idea. Think about it. They don't know you, they wouldn't like you if they did, they certainly don't like your looks – *but they figure you wouldn't be there unless you belonged there.*"

"What about my tattoo?" I said. "That ought to be enough to alert them."

"You see," said Dicken, "you're disappointed because it

doesn't. Raskolnikov again. These rich generals figure you're a rich admiral who worked his way up from able-bodied seaman and can't get rid of the tattoo on his arm without getting rid of the arm. You won't be caught on that one unless you persuade them to ask you what your flagship was."

I'd get myself caught, all right, and without trying. Soon or late one of my Pool-fellows would say to another, "Funny thing about that Professor Mayer, have you noticed? I see him at The Pool every day, and never anywhere else." And the other would say, "First time I met him – he seemed to be anxious to introduce himself – he said he was Mrs. Huddleston's Resident Guest. But that was weeks and weeks ago. Funny." "I'll just check with the Administrator. It's impossible that the man doesn't belong here somehow."

And if I got myself caught – what then? Mrs. Huddleston would be embarrassed – but that's what she'd get having friends like me. I'd pull rank – professor, not admiral – combined with the pretense that I didn't know about the fifteen-day limit. They'd shag me, that's all. I've been shagged before, but this time I'd go out glowing with good health and happy memories.

I wasn't ever caught. I swam and jacuzzied for three months and more at Hidden Hills – I don't know if "Dora" ever did get back – and I wasn't caught. Then Ms. Baby and I – she's ashamed of me, she really is – left town on an extended trip. I suppose we won't see much of our benefactress when we return. And I'll be back to sneaking into the Holiday Inn pool draped in the Holiday Inn towel which (if I remember right) I found on the road one day. And back to patronizing our darling Virginia Fry's leaky little old jacuzzi in her back yard.

I'd like to toodle up to Hidden Hills every day the rest of my life and swim in that great big pool and cook my shoulder, my back, and my spavined metatarsal arch in that great big jacuzzi. What I'd really like is not to toodle up but to *be* up in Hidden Hills every day the rest of my life and saunter across the bowling green to The Pool, twice, three times, a day. All I'd have to do – .

All I'd have to do would be to be rich, white, childless, dog-less, niggerless, sheenieless, healthy, and maybe Protestant, and roll over and play live under a sky that was cloudless all day, and never hear a discouraging (or an encouraging) word or see a cutpurse or a whore or a druggie or a cripple or a corpse or a junkyard or a pigsty.

A too well-preserved lady to be true got into the jacuzzi with me. "I hope," I said, seizing whatever I could, which happened to be the initiative, "that that watch of yours is waterproof." The lady who was too well-preserved to be true said, "It ought to be – it's a three-thousand-dollar Rolex." The waterproof life: When Crito came to Socrates on death row and told him the fix was in to get him over the wall in a basket of dirty laundry, Socrates said, "And then what?" "We can get you into Thrace," said Crito. "And if I get into Thrace," said Socrates, "will I live forever?"

If the purpose of life is to get away from it all – not for a weekend, or a month, or a cruise, but for keeps – these Rolex ladies, these generals, these Arbuthnots are the overachievers of the age. They are the Gracious Dead who made it across the Great Divide under their own steam with their own hamper of goodies such as the Egyptians interred with their Pharaohs to sustain them en route to a better world still. The denizens of the Adult Community give the lie to the adage that you can't take it with you. They already have.

:   :   :   *Last Man at the Depot*   :   :   :

She wrote Girls' Athletics for *The E Weekly* – *E* for Engle-wood High School – and I did "The Vertebral Column – The Backbone of the Paper." (" 'There's something in that, too,' said the burglar as he stuck his hand in the cuspidor.") She was captain of the girls' swim team (gloriously) and I was a miler (barely). And we were both in the cast of *Seven Keys to Baldpate*.

We would finish our after-school stints around four o'clock and walk over to the Englewood Union Station, on 63rd Street west of State, in Chicago, and sit on the baggage wagon on the platform and swing our legs and hold hands.

We would sit there, swinging our legs and holding hands, until all the Limiteds, outbound for the East (*and* the South-west) had come and gone and the Rock Island suburban trains to Morgan Park (where she lived) had got fewer and fewer and it had got to be six o'clock, 6:15, 6:30, and it had got dark and the spooky platform lights went on, and I'd say, "What will mother say?" and she'd say, "Need mother know?"

She was my girl, and the baggage wagon at Englewood was our trysting.

For train buffs – the expression had not yet been coined in 1925 – the Englewood Union Station was the One and Only Wonder of the World. It was a seedy little brick overpass struc-ture straddling the 63rd Street car line, with a narrow driveway curving up from the street; unprepossessing, unpolished, and unswept (except by a gnarled old black man who followed, rather than pushed, his broom around, and that maybe once a week). It was nothing more than a one-window ticket office, a vintage toilet, a no-account newsstand, and a miserable snack bar (another not-yet-coined expression).

From *The Progressive*, January 1983.

But it was truly a Union Station.

Along its long uncovered platforms – preternaturally long for a suburban station – the great trains of three great railroads converged on their way out of Chicago, twelve minutes after leaving their downtown terminals. Englewood was for Boarding Only – "Passengers for Toledo and beyond," "Detroit and beyond," "Harrisburg and beyond." And beyond and beyond. The New York Central to Cleveland and Buffalo and New York and Boston, the Pennsylvania to Pittsburgh and Philadelphia and Washington and New York, the Rock Island southwest to Oklahoma, Texas, and California, all from the outbound stop (no Arrive and Depart, just a stop) at Englewood.

It was a grand grimy place to sit on the luggage wagon – there was only one, for passenger baggage – and swing your legs, with or without your girl. In the late afternoon, one after another, the beautiful shiny all-Pullman monsters came hissing in with their air-brakes on, carrying their shiny all-Pullman corsage-chested cargo, and with pink roses in the bud vases on the dining car tables covered with, yes, sir, napery and set with, yes, ma'm, silver chased with the railroad's crest. They paused huffing heavily, as if to catch their breath, while the beautiful people (not yet coined) boarded. Then the crack trainman at the back gave the crack engineer the highball and the crack porters, not yet changed from their blue coats to their white jackets, scooped up their steps and the all-Pullman Pullman doors went shut and the monsters grunted their belly-bursting grunts and took majestically off for And Beyond.

One after another the Name Trains pulling in, and then out – Limiteds all, the Rock Island's Golden State and Rocky Mountain, the Pennsy's Gotham, Golden Arrow, General, Liberty, the Central's Wolverine, Commodore Vanderbilt, Lake Shore, New England States, Motor City. . . . Have I forgotten something?

I have not forgotten something.

I have not forgotten the Century and the Broadway.

The Century and Broadway were the respective flagships of

the New York Central and the Pennsylvania Railroads which (having long since euchred the B&O out of a New York terminus) competed for the passenger business that connected the country with New York via Chicago. Not excepting the fabled Orient Express out of Paris for Istanbul – walnut car interiors as an elegant setting for factual and fictional murder, espionage, regal robbery, and royal jiggery-pokery – the Century and the Broadway were over all the two most splendidly appointed trains in all the red-carpet history of railroading, with their barbers and manicurists and stenographers, their shower-baths and their $1.50 Kansas City Sirloin Steak dinners and vintage wines and whiskies, and their telegraph and (some time later) telephone service en route. They were the (not yet coined) superstars of earth travel, collected as train cards and sun pictures by every kid who collected anything, hung on office and residential walls as paintings, photographs, calendars – "The Horseshoe Curve at Altoona, Pa.," "Coming Down the Hudson."

They rolled out of their Chicago stations at exactly the same time (just, it seemed, for the hell of it), sidled up to each other as they left the yards, and came steaming into crummy, comical little old Englewood (at, of course, the same time) on adjacent tracks. And then, as soon as the genteel porters could genteelly hustle the boarding gentry aboard, they pulled out side by side, their passengers waving and sedately hooting at the windows as the iron thoroughbreds ran firebox to firebox and picked up their transcontinental speed, now the Broadway, now the Century leading by never more than a locomotive length or two until, a few miles out of Englewood, in East Chicago, they curved away from one another for the twenty-hour hurtle to New York, with only enough stops for coaling and watering between Englewood and the cathedrals of Penn Station and Grand Central. Not yet jacketed as streamliners, they had fins sticking out of the pre-air-conditioning windows of their passenger cars to keep the soot from coming in at eighty miles per hour even when the windows were (as they always were) closed; the crack trains had ceiling vents similarly shielded and small fans in the berths and drawing rooms.

The Broadway never achieved the cachet of the Century. It was never as fashionable and never as crowded. It almost always, except on an occasional Friday and Sunday, ran in one section, while the Century commonly ran in two or three, five minutes apart. Christmas Day was characteristically the Century's only single-section run of the year, and by 1929 its sixteen-wheeled Niagaras were pulling five or six twelve-, fourteen-, or sixteen-car sections daily, with an Advance Century besides (a half hour earlier). The Broadway was second fiddle because the Pennsy, first of all a freight line, had to haul itself through the industrial Alleghenies and around the middle-of-the-night Horseshoe Curve outside Altoona, while the Central justifiably boasted its Water Level Route through Cleveland and Buffalo and down the storied Hudson; to maintain the Century's pace the Broadway had to provide a jerkier and altogether less than toothsome ride.

Everybody Who Was Anybody took the Century, with its $9.60 extra fare (refundable at $1.20 an hour for every hour it ran late). I never knew it to run late except once, when I was on board (on an expense account). An icy curve going into Utica flattened a wheel and there wasn't an extra car available to replace it. (It was 1943 and there was a war on.) The Train of Trains limped humiliated into Grand Central in mid-afternoon, with the passengers having got (in addition to their $1.20 an hour) a wartime under-the-counter steak for lunch on the house.

All this and more, more, more was the old Englewood Station, and the baggage wagon on the platform was warm and smoky in the springtime, hazy and smoky in the fall, and wind-whipping cold and smoky in the winter. And my girl and I sat there, sooting up, swinging our legs and holding hands and the majestic Name Trains pulled majestically in and out (and the no-name Rock Island suburban trains to Morgan Park sort of sneakily in between) and once in a great while the

Last Man at the Depot : 25

grizzled old station custodian-cum-redcap needed the baggage truck and we had to get off and he always said, "Sorry," but not, as I remember, "Sorry, kids." (I don't remember what he, or anyone else, addressing teen-agers called them in 1925.)

:

Her name was Susan, Susan Bennecke. I don't remember what her father did, or why they lived 'way out in Morgan Park in those pre-suburban days. I went to their modest frame house once – I don't remember why; maybe something to do with school work, or books, or notes, or maybe there was only a pretext – and met her mother and father and her two big brothers, Hank and Fred. They were big/older and, like their father, big/big; they must have been on the teams at (I suppose) Morgan Park High. (Why hadn't Susan gone to Morgan Park?) Mrs. B. was certainly chunky and Susan's father probably had some up-from-the-blue-collar occupation, head of a shipping room, maybe, the kind of man you thought of as an own-furnace-stoking Householder. (Mine was an Apartment-Dwelling paper-box salesman with a turned white collar.) Swimmer Susan, though she wasn't heavy, was firm, firm and broad-shouldered. The whole Bennecke family exuded physical competence.

Whatever I exuded, it wasn't that. I was too skinny and stringy to do anything but tag along behind the track team as a spare miler. Not that I didn't, in the event, justify Coach Rosie Rosenbaum's unenlarged faith in me. The event was the City Meet in my senior year. Toward the end of the afternoon Rosie summoned me ("Who? Me?") from the dugout and said, "I want you to run the two-mile." I said, "But I'm a miler, Rosie," and Rosie said, "You're not a miler *or* a two-miler, but there are only two men entered in the two-mile and there's a point for third. Go in there and pick up that point for us. All you have to do is finish – I don't care when." All I did was finish, after dark – and Englewood won the Meet *by one point*.

Maybe it was merely their lustiness that worried me about the Benneckes – or about Hank and Fred. I wasn't a passionately four-eyed Jewish boy, but I was an intelligent Jewish boy with an intelligent Jewish disdain of the hairy-chested virtues and the whole *corpore sano* bit (*another* not-yet-coined). In their dumb chestiness Hank and Fred might suspect me of Wronging their little sister, and in my intelligent Jewishness they might suspect me of Wronging her in some vulpine, vampiric fashion. But their little sister wasn't the to-be-wronged type. In long, long retrospect I'd say that I was likelier to be Wronged than she – she with her frisky self-possession ("Need mother know?"), her rough healthy skin, her coarse yellow hair, her roguish gray eyes that did a lot of dancing (as did she), her slightly protuberant lips. All right: We are talking about, not fifty, but fifty-seven years ago; if I ever so much as kissed her, I don't remember and don't want to.

The Benneckes, all of them, Susan, too, seemed to me to be a bit beneath the Mayers, cut from some imperceptibly rougher stuff. Why was it? Was it their physicality, their bodiliness? Their being gentiles? (Jews did not think too well of gentiles generally.) Susan was not what the lady novelists called common, but she was a little less ethereal than I, a little lacking in *Fingerspitze gefühl*, fingertip-feeling. For one thing, she was less choosy. Her closest friend at Englewood was a head-tossing redhead named Jean who may or may not have been up to monkeying around above the knee and who herself had a large round friend named Muriel who was widely, and, I think, fairly, suspected of being a really hot and scandalous number in my virgin world. But no – it wasn't the company Susan kept, or this, or that: It was the trifling gap that doesn't quite separate and doesn't quite close and may some day mean trouble.

Miss Pierce, the faculty adviser of *The E Weekly*, never gave over trying to break up the Affair between us, on the ostensible ground, talking to my mother, who she'd asked me to have come to see her, that she thought that both families would object to the association, which was "becoming serious," because of the difference in religion. There was no apparent anti-Semitism there, and, I think, no real; what spurred Miss Pierce, and kept her alive, was the tortured vision of what boys and girls of any religion, or none, might or might not be up to. At seventeen, and without benefit of Freud, Jung, Hegelschlegel, or Dear Abby, even Susan and I knew *that.* (My mother was sedate; Miss Pierce didn't ask chunky, gentile Mrs. Bennecke to come to school.)

Mrs. Manley was something else again. Mrs. Manley was everything else again. I had not seen her likes before. I have not seen her likes since. I shall not see her likes again now. Mrs. Manley was our Latin teacher and she was on the right side right down the line; when I complained because Johnson got an S (for Superior) in Virgil and I got an E (for merely Excellent), Mrs. Manley said, without saying that Johnson was the only Negro in the class, "When you've come as far as Johnson has, you'll get as good a grade as he gets." Since Mrs. Manley was on the right side, she was on Susan's side and mine – and on love's. And on Latin's, Latin's, Latin's; in 1925 high school teachers were real graduates of real universities (Mrs. Manley's was Chicago).

We "had" Mrs. Manley for the four years of Latin which, a lifetime after I'd forgotten it all, enabled me to stumble around in the dark in Italy, France, and Spain. Susan was the best student in the class (and in any class). She was bright, was Susan, really Superior. I was bright, too, but not as bright as Susan and I didn't have to be; with her help with home-work on the 'phone every night ("nickel, please") I was really Excellent, and the two of us, members both of something called the National Honor Society, were sent one Saturday morning at the end of our junior year to the magic campus of Mrs. Manley's University of Chicago, and to the magic ma-hogany banisters, come, come, balustrades, of Ida Noyes Hall to take the National Scholarship Examinations. Susan got a First and I got an Honorable Mention.

She was so chipper, so "fat and sassy" (my mother would say) in her cap and gown on the Englewood stage in June of 1925. And we were both accepted at Chicago, and I ran away from home that summer, like Stendhal's hero who joined Napoleon in order to escape the sorrows that poisoned his life, especially on Sundays. I hitchhiked to California, where, on the Embarcadero in San Francisco, the man called the coppers when I tried to ship out to China and my father's cousin Morry showed up and said, "You're all right, kid," and, to the coppers, "The kid's all right," and gave me money to get home in time for college.

                                        :

We saw each other our first day on campus at the Freshman Mixer – do they still have mixers, at Chicago or anywhere else? – and we danced, my girl and I, and as the dance was winding up she said, boltish-from-the-blue, "I think we shouldn't see each other for a while." Among the things I disbelieved in those days were my ears, and I said, "What?" And she said it again, and, without waiting for me to say "Why?" she said, saying something rehearsed, "Rushing for clubs" – Chicago had men's fraternities but women's *clubs* – "begins next week and," her rehearsal collapsing, "well . . . I'll be rushed by . . . the gentile clubs . . . and. . . ." I hadn't planted the dagger, but I turned it: "And?" "And . . . well . . . if they see me going around . . . going around. . . ." I turned it again: ". . . with a Jew." "Well . . . it will only be for a few weeks, until. . . ." And again: ". . . until you're initiated into a gentile club."

It would only be for fifty, fifty-seven years, or (for all I know) forever. Like a diamond. Or a Toledo blade. (Or a true love on the baggage wagon at Englewood, at the dances in the school gym, gray eyes dancing.)

Chicago was a small campus, and we passed each other frequently. I can't remember that I cut her completely. I wouldn't have done that. I'd have nodded to her, or dipped my head a trifle – as if furtively, to mock her. Or doffed my freshman beanie elaborately, to see her blush. I don't remember. But she said hello to me always, affecting offhandedness.

And she wasn't rushed by any of the big clubs and finally accepted Tri Sig, which wasn't the least craved club on campus, but almost. And she went through college unsung and unsinging. And I, flinging roses, roses, wound up one of the Big Men, one of the Very Big Men, with a long list of roses flung and a long list of Incompletes (and a scattering of As and Fs) before I was given the snowbank treatment by Dolorosa Mater and pulling my 'coonskin coat around me got into my twenty-five-dollar Model T and swished off into the sunset, a Living Legend.

It was twenty years after the Freshman Mixer, twenty, or twenty-five, or thirty, and I, I was under contract, as always, to do my autobiography, and I dropped in at the Alumni Office and got Susan Bennecke's – Susan Bennecke Shoemaker's – address and 'phone number and 'phoned her and asked her to have tea with me on campus and we had tea. I was still stringy and still (a whited pillar of the Religious Society of Friends) a Jew. Swimmer Susan was heftier at last, as the mother of two or three children should be. Her rough skin was rougher, her yellow hair fading, but she could still smile her sassy smile and set her gray eyes dancing. I didn't gaze reproachfully, ruefully, or regretfully at her, nor she at me. Her husband, Mr. Shoemaker, of, of all places, Morgan Park, was in linoleum, or widgets, or (no, not that) paper boxes. She knew this or that about me, from the public prints.

So we talked, without hesitation and with animation. We talked about Englewood and Englewood people, and about Mrs. Manley (but not about Miss Pierce, who tried to break up our Affair). Nor did we talk about our Affair, or the Freshman Mixer, or about college (and we were sitting right there) at all. (Or about the Englewood Station.)

And then we said goodbye and I made a few autobiographical notes about Englewood, things I'd forgotten, like the time ponderous Mrs. Manley walked ponderously down one of the classroom aisles carrying her wastebasket and held it in front of a classmate who was chewing gum. That was the first day of our freshman year in Latin and Susan and I didn't know each other.

(Or about the Englewood Station.)

The railroads began fading after the war, and Englewood faded with them. The Name Trains that had raced each other out of Englewood when Susan and I sat there swinging our legs and holding hands got lightweight aluminum equipment, with bedrooms and roomettes in addition to the old-time compartments and drawing rooms and the upper-and-lowers. They were air-conditioned now and in those that carried coaches the coaches had overnight lean-back seats. There were dome cars and the brass-railed observation platforms were enclosed and streamlined. Streamliners were pulled by streamlined locomotives burning diesel oil. Developing greater horsepower than steam, they made 100 miles per hour on the straightaway. With coaling, watering, and section-point servicing as good as eliminated, the New York–Chicago run was cut from twenty hours to sixteen (and with smoother acceleration and deceleration). But nothing helped: nothing.

The Century – the *Century* – carried coaches for the first time and was down to one section, combined with the Advance Century and then with the Commodore Vanderbilt. The Pennsy cut ruthlessly. Nothing helped.

And then the name trains disappeared. *The Century disappeared.*

The plane killed off the passenger business and the truck and the Interstate cut the freights by three-quarters. And then came the bankruptcies and the mergers and the mergers and the bankruptcies and the Central and the Pennsy became the Penn Central and the Penn Central became a part of the great new nationally financed Amtrak system. And disappeared? Not on your tintype: A couple of years ago, this in the newspapers: "The Penn Central Corporation is divesting itself of the last of its rail properties." And doing what then? Something entrepreneurial, you may be sure, in conformity to the Mixed Economy: Whatever is profitable is private, whatever loses money (waging wars, carrying the mails, schooling the young) is communized.

The *railroads?* The *railroads* gone? When I was little Ma and Pa jabbered away many and many a summer evening in the breeze off the lake at the Iowa Pavilion in Jackson Park – a remnant of the Chicago World's Fair of 1893. They sat and rocked in the big dark-green cane rockers and jabbered away with the Degens and the Bruckers and the Kaplanskys and the Doc Springers, the men smoking cigars, the women lighting punk, and Pa said: "If I had any money" – he hadn't – "I'd put it in the railroads. Believe me – when the railroads go, the country will go." And they believed him.

The railroads went, but not altogether. I was waiting, quite recently, at the Newark station, for the two-car rambling wreck to Princeton, and I discovered that the Broadway Limited was still running. Did I say running? The day I waited at Newark it and all other trains out of Penn Station were "indefinitely delayed" and the unbeautiful people of Newark with their unbeautiful luggage cussed out what one of them repeatedly referred to as damn Amtrak. I talked to the dispatcher and learned that the Broadway wasn't For Boarding Only or for And Beyond but was scheduled for a Discharging and Boarding stop every fifty feet or so, twenty hours from New York to Chicago. ("Washington–Chicago service is temporarily suspended.") "Does it run late much?" "It always runs late." "How late?" "Two–three hours, depending on the weather and the track and the traffic and the equipment."

On the enchanted Water Level Route – "The Twentieth Century Limited Coming Down the Hudson," and I reading Rip Van Winkle to my enchanted children – there was likewise one train left, another mockery of one of the great Name Trains gone, this one the Lake Shore Limited. The new Lake Shore was a lulu. Where the Broadway still served a small portion of the through traffic between New York and Chicago, reaching Chicago at 9:05 A.M. (though it had to leave Penn Station in early afternoon to do it), the Lake Shore did not even pretend to provide long-distance service: It left Grand Central at 6:45 P.M. Eastern Time and, with a tail wind, reached Chicago at 3:10 P.M. Central Time the next day – twenty-three hours and twenty-five minutes to make the Century's sixteen-hour run, stopping everywhere but Englewood.

When Susan and I sat on the baggage wagon, watching the Rock Island suburban trains pull out, one after another, for Morgan Park ("Need mother know?"), the *Railway Guide* was a massive volume of maybe a thousand pages. A puny affair nowadays, it lists Englewood as a Rock Island suburban stop, but the Rock Island doesn't stop there. Nothing stops there.

:

A while back I got on the 'phone between detestable planes at the detestable airport in Chicago and tried to find out something, anything, about Englewood. It wasn't in the 'phone book, and the 'phone company had no number for it. Nobody I could raise at Amtrak, the Chicago Union Station, *or* the Rock Island knew where it was or whether it still existed. And then I got on to the Customer Information Service of Conrail, the consolidated rail freight line. "Never heard of it, myself," said Customer Information Service amiably, "but I've only been here six years. I'll ask some of the old-timers around the place. Call me back." I called him back: "You're right," he said, "there was a station at 63rd Street, but they stopped using it years ago, nobody remembers just when. It's sort of a mess out there – seems they had a fire, maybe five, ten years ago and the ceiling caved in. But nobody's been there lately. It's not a real good part of town to go to, even in the daytime – you know what I mean?"

Oh, but it was, it was, it was a real good part of town to go to, even in the daytime.

But it has been a long time. I moved away twenty-seven years ago and I've lived a lot of places. *The University of Chicago Magazine* – alumni magazine – has followed me around and I've always gone through it, with progressively decreasing attention to the front and progressively increasing attention to the back: John Howe used to say that he opened *The Times* to the obits every morning to see if he was in them. (And one day he was.) Chicago is a relatively young institution, established in 1892, and for many years there was room in the Class Notes at the back of the magazine for a little something about anybody who did anything (such as die). No more; too many alumni – or, more exactly, too many alumni dying. So under each year's Class Notes, at the end, there is simply a section called Deaths, with the names.

And there, under Class of '29, was Susan Bennecke Shoe-maker.

I was still going to the Englewood Station, the Englewood *Union Station*, years and years after the Freshman Mixer, taking all four of my kids there of a late Sunday afternoon to see the Limiteds, always fewer, pulling out for And Beyond. I told them about all the great Name Trains, and how it all (or almost all) was when I was – . When I was.

Once I was out there with Little Amanda, she was four, maybe, maybe three-going-on, and it was getting on for the end of the Englewood Station altogether, and there wasn't much to see any more. It was getting dark and late and the spooky platform lights came on and we had to go home – mother need know – and a switch engine came lumbering by and Amanda said, "It forgot its train."

: : : *The Tomb* : : :

The next best thing to eternal salvation is temporal salvation, and you can't blame a man in the prime of life, or a little past, for wondering what he might do for himself in case of nuclear war. I'd spent some time wondering lately, until I saw a headline in the local paper: "County Man Builds A-Bomb Shelter." The second paragraph of the story went like this:

Eager to share his experience in building a shelter for protection from nuclear blast and fallout, yet reluctant to pinpoint the location of the shelter, its owner declined to be named. In event of nuclear attack, or even panic due to rumor, he does not wish his family shelter mobbed by persons less well prepared.

Within an hour and a half – never mind how – I had the name and address of the man with the shelter. It was Henry T. Babcock, and he lived about two miles away from me. Professor Edward Teller, the "Father of the H-Bomb," says that there should be a shelter for everybody within ten minutes' walk. (I used to be a miler, took a third for Englewood High in the City Meet in 1925, and there's nothing to keep a man of my age from getting back into trim.) I tossed little Dicken into the car, got in myself, fastened the safety belt, and drove over to Babcock's without ceremony. Babcock and I were acquaintances, as people are in small towns, but just acquaintances. I knew he was scientifically trained and a successful, respected practitioner of his profession. Nice fellow. We didn't meet at the same parties, but, then, I don't get out much any more.

He was working in the garden, and he said he was glad to see me, and I said I was interested in his bomb shelter. "Everybody is," he said. "There doesn't seem to be any way to keep it quiet."

From *The Progressive*, September 1961.

"I guess it's the only one in the County," I said.

"I guess so," said Babcock. "I've asked Civil Defense, but they don't know. They don't know anything. I've been trying to get a Geiger counter from them for the past three years. I've got a ten-year-old counter, and I don't know if it's any good. Now that I think of it, I'd better put it down in the shelter. That's where you're supposed to keep it."

"You'd think other people would build shelters," I said.

"You would," said Babcock, "but you know how people are. They just don't want to think about it. But it stands to reason that there will be war. There always has been."

"I suppose the cost is a problem," I said.

"I suppose so," said Babcock. "It cost me four-thousand-some dollars just for a hole in the ground."

"You could have a nice swimming pool for that," I said.

"You can say that again," said Babcock, but I didn't. I was beginning to think that Babcock wasn't completely happy about the whole thing, though I couldn't see why. Here was his family – nice fellow, nice wife, three nice children – nicely sheltered from nuclear attack. But it's as Babcock himself said: "It's like insurance. If you have it, you don't need it. If you need it, you don't have it."

"Well, you've got it," I said.

"Well, I guess so," said Babcock. "But there are problems, lots of problems."

"You bet there are," I said.

Babcock excused himself to get the old Geiger counter and a pick, which he said he thought he might as well put down there because he had no use for it in the house and you're supposed to have some tools in the shelter. Dicken and I were left in the living room. The house was one of those new ranch-style affairs with merging "areas" instead of rooms. There were no bookshelves visible, but the coffee table had a book on it, dealing with Babcock's profession, and several copies of *Life*, *Time*, and *Reader's Digest*. Our host returned with the pick and the Geiger counter and said, "Well, let's go." We followed him out of the house and across the yard in the rear.

"I should have built it under the house," said Babcock thoughtfully, as we crossed the yard.

"Did you build it yourself?" I said.

"No," said Babcock, "it was built by a contractor."

"But you designed it," I said.

"No," said Babcock, "we had the architect of the house design it."

The shelter was about forty feet from the house (which was made of wood) and ten feet from the wooden two-car garage. There were three protrusions from the ground, an air-intake pipe (capped with a filter), an air-exhaust pipe, and a tilted entrance hatch. The intake was about five feet from the wooden fence surrounding the house and garage, and the exhaust was surrounded by a large pile of kindling. "Well," said Babcock, "this is what it looks like from the outside. Here," pointing to the capped intake, "is where the air goes in. We draw it in with a blower in the shelter."

"What if the fence was on fire?" I said.

"What if what?"

"What if the fence was on fire, or the garage, or the kindling?"

"Oh," said Babcock. "Yes. That would be bad. We'd be drawing the smoke right down into the shelter. That would be bad."

"What's the kindling around the vent for?" I said.

"That's just our kindling pile," said Babcock. Then he said, "I suppose I ought to move it away, but there's so darned much to do all the time."

"Of course," I said, "if you had a real fire storm above ground, with everything burning, I suppose the fire would suck the oxygen right out of the shelter. That's what happened in the ten-night raid on Hamburg." "Is it?" said Babcock. "Yes," I said. "The people in the shelters were asphyxiated." "That would be bad, all right," said Babcock.

We went over to the iron hatch-lid set in concrete. It took a lot of lifting. "Pretty sturdy," I said. "Yes," said Babcock, "pretty sturdy." The lid had a heavy hasp for a padlock on the outside, but there was no padlock. I asked if the hatch could be locked from the inside, and Babcock said it couldn't be. I thought about this and said, "Then the whole town could follow you into the shelter, couldn't it?"

"Well," said Babcock, "that's a problem, all right. Of course, there's an inside lock on the door at the bottom of the stairs. Once we got into the shelter itself, we could lock ourselves in."

"Then somebody might snap a lock on the hatch from the outside," I said, adding, "but nobody would do that."

"I hope not," said Babcock.

"Of course," I said, "you couldn't let *everyone* in."

"No," said Babcock, "there's just room for Nettie and me and the kids. It's not much more than a five-man shelter, really."

"I suppose you might have to stand off some of the people who wanted in," I said. "You know how people are," I added.

"Well, that's a problem," said Babcock. "Everybody would want to get in. I don't know what we'd do about that. One fellow said I'd need a gun."

"It might take a lot of shooting," I said. Babcock didn't say anything for a bit, and then he said, "The trouble is, you can't figure out everything."

"You can say that again," I said.

The inside of the hatch-lid was lined with sponge, and I asked Babcock why. "Well," he said, frowning, "theoretically it's to keep the lid from sweating. He emphasized the "theoretically." The wooden stairs to the floor of the shelter were steep but the stairway had an iron handrail. I was surprised to learn that the roof of the shelter was covered by only three feet of earth, but Babcock explained that the deeper you dig the more it costs. With its seven-foot ceiling, and its foot-thick floor, the bottom of the hole was eleven feet nine inches deep. (The roof was nine inches thick.) The construction was all steel-reinforced concrete except for the hatch-lid, the stairs, and the door at the bottom of the stairs. At the foot of the stairs was a 180-degree turn to the shelter door. Babcock said that

that was the only idea he had ever been able to get from Civil Defense, and that every time he ever tried to find out anything from Civil Defense he ran into a stone wall of red tape. Whatever else made him unhappy, there was no doubt about Civil Defense. But there seemed to be something more than Civil Defense weighing on him. The local paper had described him as eager to share his experience; I found him willing rather than eager. His manner was that of a real estate agent showing a property he'd just as soon the client didn't buy.

"What was Civil Defense's idea about the 180-degree turn?" I said. "Well," he said, "the radioactivity is supposed to travel in straight lines, so it can't turn the corner. I suppose that's so," he added. I thought that was interesting and said so. Babcock said nothing.

The door of the shelter itself was made of wood, with steel trim. I opened and closed it a few times and asked if it was airtight. "I don't know," said Babcock. "It's snug, but I guess you wouldn't call it airtight." "I was just wondering," I said. I was just wondering about poison gas, and whether bacteria, once you took them off the leash, would turn 180-degree corners.

I don't know why, but I had thought that the shelter would consist of two or three rooms, at least. It consisted of one clammy concrete bunker eight by ten feet. Very clammy. My host began mopping up the dew with small bags scattered around the floor. "They're filled with chemicals," he said. "They're supposed to absorb the moisture, and then you bake them out in the oven." I said they didn't seem to work too well, and he said No, they didn't. He'd heard there was some cans of stuff that worked better, but he didn't know what it was called or where you got it.

The decor of the shelter was simplicity itself. There was one naked light, shelves of tinned and packaged food, a bunk spring (without legs) leaning upright against the wall, a plastic garbage can, a slender cylinder of oxygen about two feet tall and six inches in diameter, and one metal cleat in the ceiling. And, of course, the Geiger counter and the pick. Nothing else.

The Tomb : 39

No furniture of any kind, no hooks or hangers (or clothes to put on them), no copies of *Life* or *Time* or the *Reader's Digest*.

I asked Babcock how long he figured they might be down there. "You mean," he said, "in case of———?" "Yes," I said, "in case of———." "There doesn't seem to be any way to find out. Some people say weeks, and some say months, so you don't really know. It's a problem." I agreed that it was and asked him how the family planned to occupy itself in the shelter in case of———. Babcock said they hadn't really thought about that. I asked him how he'd know when to come out. "You mean – afterward?" he said. "Yes – afterward," I said. "Well," said Babcock, "we've got a plug-in here for a portable radio, if we remember to bring it down when we come, and an antenna up through the vent." "So, then," I said, "you'd find out over the radio." "If we remember to bring it down," he said again, and then, "I guess we'd find out that way, un-less———" "Unless———?" I said. "Well," he said, "unless the station is knocked out, or the current goes off. Of course," he added, "we've got this old Geiger counter, if it works, but we'd have to go outside to use it, so I don't know what we'd do about that. I guess it isn't much use, when you come to think of it."

"And where," I said, "is the Gents' Room?" "There," said Babcock, indicating the plastic garbage can, which was four feet tall. "And the garbage can?" I said. "There," said Babcock, indicating the plastic garbage can. I thought that the place ought to be pretty spicy after a week or so, and Babcock said, "The CD literature says to have a chemical toilet, but I can't find out where to buy one or how to build one. And I'm afraid to use chlorine, in case the fumes are poisonous. So we got this plastic garbage can. But we haven't been able to figure out———"

By way of changing the subject, I asked him what the single cleat in the ceiling was for. He said, "We thought we could get those cleats into the walls, to hang the bunks on, but for some reason we couldn't," and he pointed to the pockmarks in the concrete. "This is the only one we could get to stay in, so we haven't been able to put up the bunks." I said that the concrete must be pretty hard, and he said that I could say that again.

I asked him about the food, and he said that that was a problem. "The trouble is," he said, "that it spoils. Rust. I guess it's the damp, or something. I opened a can of tomato juice a while back, and it was spoiled. Somebody said you should rotate the food every two years." "Every year," said his little boy, who was with us. "Every year," said Babcock. "Here," he said to his little boy, handing him a can, "take this spaghetti up to the house, and we'll have it for lunch." "Every year," said the little boy, going out with the spaghetti.

Besides the canned and packaged foods, there were twenty-four beer-sized cans of water for a family of five. I asked Babcock if he thought it was enough. "I guess not," he said. "I ought to get some more. Of course it depends on how long———" "But," he went on, "we have some other stuff to drink," and he pointed to maybe a dozen cans in all of ginger ale, root beer, and juices, and two bottles each of king-size Coca-Cola and Seven-Up. He said they had instant coffee, too, and he thought they had a hot plate somewhere. "I guess we'd have to drink it cold, if the current went off," he said.

I asked him what they would do for light if the current went off. "Well," he said, "I don't know, exactly. If the current goes off, we've got this flashlight, of course." He showed me the flashlight, of the sort that burns out in a night. I asked him about candles. "I don't think they'd do," he said, "they'd use up the oxygen." "But you'd be getting fresh air through the blower," I said, "so you'd be all right." "Well," said Babcock, "that's the biggest problem, I guess you might say. As long as the current is on, the blower works fine." He turned it on. It worked fine, but it roared. "It's a little noisy," said Babcock, "on account of the concrete, I suppose. But you can see for yourself, it works fine. The trouble is, it might be drawing the radioactive particles right in through the filter from outside. I haven't been able to find out if the filter would keep them out. Another thing is that you're supposed to change the filter, but you'd have to go outside to do that." At this point, he seemed to become thoughtful, and so did I.

"And if the current goes off?" I asked. "Oh," said Babcock, brightening, "you can operate the blower with the hand crank. Here, try it." I tried it, for twenty to thirty seconds, and it nearly broke my arm. "It goes a little hard," said Babcock. "I guess we'd have to do it in shifts if we were going to do it all the time. Of course it depends on how long———" "And," I said, "on whether the filter was drawing radioactive particles in, or napalm, or gas. They" – I meant the Russians – "might use napalm, or gas."

"Gas," said Babcock, without any tone or emphasis. "If they use gas and we use the air pump, I guess we've had it." Neither of us said anything, and then Babcock said, "You know, I guess the pump isn't really much use, except the blower part, to circulate the air you've already got." Neither of us said anything again, and then Babcock said, "We might be better off to depend entirely on the oxygen tank," and we walked over to the tank, which was as I've said, a cylinder about six inches in circumference and two feet tall. "How much oxygen is there in it?" I said, thinking of his scientific training. He looked at the tag on the cylinder. "I don't really know," he said.

"They give you a formula to calculate – by the cubic feet and number of persons and so on – but I haven't had a chance to calculate the formula, there's so darned much to do. The darned thing's on my desk in the house. It's pretty complicated." I asked him what it said on the tag. "It says two thousand pounds pressure," he said, "but I don't know what that means. If I knew the *weight*," and he turned the tag over. It was blank. I asked him if he had any idea how long it would last in case———. He shook his head and said, "Several days, maybe. I don't really know. I ought to calculate that formula." He shook his head slowly and said, "My wife's a chain smoker. I guess that affects it, too."

It wasn't getting any warmer in the shelter, and I asked

Babcock what they'd do for heat in case————. Babcock said that would be a problem, he guessed, but an old Navy man told him that with enough bodies down there it would be warm enough. I said, "Of course, there's such a thing as too much heat in a shelter. The people in those deep shelters in Hamburg died of asphyxiation, but their bodies were charred from the heat above the ground."

Babcock was frowning, and there didn't seem to be anything more to say or to see, and we went on up and out into the summer day. "It's nice outside," said Babcock. "It will be nice to come out after————" I said. "I don't know," said Babcock, "I just don't know. It's a problem." "*It's* a problem?" I said. Babcock nodded. "Food and water," he said, "what if they're contaminated?" "And air," I said. "Air," said Babcock. "And people," I said. "I suppose," I went on, "that you'll have to keep away from contaminated people." Babcock nodded and said, "But maybe they won't keep away from you." "Well," I said, in a tone with which I might have slapped another man on the back, "keeping away from contaminated people has always been a problem, socially." He was still frowning.

If I had to put an adjective to Babcock, I suppose it would be "apathetic." He had certainly lost interest in the shelter. (Had he ever had any?) But there was something more than apathy there. I seemed to be making him actually miserable by asking him the questions that anyone would ask about it. He had done his duty by showing me the shelter; he had done his duty by building it; but doing his duty appeared to have touched him with a deep melancholy. Even when he said, "It's nice outside," he said it without much zest.

We stood there in the summer day and said good-bye, and he said, "If there's anything else you'd like to————" and I was still trying to figure out how he felt. Babcock's trouble is that he doesn't want to die and he knows he's going to die and where he's going to die and where he's going to be buried.

I put Dicken into the car and got in myself and fastened my safety belt, and we started home. Now Dicken may not think a lot – it's hard to tell – but he doesn't say much. He didn't say much on the way home. He didn't say anything until I asked him what he thought about it, and then he said, "It's a tomb, if you ask me." "You can say that again," I said, and Dicken said, "It's a tomb, if you ask me."

: : : *In the Swim* : : :

My club has a great swimming pool, with six wide lanes separated by floats. Each wide lane is divided by a bottom-stripe so that two clubfellows, with a little mutual consideration, can swim laps in one lane. My club, this spring, is the University of Louisville, in Kentucky.

Now, Louisville is a border town, for all its magnolias. We got rich in Louisville (pronounced "Lou-uh-vil," the only two-and-a-half-syllable word in the English language) by doing business with the Nawth'n armies, distilling whiskey, curing tobacco, and racing hosses. Right nice town, maybe the country's nicest. But a border town.

We border people don't know what to do about the Nigras. Can't lynch 'em, 'cause we're Nawth'nrs. Can't mix with 'em, 'cause we're South'nrs. So we give 'em the snowbank treatment. Kind of stay away from them, and they kind of stay away from us, from our churches and our schools and our clubs, and, yes-ma'am, our cemeteries. They know which side of town to live on, and so do we. Wouldn't of had no trouble with busing – *we're* not shanty Irish like the Boston people – if it hadn't been that we're neither Nawth'n nor South'n but border. Uneasy.

The University of Louisville doesn't discriminate, but, the way things are, and Kentucky being something like forty-ninth in per capita expenditure on education, the Nigras don't much make it to the university. They're about 10 percent of our student body (110 percent of the basketball team). Quite a few of them at my club, in the locker room, but almost none in the pool; you know how it is – young Nigras never had much of a place to learn to swim before.

My club is crowded, and it is usually two to a lane. The

From *The Progressive*, June 1977.

other day each of the six lanes had two swimmers in it, so I jumped into the handiest. Its two occupants were one white and one Nigra – the only Nigra in the pool. It's a little tricky with three in a lane, but pretty soon the other honky got out and then there were two of us, the Nigra and I. But not for long.

Another Nigra entered the natatorium, looked around, saw that each lane had two swimmers – and jumped into ours. Two Nigras, one honky. And then two more Nigras entered the natatorium, looked around, saw that each lane had two swimmers except ours, which had two Nigras and one honky – and jumped into ours.

Why did they jump into ours, or, perhaps more suggestively, why did they *have to* jump into ours? (Why did *both of them* have to jump into ours?)

Five swimmers in one lane isn't impossible. Only almost.

Meanwhile, as one clubfellow in one of the other five lanes got out of the pool, a newcomer got in. The population held steady, two each in each of the five lanes, five in the sixth.

And then, in the lane next to ours, one of the swimmers got out, and nobody got in.

If one of the five of us in our lane had gone over to that one, it would have been two in that one and four in ours. Or if two of us had gone over, it would have been three in each.

None of my four Nigra clubfellows went over.

Neither did I.

I reckon – Ah reckon – I understand why *they* didn't. Our lane was their ghetto, their aqueous turf. They hadn't planned it that way, anymore than they had planned to live on the west side of town. But there they were, and so it was theirs.

But why didn't I, then? It wasn't *my* turf. But, like them, I hadn't planned to swim there or carved out that lane for my own. I was there, and so it was mine and anybody else's who got in it, all clubfellows being created equal.

They wanted me to get out of their lane – or did they? I didn't know. If I'd known, I'd have got; that one's easy, all the easier because the five of us were having a hard time swimming and I'd have relieved them and myself of some of the congestion. But I didn't know.

Maybe they wanted me to go, but if I'd gone they'd still have supposed it was because I didn't want to swim with Nigras. Maybe they didn't want me to go, and if I'd gone they'd have been sure it was because I didn't want to swim with Nigras.

So I couldn't go, and none of the four of them went, and the five of us swam in that lane like the dead in the famous old Jewish cemetery in Prague, who, for want of any other place to be buried, had to be buried in layers. Only ours, at my club, was an interracial ghetto.

I couldn't go over to the next lane because (a) I was afraid they were racists and/or (b) I was afraid that they would take me for a racist. Maybe they weren't thinking about it at all, or about me, or about anything in particular. I didn't know. I reckon – Ah reckon – I never will.

A Man with a Country

: : : : : : : : : : : : : : : :

: : : *The Trouble with the ACLU* : : :

I grow – if grow may be said of a biodegradable man – I grow daily more desperate as I see my own, my native land trampled into the dust under the hooves of the four horsemen of the age – capitalism, racism, nationalism, and war. Nor do I see salvation in either my fellow Americans or in the American Civil Liberties Union.

As for my fellow Americans, they live, a comfortable majority of them, in nice – that is, Jim Crow – neighborhoods or, better yet, in Jim Crow towns like Carmel, California (where I live), from which non-Caucasians do not need to be excluded by statute or subterfuge as long as they can be excluded by poverty inflicted by prior racism. Most of them voluntarily pay their income tax, the preponderance of which is used for past, present, and future genocide. More and more of them spend their last days fallen among lawyers and racing between the bank and the bucket shop trying to maximize their unearned increment. When they are not ossifying in front of the television set, they idle away their leisure eating, drinking, and writing to Dear Abby to find out why they aren't merry.

So much for my fellow Americans – always excepting thee and me – and by way of biting the hand that feeds me a buffet lunch, I am tempted to say so much for the ACLU.

What is wanted in these parlous, perilous times, is equal justice. The ACLU is not interested in equal justice. The ACLU is interested in equal justice *under law.*

But all the most execrable and epidemic injustices are constitutional. As constitutions go, the American is a pretty good one. But so was the Weimar, under which the Nazis came to power. So was the Masaryk constitution under which the Communists came to power in Czechoslovakia.

From *The Progressive*, February 1980.

There is no constitution, however valiantly defended, which will sustain the liberties presently trampled by the four horsemen. Our own is valiantly defended by the ACLU, but the horsemen laugh at courtrooms. On occasion – and with laudably increasing frequency – the ACLU turns its attention from the courtroom to the legislative chamber and does what it can to forestall the enactment of a bad law or to overturn one. But as long as the bad law is on the books, the defense of the Constitution requires the citizen – the sovereign citizen, mind you – to perform the bad actions the bad law commands or abstain from the good actions the bad law forbids. In so far as the four horsemen are encased in the armor of the Constitution, they are untouchable.

Nationalism, for instance, is no proper business of a national organization interested in equal justice under national law. But nationalism is a monstrosity – an archaic monstrosity at that – which asserts the particular welfare of the tribe over the general welfare of the race. Nationalism, recognizing no authority but its own, sets every tribe against every other in perpetual warfare in the tribal, or national, interest. It permits alliance but not community and truce but not peace.

So, too, war, the full flower of nationalism, consuming the tribal substance along with the lives, the fortunes, and the sacred honor of every citizen of every nation. As long as American law refuses to put an end to American aggression in Indochina or to proclaim the self-evident illegality of an undeclared war in Korea, the ACLU is helpless to say a mumbling word. It can maintain the soldier's right to wear his hair long; it can not maintain his right not to be a soldier and kill as many of his fellow-men who have never offended him as he possibly can.

The same Constitution which legitimates nationalism and war – the twin monstrosities which condemn the tribes to fight to the death – this same Constitution permits and prospers the consummate abomination of capitalism, pitting man against man out of the tribe and in it. Aristotle tells of the stranger in Athens who was asked what country he belonged to and replied, "I am one of the rich." Every man against every other and each against all, one eating four meals a day while another eats two, or none.

Impotent, irrelevant, the Constitution, and, if the Constitution, the ACLU, when within two weeks of each other the Christian John Paul and the Communist Castro rise on the same platform in the great metropolis of the nation which consumes 40 percent of the world's produce and plead with the rich to share with the poor. Never a mumbling word from the Constitution; only the *tu-quoque*, or you-too, alibi that socialism perverted in Russia is as heinous as capitalism pure in America.

So, too, in so far as we represent an organization operating *under law*, are we members of the ACLU incapable of any least action against the ageless atrocity of racism unless and until the law does not forbid it.

The lovers of liberty – the ACLU foremost among them – cheered when *Brown* v. *Topeka* permitted them at last to exercise the right of free association. But they had had to wait fifty-eight years after the inhumane separate-but-equal decision in 1896 until, at longest last, the juridical wind blew fair instead of foul.

The Constitution is the law, but the law is what the judges say it is. And, as Robert Hutchins observed, what the judges say it is may depend on what they had for breakfast. If, like the Germans of the 1930s, we are law-abiding citizens, we are at the mercy of good and bad legislators who make the laws, of good and bad judges who interpret them, and of good and bad executives who enforce them.

It is "in vain," says Justice Story, in his classic *Commentaries*, "to oppose Constitutional barriers to the impulse of self-preservation." Confronted with the claim of national security, the courts are loath to challenge the emergency powers granted the executive by the legislature in time of war or impending war. In these marvelous days of the black box and the red button, the national security is ever more clamant and the national emergency ever more instantaneous: As the technology of "first-strike capability" proceeds, we may look to ever greater incursions on our liberties in the name of survival of the tribe at the expense of its members.

:

I need hardly remind the survivors of the Nixon Administration of the three terrible years in which the writ of *habeas corpus* – the most sacred of secular liberties – was in suspension in this country by virtue of the President's arrant exercise of executive privilege. This unconscionable act of a President who exalted liberty at every oratorical turn was performed under wartime emergency in the year 1863 and was not nullified by the courts until 1866 – two years after the American Civil War was over.

Nor need I remind a post-Nixon audience of the so-called wartime emergency in which a supine Supreme Court foreclosed freedom of speech in an opinion which held that "when a nation is at war many things that might be said in time of peace are such a hindrance to its effort that these utterances will not be endured so long as men fight and no court could regard them as protected by any constitutional right. . . . Conviction affirmed." This opinion of this supine Court was not delivered by a Nixon appointee. It was delivered by Justice Oliver Wendell Holmes in *Schenk* v. *The United States* at the time of the first World War.

Neither need I remind my fellow-Californians of the Supreme Court decision that "compulsory exclusion of large groups of citizens from their homes, except under circumstances of direct emergency and peril, is inconsistent with our basic governmental institutions. But when under conditions of modern warfare our shores are threatened by hostile forces, the power to protect must be commensurate with the threatened danger. . . . Conviction affirmed." That, of course, was the Court's decision flouting due process *and* equal protection in upholding the military seizure, in March 1942, of 110,000 of our unoffending Japanese-descended neighbors and their deportation into what the dissenting minority of the Court called concentration camps. The opinion of the Court – *Kore-*

matsu v. *The United States* – was not written by one of the "nine old men" of the Harding-Coolidge-Hoover era – it was written by Justice Hugo L. Black.

Black, Holmes, Lincoln (he of the *habeas corpus* suspension): If there have been three paladins of the rights of man, three watchdogs of American liberties since the storied days of Jefferson, it is these three. But it was precisely these three watchdogs who were prepared to strike down those rights and liberties in the name of the war-making State.

Who – as the Romans used to say in their broken English – who will watch the watchdogs? In the last resort, only the American Civil Liberties Union. We may be sure that the ACLU, had it existed in 1863 and 1917, would have tackled Lincoln and Holmes on behalf of the supposed traitors of the day just as, when nobody else would, it tackled its great friend, Hugo Black.

I have deplored the nonfeasance of the ACLU with regard to the four transcendent, but Constitutional, evils of nationalism, racism, capitalism, and war. Now, in the light of the melancholy conduct, not of a Nixon or a Nixon court but of men like Lincoln, Holmes, and Black, I begin to understand that nonfeasance. The American Civil Liberties Union has been busy not about other things but about one other thing. While the rest of us are running around like heads with our chickens chopped off, the ACLU is sleeplessly minding the American store whose stock in trade is liberty – not the liberty of the Junior Chamber of Commerce Young Man of the Year, who is not in jeopardy, but the liberty of the unpopular and the obnoxious, of the depreciated and the disadvantaged.

It is the single and singular mission of the ACLU – a mission that is usually thankless and often detested – to make the liberties of the least among us as secure as liberty can be made under law. Right now, the ACLU is in court in Carson City, along with the Episcopal bishop of Nevada, challenging the constitutionality of the death penalty on behalf of a convicted murderer. This hand-to-mouth organization commands the unpaid services of the genuinely best and brightest men and

The Trouble with the ACLU : 55

women of the bar all across the country. But its extraordinary effectiveness lies, I think, in its steadfast single-mindedness – a single-mindedness which always makes me think of the last line of a gospel hymn called "The St. James Infirmary": "Put a twenty-dollar gold piece on my watch chain, so the boys will know I died standing pat."

:

The ACLU stands pat. It stood pat thirty-five years ago in the landmark *Terminiello* case in Chicago to support free speech for fascists, and it stood pat two years ago in Skokie when it supported freedom of assembly for Nazis and, in doing so, lost almost half of its financial support in Illinois. It stood, and stands, and will stand pat for freedom of speech and assembly and the press for Communists in the United States and (with some logistical difficulty) for anti-Communists in the Soviet Union. It has supported blacks against whites and whites against blacks; unions against bosses and bosses against unions; citizens against police and police against citizens; poor against rich and, yes, rich against poor. But going wherever its single-minded mission calls it, it has usually found itself on the side of those who have nobody else on their side, the publicans and sinners, the rejected, the desolate, and the dispossessed.

This habitual association with the unloved or forgotten of the world suggests to me, and to my amazement, a profoundly religious, and a profoundly Christian, wellspring in a rigorously secular institution.

After all these decades of unrelenting struggle to maintain the separation of church and state, what a shock it would be to the ACLU to discover that it itself is a church, moved to care for the uncared-for by a power which exceeds its nature and ours.

This organization may be mistaken for a church. There is no danger of its being mistaken for a state. In season and out it carries the fight to City Hall and endures the contumely of all those upright persons and personages who seem to believe that there would be no hell if the ACLU didn't raise it, no trouble if the trouble-makers didn't make it.

56 : *A Man with a Country*

These do be parlous times, parlous unto tindrous. So far is the peculiarly American commitment to progress from being axiomatic, it is not even spoken of any more. Our fondest hope is that things will grow worse no faster than they are growing worse now.

But here and there a good sign is seen. A little headway has been made, if not against nationalism, capitalism, and war, against racism in this, the homeland of racism. And while it is true, thanks in part to free-enterprise television, that our society is plunging headlong from literacy to illiteracy – another first in human history – it is also true that recently the denizens of Elk City, Oklahoma, could, and some of them did, see and hear James Earl Jones in his public television portrayal of the magnificent life of Paul Robeson.

And along with the sweep of hedonistic materialism, the material insecurity of our old and our ill and our poor has been slightly, if only slightly, alleviated by national insurance. There have been other small gains and wavering intimations that the rising generation may yet fool us by turning out better than we are, just as we fooled our elders by turning out worse than they were. The end, in a word, is not yet.

:

Civil liberties do not civilize a society; the Bill of Rights was amended into the Constitution and it can be amended out. What civilizes society is the determination above all else to be civilized. It is not too late – it is never too late – to hope that ours will one day be such a society and once again be, as it once was, a beacon to mankind.

When, and if, it is, it will surely be because the example of a very few single-minded Americans from generation to generation perpetuated the singular heritage of liberty passionately prized – a heritage whose very existence once struck tyranny into the hearts of tyrants everywhere and raised the hopes of a suffering and sorrowing world.

: : : *Pledge in Pomona* : : :

Like 16,811 other American cities of less than 50,000 pop., Pomona, California, is known as The City of Churches. And no wonder; it has fifty-two of them, or one for every 730.77 Pomonans. It is also the Site of the New $50,000,000 Home of the Convair Guided Missile Division of the Consolidated Vultee Aircraft Corporation. Everything holy and profane that man can do to protect Pomona has been done. And yet there is fear in Pomona.

One evening recently I was scheduled to speak at Pomona's Junior High School on "The Struggle for Europe." On the platform with me, as panel discussants, were Professor Albert Britt of Scripps College; Professor Philip Merlan of Claremont Graduate School; and Mr. Herbert Tay, the Junior High School history teacher. There was also, as chairman of the meeting, Ferner Nuhn, distinguished authority on American culture. On the platform, also, was an American flag. Admission to the meeting was free. An offering would be taken for the work of the American Friends Service Committee, whose work, in small part, consists of sponsoring such meetings in the interest of peace.

A goodly crowd, around three hundred, was there. But the auditorium seats eight hundred, and the crowd was too thinly scattered for that pleasant packed-in sense that goes, on both sides of the apron, with a full house. But the brightly lighted auditorium disclosed a few people at the far sides, both front and back. Mr. Nuhn opened the meeting. Or tried to.

No sooner had Mr. Nuhn said, "It is my pleasure, this evening, to welcome – " when a man at the right side, in the front row, called out, "Let's all take the pledge to the American flag."

From *The Progressive*, January 1953.

Mr. Nuhn said, "I beg your pardon, sir, but you are out of ———" and a man at the left side, in the back row, called out, "Come on, everybody, take the pledge of allegiance."

And then, when Mr. Nuhn said, "I beg your ———" a man at the left side, in front, called out, "Everybody who isn't a Communist get up and take the pledge to the flag," and then a man at the right side, in back, called out, "Don't be afraid of the Commies, folks – get up."

"I'm sorry," said Mr. Nuhn, the distinguished authority on American culture, "but ———"

"Come on, everybody," an elderly man in the middle called out, "we're not Commies in Pomona."

"Please ———" said Mr. Nuhn, in his cultured American manner.

"Ah, come on," one of the earlier callers in front called out, and at the same time, another of the earlier callers in back called out, "Let's go, Americans – the pledge to the flag," and then still another of the earlier callers, with an overseas cap tucked into the shoulder strap of his army shirt, went to the front, faced the audience, and started reciting the pledge of allegiance to the flag, with his right hand over his heart.

Mr. Nuhn sat down. The other four of us on the platform were already sitting.

When the man with the overseas cap began reciting the pledge, perhaps twenty persons, of the three hundred in the auditorium, stood up to recite it with him. As the recitation proceeded, others got to their feet, slowly, in ones and twos and threes, and joined in. A few, at first, and then more and more, but ever more slowly, all over the auditorium. By the time the recitation ended, there were not more than twenty persons, of the three hundred in the hall, who were still in their seats. The five men on the platform, including me, were still in their seats at the end, too.

I don't know about the other four – and I haven't seen them since – but my heart failed me for fear. I doubt that I could have got to my feet if I'd wanted to, I was that afraid. I knew that the people who had got up were afraid; that was clear, not only from the way they stood up, but also from the way they sat down, just as slowly, at the end. But I hadn't suspected how afraid – how unprepared – I would be to do what was right the first time in my life I ever had to do what was right in the presence of fear all around me.

:

I was the reason for the outbreak and its prime object. At a meeting in Syracuse, New York, in 1947 I had said that some of the people who oppose world government believed that the advocates of world government wanted to defile the American flag. A local newspaper reported that it was *I* who advocated defiling the flag. Although the newspaper subsequently published the finding by the district attorney that I had been misquoted, the canard kept appearing in (and only in, as far as I know) Southern California.

The evening preceding Pomona, at a similar meeting in a Pasadena church, people outside the church distributed handbills reading, "Milton Mayer said: 'HAUL DOWN THE AMERICAN FLAG . . . HAUL IT DOWN, STAMP ON IT, AND SPIT ON IT!' This man is a subversive sponsored by a subversive organization, the American Friends Service Committee. WHY is he allowed to speak in a Christian Church or Public School?" The cards were signed, "KEEP AMERICA COMMITTEE, BOX 3094, Los Angeles 54, Calif., H. W. Courtois, Sec'y." Outside the Pasadena meeting sample ballots also were distributed for the MacArthur-Tenney presidential ticket of Gerald L. K. Smith's Christian Nationalist party, along with copies of Smith's pamphlet entitled *Is Communism Jewish?*

The church in Pasadena had been filled. A lady in front – H. W. Courtois turned out also to be a lady, who was afraid if General Eisenhower were elected, Rabbi Silver of Cleveland would run the country – succeeded in diverting the discussion from the struggle for Europe to the honor of the American flag, but nothing serious had happened. I had been rattled a bit; the man on the platform is supposed to handle this sort of thing with an iron hand, and I am not the iron-handed type.

But the Pasadena meeting was never in danger of disruption. After all – Pasadena.

:

But Pomona, away out in the citrus groves, is a good bit spookier, by night at least, than Pasadena. Or so it seemed, while I sat in my seat, along with the other four men on the platform, and two hundred eighty of the three hundred people in that great big big brightly lighted auditorium took the pledge of allegiance to the American flag.

I didn't know, as I say, how the other four felt or whether, indeed, they would stay in their seats to the end. I was afraid to look at them. I was afraid not to look straight ahead at all those people in the auditorium with their right arms stretched out toward the flag on the platform. Ferner Nuhn, the chairman, was a Quaker; maybe he was prepared for what was happening, because Quakers are supposed to be prepared (according to an old engraving) to go on with their worship even when Indians with tomahawks break into the Meeting House. Professor Britt of Scripps, a small, spare, elderly man, had been president of Knox College, in Galesburg, Illinois; I didn't know about him. Professor Merlan of Claremont had a strong foreign accent; I didn't know about him, but I suspected that he might be a refugee and, like so many refugees, afraid of ever having to be a refugee again. Teacher Tay hadn't said much at dinner before the meeting, and the meeting was taking place in the very school where he was employed. Certainly the other four – except maybe Ferner Nuhn – hadn't bargained for trouble. But here trouble was.

What was the trouble?

What were the people in the auditorium – including those who had called for the pledge to the flag – afraid of? Why did a few, so widely scattered, call out so wildly, like people in a burning theatre, and why did the rest get up so submissively when these few called out, "Get up"? What was the matter? What was the matter in sunny Pomona, The City of Churches, Site of the New $50,000,000 Home of the Convair

Pledge in Pomona : *61*

Guided Missile Division of the Consolidated Vultee Aircraft Corporation? What was the matter – for that matter – in me?

The few who had called for the pledge appeared to be afraid of Communists; afraid of Communists in a land flowing with grapefruit juice and guided missiles. The many who had got up, reluctantly, appeared to be afraid of the few who were themselves afraid. If the many had remained in their seats, wouldn't fear have melted away in sunny Pomona, the fear that had seized both the few and the many, and from Pomona wouldn't fearlessness have spread through the land? Why were people afraid in, of all places, Pomona?

Why was I? Was I afraid of being hurt? I don't think so. I've been hurt before; it doesn't hurt much. Of being shamed in Pomona? I don't think so; I hadn't been shameful, and the world is wide. Of being thrown out into the street? What's that, when a man has, as I have, a clothesbrush? Of a general disturbance, with the police coming in? Why, they would protect me; "Pomona," says the Chamber of Commerce, "is virtually crime-free. Led by FBI-trained Chief Ralph E. Parker, one of the youngest and ablest police chiefs in the State, the Pomona Police Department has been recognized by the Federal Bureau of Investigation as. . . ."

What was it I was afraid of? Was it only because the man on the platform is naked, unhidden? I wondered – even in my fear – if Ferner Nuhn was afraid of American culture. *I* was. This was *my* country, *my* people, *my* home, rich and strong and not, like old Germany, stripped and impoverished. I was just back from Germany, where, when it happened there, beginning with the way it was happening here in Pomona, people said, "Oh, well – Germans." I was afraid of American culture.

But that was secondary, and I can't say I really thought of it while we five sat in our seats on the platform and the people below, their arms stretched out, palm upward, recited in unison the pledge to the flag. Primarily I was afraid because I felt fully, for the first time in my life, the power of fright over people of my own kind, of my own country and condition. In their capacity for fright, for being carried away from their reason and their training, I felt fully, for the first time in my life, my own. The bright lights of the auditorium didn't help; on the contrary, it seemed all the harder to hide. Congregation didn't help, either; all seemed to be adding their fright to the fright of each.

When the recitation of the pledge to the flag was finished, everybody sat slowly down. There was a quiet in the auditorium. Nobody, including those who had called for the pledge, knew what to do next – or rather, what was going to be done. But nameless anticipation was not the only ingredient of the quiet; there was catharsis, too. The fear had called out – to a flag, to be sure – and was quieted. Why? Weren't the five men on the platform, and the twenty below them in the auditorium, as dangerous now as before? They had refused to take the pledge, hadn't they? But they appeared – paradoxically enough – to be less dangerous, for the time. At least the meeting was allowed to proceed.

I wanted to address myself to "The Struggle for America," but I had been billed to discuss "The Struggle for Europe" and I discussed it. When I finished (to uncertain and mild applause), I was scheduled to call upon each of the panel discussants to discuss the discussion, and I did so.

Mr. Tay, the history teacher, discussed free enterprise, favorably, as the basis of American strength in the world. I didn't think I had discussed free enterprise, but Mr. Tay, who had not taken the pledge of allegiance, was a public school teacher in Pomona, in the very school where he had not taken the pledge. Mr. Tay was in a tight spot. I admired him.

Professor Britt of Scripps, the retired president of Knox College, did not discuss the struggle for Europe any more than Mr. Tay did. He discussed freedom of discussion, and the respect of every American for the freedom of every other, as the basis of America's strength. Very briefly, very sharply. Professor Britt seemed to surprise the audience; to me he simply revealed himself as one of those ordinary great Americans to whom the Americanism of the founding fathers is simply the natural state of human society.

Then Professor Merlan of Claremont rose to discuss the discussion. Now up to that point no one (at least, not I) had considered anti-Semitism as an element in the meeting. We should have, I suppose. And we most assuredly should have assumed anti-foreignism. When Professor Merlan stood up – uncertainly, I thought – I saw suddenly that this was the deadly moment. Professor Merlan was clearly a foreigner, and, I was sure, a Jew. Professor Merlan's spot was tight in the extreme.

"You must excuse me," said Professor Merlan, in an accent which frightened me all over again, "if I do not discuss Professor Mayer's analysis of the European situation except to say that, in general, I agree with it. I must discuss something else. I must discuss loyalty to America." He paused – again, I thought, uncertainly. The quiet in the hall was dreadful anticipation now, unmixed with relief. "Yes," he said, "I must discuss loyalty to America."

I heard him breathe a deep, uneven breath – he was almost next to me – and then say in his foreign accent: "I try to be loyal to America. I think I owe more to America and also to the people of America even than most of you do. I owe not only my happiness and my good position, but I owe also my life. If it had not been for America, I would have been killed in Europe long ago. And so you see, it is natural that I try to be loyal."

Professor Merlan looked around, through his thick glasses. "If I try to be loyal," he said, "I must do all that I can to keep harm from coming to America. Terrible harm came to Europe. Part of this harm, perhaps much of it, came because people became afraid to be thought disloyal. In the end, everyone was afraid. Everyone wished to be sure to do what every other one was doing, and especially to say how loyal they were, and to take pledges like the one I could not take this evening."

He paused again, and took another long, uneven breath. "These pledges do not prove that one is loyal. Loyalty is in one's acts and in one's life, and also in great ideals, and not even in the symbol of great ideals. And when these pledges are taken under compulsion, because someone, anyone, says, 'You must take them,' then they prove that everyone is afraid only. An America which would be afraid, afraid of freedom, would not be an America to which I would wish – to which I would wish to be loyal with my life. As long as America is good, and as long as we have the wish to be free with ourselves, here in Pomona, in Claremont, in every city, America need not be afraid."

The applause did not start at once. Then it started slowly – much the way the people had got up out of their seats to take the pledge – and then more and more people joined in. And it went on, and the earth shook in Pomona. Professor Merlan looked around, still, I thought, uncertainly, as if to say, "What do you think of what I have said? Would you say it was correct? Would you agree?" Then he sat down, and in the presence of one who had been prepared to be crucified, the fear of all fell away.

There wasn't anything more to say, but, as the speaker of the evening, I had to discuss the discussion of the discussion. I didn't. I said thank-you to Professor Merlan – I didn't say what for – and then I said that most of us in the auditorium had been brought up to take the pledge of allegiance to the flag, and that I had never before supposed that it might do any harm. I did not think it made men loyal or illuminated treason, but neither did I find it objectionable. But, I said, those of us who did not mind taking the pledge of allegiance could not, as good Americans, believing in freedom of worship, compel others to take it who believe literally in Christ's injunction against taking oaths to human beings or to human institutions. The freedom of conscience of our Christian countrymen, I said, was more important for the safety of our country even than the pledge of allegiance to the flag.

That was very good, but there was not much applause.

Then Ferner Nuhn added an anticlimax of his own. He called – doubtless in the interest of American culture – upon an elderly man in the middle of the auditorium who had been demanding all evening, and always out of order, to be heard. Mr. Nuhn asked him if he would like to come to the platform and speak, though it was late, for five minutes.

He was Joe Higgins, candidate of the Liberty party for President of the United States. His ancestors, he said, came over here in 1532 – really early, when you think of it – and he and his ancestors had been fighting ever since against the world conspiracy of the Rothschild international bankers. His ancestors had fought, he said, in every American war and on both sides of the Civil War. Then Joe Higgins poured it on, on the mess in Washington, the perfidy of the UN, Mrs. Roosevelt, the English.

People in the auditorium were laughing, more and more. Ferner Nuhn, as chairman, rose frowning to his feet and the laughter subsided. But it began again. Some people left. More and more who remained were laughing. Ferner Nuhn stood up again, frowning. "All right, Joe," called one of the men who had earlier called for the pledge of allegiance, "that's enough." Nobody was afraid now. Everybody was having fun with Joe Higgins. And when Joe Higgins finished, Ferner Nuhn thanked him for his contribution to the discussion, and the meeting ended.

:

There are just four footnotes.

Before we left the hall, a pastor from nearby Claremont came up to the platform and said to me, "I needed to have this experience tonight. I needed to realize that what can happen anywhere can happen anywhere else. I hadn't believed it."

A Republican advertising man from Los Angeles, one C. Richard Creamer, got hold of the man who had led the pledge of allegiance to the flag, shook hands with him, and thanked him for letting the meeting go on after the pledge was taken. "I think," said Republican Creamer, "that it's a darned good idea to let everyone talk, don't you?" "I guess so," said the leader of the pledge, "but I was wounded in Korea and I don't like these fellows. But I guess you're right, I'm glad they had a chance to talk." "Me, too," said Republican Creamer,

"I'm a veteran myself, but I'd a lot rather talk than fight."
"You bet," said the leader, and shook Republican Creamer's hand.

Outside the school – I was one of the last to leave because some college youngsters had come up to talk to me – two very little thin ladies broke away from a conversation they were having with Joe Higgins and came up to me. "You're not a Christian," one of them said, "you're a Jew." "That's right, ma'am," I said. "What right have *you* got to talk about Christianity?" asked the other one. "Why," I said, "Jesus said He came to fulfill the Jewish Law, and Paul said there would be neither Greek nor Jew – don't you believe that?" "You get away from me, you Jew," said the first very little thin lady, and they both rejoined Joe Higgins, leaving me standing there.

A little later, while we were having a council of peace at the home of Dr. Joseph Griggs in Claremont, another lady came in, with her young daughter. "My daughter stood up in the meeting when I did," said the lady. "I did wrong, and she did it because I did it. But I wasn't expecting anything like that. I had never given a second thought to taking the pledge of allegiance to the flag. Now I think I'm better prepared when it happens again, so I'm glad I had the experience. And I think that most of the people who were at the meeting won't be afraid the next time."

"Be ye unafraid, for I am with you always," said somebody in the room.

"With a foreign accent," said somebody else.

: : : *A Man with a Country* : : :

Mrs. Mayer and I stood fidgeting in the plenipotentiary presence of Mr. Robert C. Ode, the American consul in Berne. The date was January 18, 1963, and the weather was the reason we fidgeted (though Mr. Ode may have thought we had other reasons). We had half an hour to get the last train to connect, via Meiringen and Brünig, with the postbus back to our mountain; and Switzerland, including Berne, was disappearing under the heaviest snow in a hundred years.

We had each slipped Mr. Ode ten dollars for a new passport. Ours would expire while we were making a quick trip home in March, and we figured we'd get the new ones now and have it over with. We had completed the application forms and handed them to Mr. Ode, who bade us swear solemnly that we would support and defend the Constitution of the United States. We said that we swore neither solemnly nor jocosely nor, indeed, at all, but we would affirm, in the fashion permitted people who follow the biblical injunction against swearing; and affirm we did. Whereupon Mr. Ode should have handed us our shiny new passports.

Whereupon, instead, he handed us a sheet and said, "Now, if you'll just sign this. . . ." The sheet contained the following mimeographed words, and no others:

WARNING

Section 6 of the Internal Security Act of 1950 (50 U.S.C. 786) prohibits application for or use of a passport by and issuance or renewal of a passport to a member of an organization registered or required to register as a Communist organization under Section 7 of the Act. The following organizations are registered under Section 7:

From *Harper's Magazine*, March 1964.

The Communist Party of the United States of America.

*   *   *

I am not and have not been at any time during the period of 12 full calendar months preceding the date of this application (and no other person to be included in the passport is or has been at any time during the said period) a member of any organization registered or required to register under Section 7 of the Subversive Activities Control Act of 1950, as amended. (50 U.S.C. 786).

_____

Signature

"Who issues this?" I said.

"The Department of State," said Mr. Ode plenipotentiarily.

"Since when?"

"Oh, quite recently."

"And it has to be signed?"

"If you want a new passport."

"But not sworn to?"

"Apparently not."

"And what organizations besides the Communist party are _required_ to register?"

"I'm afraid I don't know."

"But how am I to know that I am not a member of any such organization when I don't know what the organizations are? Aren't you asking me to sign a blank check?"

"Well," said Mr. Ode, "I'll go upstairs and get the regulations. Nobody has raised any objection before"; with which he gathered up all the papers on his desk, put them in the safe, locked the safe, and went, I suppose, upstairs.

He returned with a sheaf and went through it. "I can't read you all of this," he said finally, "because some of it is classified. But it says here that any person who objects to signing the statement may submit his reasons to the Department for its further determination. Do you object to signing the statement?" I said I did.

"And you, Mrs. Mayer?"

All of our papers and most of our books, clothes, and fur-

A Man with a Country : 69

nishings, our car, and two of our children were in Switzerland;
somebody would *have* to have a passport to return from the
Free World to get them. And time was wasting and the snow
getting heavier. Mrs. Mayer signed and got her passport. I got
nine of my ten dollars back (the house taking its usual commission), and we went out into the glittering dusk and got
back to Brünig in the frozen-fingered dawn.

.

I warmed my fingers and submitted to the State Department
my reasons for refusing to sign the statement, sending a copy
to Attorney Francis Heisler of Carmel, California, who spe-
cializes in supporting and defending the Constitution of the
United States against attack by anybody (including the United
States government). I explained that I had assignments in
Europe for two religious organizations (the American Friends
Service Committee and the Fellowship of Reconciliation, to
attend the Christian Peace Conference in Prague) and four
publishers (the *Christian Century,* to report on the conference;
Harper's, to report on life in Prague; *The Progressive,* to report
on Eastern Europe; and the Encyclopaedia Britannica, to report on the Americanization of Europe). Thus my freedom
of press and worship was involved. My freedom of assembly,
too, in that the requirement would penalize me (if I *were* a
Communist) for association. And of course there was Article 13, Section 2 – but who cares? a member nation? – of the
United Nations Declaration of Human Rights: "Everyone has
the right to leave any country, including his own."

I forgot to invoke the Old Fifth, but I remembered to say
that it looked like cruel and unusual punishment to me to de-
prive a man of a passport who had never been charged with or
convicted of an offense against the United States or any State,
Territory, or Insular Possession thereof. In conclusion I shot
my cuffs at posterity: "I am willing, indeed eager, to witness
openly to all of my personal and organizational beliefs and
associations past and present; but I am unable to do so under
duress. The test oath – and the Warning sheet in question is
tantamount to such oath – requires a man to deny a crime with

which he has not been charged. It is the historic instrument of tyrannies for the reduction of free men to servility. It is unworthy of my country and my government, and I hope that my protest will weigh against it. . . ."

Sincerely yours, and *Ruat caelum.*

A few weeks later, on my arrival in the United States, I sidled into the San Francisco passport office to see if my new passport was waiting there for me. It wasn't, but "Washington" had instructed "San Francisco" to ask me to fill out a new application form. The new form included the non-Communist disclaimer as a part of the oath that has always appeared on the application. I complied, inking out the disclaimer. I knew that the San Francisco application was meaningless because the Berne application was (1) prior, (2) pending, and (3) complete (the *Warning* sheet having been wholly separate from it). Nevertheless the State Department latched on to the San Francisco form so that it could claim that my application, with the disclaimer inked out, was incomplete. The Department was thereby estopped (I can see it rolling words like "estopped" around) from processing (more rolling) the application. It had to make that claim or admit that it was denying me a passport. And such admission would at once entitle me to a hearing under *Kent* v. *Dulles,* which in 1958 established travel as an inherent right of citizenship which may not be denied without due process of law.

The Kent case required (for the first time in the melancholy history of McCarthyism) that the about-to-be-injured party be confronted with the evidence against him. The Passport Office opposes confrontation, which would disclose the sources of its information. Mr. Abba P. Schwartz, the State Department's administrator of security affairs, favors confrontation (and Mr. Abram Chayes, counsel to the Department, supports Mr. Schwartz); in the midst of which slow swordplay I came clattering along in my dusty sandals and nailed my dusty theses to the door of the State Department. I do not doubt that I am a pawn (on whosoever side). But what "these Bernards" – as Dostoevsky would say – always forget is that this is a game in which even a pawn can play and, in the end game, play a mortal role.

But the end game was a long time developing. My lawyers – whose name was now Phalanx – decided that every possible administrative remedy should be exhausted before I sued, so that the case would be solidly bottomed (more rolling). All spring they roamed the State Department corridors in the ingenuous hope that somebody would step out of an office and say yes or no. Came June and Miss Frances Knight, director of the Passport Office, finally told me in writing that she was estopped, etc., and I buckled on the whole armor of the law which, in its impartial majesty, alike forbids the government to oppress the citizen and the citizen to oppress the government.

The issue inside the Department (so my overcover agents informed me) had gone all the way up to an assistant secretary, who overruled Mr. Chayes on "policy grounds." Mr. Chayes had advised the Department to give me the passport and get shut of me; its legal grounds for refusal were, he thought, untenable. But Miss Knight told the San Francisco *Chronicle* that she understood that this was to be a test case of the Department's passport policy.

:

So *Mayer* v. *Rusk* went to court. The lawsuit (in which I disappear now except for the title of the pleadings) goes on apace, and the pace would pleasure a senior snail. We – for I am now multitudinized by *amici curiae* – were granted a statutory three-judge court to hear the matter in the first instance and were thus assured a direct appeal to the Supreme Court. But one of the three judges was just moving to Washington, so the hearing went over from July to October. We pleaded the urgency of my situation and offered, as friends of the court, to carry the judge's piano for him. No go. October it was. On December 3, 1963, the decision was given against us, the buck being expected, in such cases, to pass to the nine-judge court above. It is now passing, sedately.

I was aware that it might be months or years before I came out the other end of the juridical process. With my new passport (if I got one) I would just about make it from the house to the old people's home. The prospect didn't please, so I thought I would try to intimidate the State Department into a quick carriage of justice. I put in a person-to-person call to Miss Knight's mouthpiece, Mr. Robert D. Johnson, deputy director of the Passport Office in Washington, and when he answered, I said, "Johnson, old boy – " "This is not Mr. Johnson," said the man in Washington, "this is Mr. Whacker [or maybe it was Tibble, or Veepings] in Mr. Johnson's office." Nothing undaunted, I tried to tell Veepings just how it was. He replied, "Mr. Mayer, the Department takes the view that it is the citizen's duty to help his government enforce the law."

I say that these words of Veepings lay the foundation for the devil's very own polity. They mean perpetual martial law and the perpetual alienation of a man's natural right (especially a small man's) to pass by on the other side of the street when one policeman is arresting a dozen thugs with blazing guns. If we do not pin back these Veepings' ears, we shall find our own amputated because we did not interpose to give the man from the municipal animal shelter a pants-leg up on a rabid dog. If we do not strike down the Veepings Doctrine, there is no limit to government, and we may as well confess that we are no better off than the Russians.

But there is no arguing doctrine with a Veepings, and I thought I would try a more primitive gambit. I wrote Miss Knight a Dear Sir letter, calling her attention to Section 6 (a) (2) (b), which forbids her to issue a passport "knowing or having reason to believe" that the applicant is a Communist. I asserted (without saying I was or I wasn't) that she did not have such knowledge or belief. Unless, therefore, she informed me that she did, I respectfully demanded that she issue me a passport at once. She did neither.

I concluded that I might fare better with a man of my own sex, namely, my adversary in *Mayer* v. *Rusk*. I directed Mr. Rusk's attention to Section 6 (a) (1), which makes it a felony for a Communist to apply for a passport. Pointing out that I had applied for a passport in Berne, not to mention San

Francisco, I respectfully demanded that he either give me a passport or charge me with a felony. He did neither.

But these Rusks, Knights, and Veepings' are only accomplices, after the fact, of the United States Congress in a fraud perpetrated, like all frauds, for gain; the gain being the defeat, in the next election, of the opposing candidate's furious anticommunism by one's own furiouser anticommunism. This is the actual "intent of the Congress" – which the courts are always trying to determine – but even its putative intent does not authorize the State Department to make me swear that I am not a Communist. The Department thought that one up itself. The accomplices are fraudulent in their own right.

Their fraud is not even impalpable.

Say that I'm a Communist agent, using my American passport to further my infamous interests. How best do I disguise myself? Best, I submit, by posing as an independent (if not wholly obscure) journalist who is able to rig up assignments taking him almost anywhere on a moment's notice, and by affecting, on the side, to be a religious man with an ecumenical outlook and an affiliation of some amorphous sort with a cheerful institution like Quakerism. And that is just what I am.

Why, then, do I blame the State Department for requiring me to purge myself of suspicion? Because where I come from (which is Justinian Rome, via Missouri), the burden of proof is on the accuser and my answer to him is, "Show me." I am paying J. Edgar Hoover a handsome wage to find out whether I'm a Communist. Why should I do his work for him at my own expense? Mr. Hoover is the head of what Attorney-General Kennedy calls the greatest investigative body in the world. If the greatest investigative body in the world cannot find out whether I'm a Communist without my help, it is not the greatest investigative body in the world.

Say that I'm a Communist agent, bent upon disguise. Would I be a member of the Communist party? I would not be, not only because I would not be so silly as to bait the trap for myself, but also (and much more crucially) because the State

Department will give me a passport if I'm a Communist agent *provided I am not a member of the Communist party.* Just listen to this, from page A-19 of Mr. Rusk's answer to my complaint: "To obtain a passport a present member need only sever his *organizational* connection with the Communist organization; he is not required to alter his beliefs or convictions" (emphasis added).

Say, then, that I'm a Communist agent. I am asked to swear (solemnly) that I am not a member of the Communist party. I do so. I wouldn't boggle at perjury – not if I were a traitor to begin with – but the fact is that I have told the truth. But say that I'm neither a Communist agent *nor* a party member. In that case I must answer the question the same way the Communist agent answers it.

Is this – as Milt Gross used to say – a system?

It is not a system but a fraud, perpetrated, like all frauds, under a false pretense: the pretense of keeping Communist agents from going abroad. As any fairly mature infant knows, there is no way to prevent the flow of information between the two worlds anyway. All I have to do in, say, Prague, to tell the CIA that the Russians are using aspirin, and not bicarb, to trigger their new device is to put three twenty- and two sixty-heller stamps in a prearranged order on my picture postcard to Aunt Kate. Everybody knows that that's how the Russians got the bomb in the first place.

So palpable is the pretense that the State Department only pretends to enforce it. On April 19, 1963, Miss Knight wrote me that the oath I declined to take "is required of all applicants." But several weeks later applicants of my acquaintance were still being handed the old forms without the oath; and this, mind you, was at least fifteen months after the State Department announced the new regulation in January 1962 (after the Supreme Court upheld the order requiring the Communist party to register) and at least twelve months after its new forms were issued in May 1962. In all that time the Department had not got around to getting its new forms to its passport application offices, and in all that time it had issued, I suppose, a half-million passports, most of them, doubtless, to Communist agents who sped to Tiflis and sent Aunt Kate a picture postcard with an interesting arrangement of stamps. Either I should get my passport or the half-million Communist agents who got theirs should have them revoked, I don't care which; I want the equal protection of the laws guaranteed by the Fourteenth Amendment.

:

The last refuge of a Department is the stall, in the hope that something will turn up. In *Mayer* v. *Rusk* the Department's hope, in its succession of stalls, appeared to be the Flynn case. Elizabeth Gurley Flynn, who *claims* to be a Communist, had her passport revoked and was suing. If the Department could get the Flynn case up to the Supreme Court before mine, the Court might hand down a careless enough opinion in her case to bolster the Department in mine – an opinion, for instance, that the national security puts travel within the sole competence of the executive power. The executive power was vastly extended by Mr. Roosevelt's emergency a quarter-century ago. The emergency is still on. Nowadays it is, of course, communism.

The defendant in *Mayer* v. *Rusk,* having no other stick to beat me with, has to use the Red Menace – the same Red Menace that the *Chicago Tribune* was using fifteen years ago to prove the disloyalty of the Rockefeller Foundation (of which Mr. Rusk is ex-president). Mr. Rusk ought to know better. He ought to know that I am not arguing that the Reds are or aren't a Menace. He ought to know that I am not arguing that the Internal Security Act is a good or bad thing. (It is as bad as it was when Mr. Truman vetoed it and said we were throwing our liberties away). I am arguing that Miss Knight is not empowered to ask me whether I'm a Communist. My political affiliation is none of a free government's business, and a government makes itself unfree when its Congress and its courts decide that communism is only a criminal conspiracy and not also a theory of man and of history to which an honest (if mistaken) man might repair. The reason that communism is outlawed in America and Germany – and only in America and Germany among republican countries – is that only Americans and Germans will let it be defined for them as a criminal conspiracy and nothing more. I reject godless communism – along with godless capitalism – but that is *my* business.

The Catholic Council on Civil Liberties condemns the loyalty (or rather, the non-disloyalty) oath in general as "un-American, coercive, discriminatory, prejudicial, and ineffective." The standard oath of allegiance required of every officeholder (and of every soldier, and of every passport applicant) may be ineffective, but it is none of the rest of the things that the Catholic Council complains of. And it is the rest of the things that stick in my craw. I can take (or affirm, in my peculiar way) the oath of allegiance without its sticking. As St. Thomas said of the lady's belief that the names of the blessed were inscribed on a golden scroll in heaven – if it does no good, it probably does no harm either.

But this is the first time that I myself have had to face the loyalty oath in all its fatuous panoply and its design to make wall-to-wall people out of us. My rejection of it in the past has cost me a couple of jobs I could do without, and I sympathize with my thirty-four million countrymen who have had to take it or be blacklisted. In a high school in my neighborhood all seventy-one of the teachers protested the oath – and all seventy-one of them took it. They do not love their country the more for having taken it, and Mr. Rusk is smart enough to know that the only loyalty is love.

My real objection has no merit in a three-judge, a nine-judge, or a twenty-seven judge court: This oath is repugnant to me as an American. If my Republican father had been told he had to take it, he would have said, "What do you think this is – Russia?" Every Sunday afternoon in Chicago he used to take me to a bosky dell called Bughouse Corner in Washington Park and listen to a succession of rabid revolutionaries, each more rabid than the last. A solitary copper named Big Tom shook his club at the kids to keep them quiet so their fathers could hear the Bolsheviks. Big Tom was the FBI, the

CIA, the Internal Security Act, and the Subversive Activities Control Board all in one, and between him and the ruin of the Republic stood nothing but my father's attachment to the Republican party. Had my father come to believe that the Bolsheviks were right, not Big Tom or the FBI or the CIA could have saved the country from him. No police power has ever saved a country from subversion or ever will.

:

Ruat caelum. Though the heavens fall, I do not intend to take that un-American, coercive, discriminatory, prejudicial, and ineffective oath. But what will I do if, some months or years from now, the Supreme Court holds against me? I don't know what I will do. But I think I know how I will feel. I will still feel like resisting.

It would be much more useful if a senator or a congressman – or a President who vetoes it – would resist a bad law like the Internal Security Act or a bad regulation like the State Department's; but they will not. They say, "It's the law. We may not like it, but it's the law." But we hanged the Nazi leaders at Nürnberg for saying that, and properly; a man who will obey the law, whatever the law, wants a form of government in which man exists for the state and not the state for man.

The great rights of man are compendent, and the vitiation of one of them, mobility, for instance, is the vitiation of them all. My sophisticated neighbor says it's a small matter, this anti-Communist jag, but a simple-minded Nazi told me, when I spoke of the persecutions in Germany, that "that was much later. At first it was only the Communists." And so, when my neighbor says, "If you're not a Communist, why not say so?" I have got to say what we say where I come from (which is where we say *Ruat caelum*). I have got to say, *Principiis obsta* and *Finem respice.*

Resist the beginnings. Envisage the end. Maybe these aren't the beginnings. Maybe they won't proceed to the end. And maybe a stand should be made somewhere further along the road. But I didn't intend to make a stand; not I. I was tending to my business when I was confronted by Leviathan commanding me to do something un-American. It is not as if I were, say, a teetotaler confronted by the Volstead Act.

I blush to say it in these supranational days, but I love my country, and I could no more leave it lightly than I can remain and stand by while it is being pulled to pieces. This is my own, my native land. I am an American. But I am a man before I am an American; not a good man, and getting no better, but a man, and a man has the overriding duty, in jail or out, to be free.

But when did expatriation ever mean freedom? Suppose that another republic accepted me. (I say "suppose" because, though they all despise the American demonology, they may hesitate to offend the American government.) What would become of me if I resisted a bad law, in, say, England? I should then depart thence for some place like Russia, where, as a non-Communist, my right to travel would be exactly what it is here as a non-anti-Communist. And I'd be short more than a few other rights besides. If I were not imprisoned (in a small jail) when I outraged a government that was not my own, I suppose I should be deported. And go where at the last? At least my own government is not threatening to deport me – just the opposite – and that is something among many things I have to be thankful for. What I want are the things to be thankful for that we have lost in this country between my father's time and mine.

On June 17, 1964, the Supreme Court held Section 6 of the McCarran Act, on which the oath was based, unconstitutional. The passport was granted (The Progressive, November 1964).

: : : *Rendered unto Caesar* : : :

I was a spavined old man of forty-three (this was ten years ago) when I realized that my Government was unlikely ever again to order me to pick up a gun and kill a man who has never offended me and who had been ordered by *his* Government to pick up a gun and kill me; each of us subject, if he disobeyed the order, to being set upon by his own Government. The last time my Government ordered me to perpetrate this abomination – for such it may be seen to be, on its very face – was in 1942.

On that occasion I had said No (as who wouldn't, to such a preposterous demand?) and the Government retired in instant confusion. I had not expected that it would stand up to me like a man; rather, I had expected it to use its brute force on me. But I appeared to have taken it by surprise. Governments taken by surprise hasten to reclassify, supposing by this device they may escape their predicament. Mine reclassified me.

It reclassified me as "indispensable war worker" because I was beating my gums in the lower depths of the one remaining peaceable division of a university engaged in a great secret war project. (The university's motto was, Let Knowledge Grow from More to More, that Human Life May Be Enriched; and by August 6, 1945, its knowledge had grown to the point where it was able to enrich human life in Hiroshima.)

When I saw that all a man had to do was say No to send the Government headlong, I lost my fear of it. I had long since lost my respect for it, as any man necessarily must for any such organization, be it Murder Inc. or Murder United. But the Government found other men to do its sorry work, and enough of them, I suppose, because it did not come near me again; not even in 1948, when it enacted universal peacetime

From *Manas*, October 31, 1962, reprinted in condensed form from *Fellowship*, September 1962.

conscription (which Woodrow Wilson had called "the root evil of Prussianism"). It sent me a classification card again, and I sent it back with a letter of regret and heard nothing more.

Others may have had another sort of experience with Government, or with Governments more purposeful than mine, but mine convinces me that Government, whatever it means to be, good government or bad, is something of a humbug. The good things it pretends to do are done by men – by free men, and even by slaves – and the one thing it is specifically designed to do, and always promises to do, it never does, namely, keep the peace.

A humbug and, like all humbugs, a fourflusher. A few years ago I was invited to Hungary on a religious mission. My American passport forbade me – quite tyrannically – to go to Hungary. But my American Constitution forbade the Government to interfere with my religion. As between the passport and the Constitution, I held with the Constitution and so informed the Government before I went. The Government waited until I got back and then threatened to take my passport away from me, and thus make me a prisoner of my own country, unless I immediately swore that I would never again disobey its regulations present and future. Again, all I had to do was say No. My religion forbade me to swear at all and my Americanism forbade me to agree to obey anybody's *future* regulations, and I said so. The Government ran away at once.

There remained one matter in respect of which I felt that the Government needed a really good licking and would not behave itself until it had one. That was money. If men for its abominations were, as it seemed, a dime a dozen, it wanted only to get the dime to get the men. I might be palsied and arthritic, but I could still hand over the dime and the Government would let me go my wind-broken way. As long as I went on giving it its annual allowance, I could no more expect it to mend its ways than I could a reprobate son. I had to say No to the dime and see what happened.

The Government was even then – this was 1952 – on a shooting spree and I was financing the spree. It was ordering men to kill other innocent men and burn down their shanties, and I was buying it the men. I was paying others to do what I would never do myself or, indeed, countenance in others in any other circumstances. This couldn't go on.

Such were my reflections when, that same season, in a German town, I saw the ruins of a hospital in which eighty-five people, their eyes bound after surgery, were burned up blind when a bomber missed the railroad station. I realized that my notion of war as two innocent men ordered to kill one another was a little refined. War meant killing people in hospitals, including whatever Jews in Germany Hitler had overlooked.

This really couldn't go on. I notified the Government that I was cutting it off without a nickel of my dime until it straightened up. It was spending at least half of its allowance on criminal debauchery and I did not see how I could be a God-fearing American and go on paying its upkeep.

Taxes are inevitable. So is death. But suicide isn't inevitable. I intend to die unwillingly and without giving death any help. The inevitability of any evil is not the point; the point is my subornation of it. Why should I, on receipt of the Government's demand for money to kill the innocent, hurry as fast as I can to comply?

My neighbor says that the Government will take the money anyway, by force and violence and other lawful means. He is right, but what's that to me? If a robber ties me up and robs me, I have not become a robber. If the wicked Russians kill me and my little ones in my (or at least in my little ones') innocence, I have not become a killer. I have become a killer only if I kill wicked Russians (or, more likely, their wicked little ones).

My neighbor says that my refusal to pay half the tax begs the question, since the Government will use half of what I do pay to kill the innocent and, in the end, with interest and penalties, get more from me than if I had paid the whole tax with a smile. Agreed. But the point is unaffected; the point is the smile.

I am told that the Government doesn't need my piddling nickel to get on with its abominations. Agreed again. But I need it. The year I first refused to pay it, the tax came to $33.94. I could buy myself a champagne supper with $33.94. Or I could send it to the American Friends Service Committee, which could buy 1,697 dinners with it for hungry children in Orissa Province in India. One way or another, the Government doesn't need the $33.94, and I do; and its characterization of the amount, when I went to court for it, as "this small tax" was contumelious.

Of course the Government can get along without my money. If it gets less from me, or none, it will get more from my neighbor. Or more from me, then less from him. It will get the money and buy the guns and give them to the Portuguese to defend democracy against the Russians by killing the innocent in Angola. Good enough. I am not the government; I haven't the power to put a stop to the abomination, but only to put a stop to my being willing to perpetrate it myself. . . .

If I need not pay my taxes because I am squeamish about the killing of men, then, says my neighbor, the vegetarian need not pay his for inspection of the killing of animals, etc., and, in the end, no one need pay his taxes for anything he doesn't much fancy, and this is Anarchy. My neighbor is not alone in saying it. When the Circuit Court of Appeals was hearing my complaint against the Government, one of the Judges said to my learned counsel, "Is the plaintiff aware that this Court, if it held for him, would itself be laying the axe to the root of all established Government?" And learned counsel said, "I think he is, Your Honor."

Is a man who is worth anything at all to be diverted from positive horrors by putative horrors? I have no primary obligation to save established Government from the axe, but to save myself from the fire. I will pay for the conveniences of Government, including those conveniences I don't use. I will pay for its inconveniences, because prudence dictates that Governments long established should not be changed for light and transient causes. But why should I pay for its madness –

Rendered unto Caesar : *83*

or my neighbor's, if you will – because the madness is established? All the more reason for cutting it off at once; all the more. The Government is anarchical, not I. It, not I, denies the kingdom of God and throws its anarchical bombs into the midst of the family of man.

I am not first of all a doctor of political philosophy, with no better business than to set terms like Anarchy in order (though I may say that if there were only one other term, and that Slavery, I, like Locke's judicious Hooker, would know how to order the two). I am first of all a man; not much of a man, and getting no better; but still a man, born with a set of terms to live by and an instinctive apprehension of their validity. My neighbor says "Anarchy" as if he were affirming the Eleventh Commandment instead of denying the Second and the Sixth. He wags his head and says that there is no other way than established Government – or even than *this* established Government – to manage human affairs.

Who said that human affairs are manageable? – Not I. Perhaps they aren't. They do not seem to be just now, nor for a long time since. If they aren't, then a man who may not live until they are must manage his affairs as best he can. The burden of proving manageability is on the managers or, as they are known in election year, the rascals. Neither my neighbor nor *the rascals* can relieve me of my responsibility by thumbing through their index of terms and threatening me with Anarchy.

But all this is by the bye. I do not mean to argue Pacifism here (another of my neighbor's terms). I mean to abide by the Aesculapian oath to do good if possible, but in no case to do harm, whether or not the doctors of medicine (or of political philosophy) abide by it. And if I can not once in a while try to be righteous without succeeding in being self-righteous, I am sorry that I am offensive and that my neighbor is diverted by the offense.

My neighbor is forever saying that the situation is pretty bad (or at least hopeless) and asking, "But what can one man do?" He means to answer his own question with, "Nothing." I tell him what one man can do, almost nothing, perhaps, but not quite nothing, and do at no more effort than it takes to keep his golf clubs polished. But when I tell him, he says, "But one man is ineffective."

I know that one man is ineffective. I know that Roosevelt, Truman, and Eisenhower were ineffective. They all hated war – so they said, and I believed and believed them – and they all made war. I hear that John F. Kennedy, as President, is the prisoner of his position. And these men are managers, and my neighbor and I are not even managers. How, then, should one of us be effective? But one of us can try to do the right thing, all by himself, and, maybe, even be effective. The United Nations has not been able to disarm the world by one man; I, all by myself, can be more effective than it has been.

"But someone must take the responsibility for Society." Is there no other way than public preferment to take responsibility for Society? If there is none, a man may have to be irresponsible. Too bad; but not as bad as being responsible for the offenses the men-turned-Government are obliged to commit in Society's name. Society, grumbling at the offenses, but assenting to them, has compelled me to choose between a bad course and a worse.

Thoreau imagined a State which would recognize the individual as a higher and independent power. He may have been whimsical then. He would be much more whimsical now. Two victorious world wars for democracy have not extended democracy even among the citizens of the victorious nations. Two victorious world wars for democracy have extended, not the black man's, but all men's enslavement to war and its preparation.

The State that Thoreau, so whimsically in his time, so much more so in ours, imagined "would not think it inconsistent with its own repose if a few were to live aloof from it, not meddling with it, nor embraced by it, who fulfilled all the duties of neighbors and fellow-men." Some of us who once pitied the Forgotten Man would like ourselves to be forgotten now, but the State insists upon remembering us each and several; not, to be sure, as men, but as cards to be slipped soundlessly into a computer. But when one of the cards does not slip sound-lessly out the other end, the computer may not know, for a moment, what to do, and so, for a moment, do nothing. The only thing a man – a man, not a card – can do now is obstruct and pray for obstruction.

"Ask not what your country can do for you, but what you can do for your country." When Mr. Kennedy spoke these words at his inaugural, I knew that I was at odds with a Soci-ety which did not immediately rebel against them. They are the words of totalitarianism pure; no Jefferson could have spo-ken them, and no Khrushchev could have spoken them better. Could a man say what Mr. Kennedy said and also say that the difference between *us* and *them* is that *they* believe that man exists for the State and *we* believe that the State exists for man? He couldn't, but he did. And in doing so, he read me out of society.

This good man, and the good men around him, can neither do good themselves nor allow me to do good if I would. They are all of them prisoners of their position – prisoners already of the Government which tries to imprison me. I offered to give the Government all the money it wanted, no matter how much it wanted, if it would use it to help my countrymen. My country's children needed schools. Its old people needed medical care for want of which I (with my own eyes, as my mother would say) had seen them die.

But the Government wouldn't hear of these needs. They were all beyond its capacity – the capacity of the Govern-ment of the richest nation in history. So straitened, indeed, is the Government's capacity to help men, at home or abroad, that it is constrained to notify the children of Orissa Province in India that they either have to make war on "our" side or starve.*

---

*"It is my belief that in the administration of these (foreign aid) funds we should give great attention and consideration to those nations which have our view of the world crisis." – President Kennedy (*Newsweek*, September 18, 1961).

Shall we say "Yes" to a Government, no matter what it asks of us? If so, men are freer in Prague than they are at home; and this would seem strange unless you hold that ours is a Government that, unlike any Government that ever was before, never asks anything of us. Our government is certainly better than many in many respects, but in the one respect of mortal wrong, the killing of the innocent, it is identical with all the rest.

There is something to practice's making perfect. I may say, "I would say *No* to Communism," or, "I would have said *No* to Nazism." But if I can not say "No" to a Government whose pains are light, what makes me think I would say "No" to a Government whose pains are heavier?

It is excruciatingly easy for me to say "No" to Communism, and I say it. I would not rather be red than dead; I would rather be neither. But I would rather be either than have the blood of the innocent on my hands. Wouldn't you? The Russians will have to answer to their Government's abominations, you and I only to ours. What our Government requires of you and me, in our dotage, is only that we give it the money to buy the gun and hire the man to carry it. What say you?

The world may end next week, or next year, and the last flash will light up the darkness in which we stumble now. We shall be able to see then, in an instant, that the Government, like us, wasn't itself very good or very bad but only, like us, enchanted, and, in its enchantment, like us in ours, turned everything it touched to iron. Between now and then we shall none of us change our wonted ways very much or very fast, and we should not expect to. But then, in the last flash, instead of saying, "What little can I do?" we shall say, "What little could I have done?"

: : : *A World Without Government* : : :

The morning of April 18, 1861, President Lincoln offered the command of the Union forces in the field to a cavalry officer named Lee, with the rank of major general. Lee was a Virginian, but he was a staunch Unionist and an opponent of both slavery and secession. He didn't hesitate: he declined the offer and resigned his commission in the U.S. Army.

That same afternoon, Virginia seceded and Robert E. Lee took command of its military and naval forces – and, ultimately, of the forces of the Confederate States of America.

Lee was a Virginian first; he believed that the nation had its authority from the several sovereign states. Four years and six hundred thousand lives later he accepted the authority of the nation at the point of the sword and became, outwardly, an American first; inwardly he never regretted his decision to "go with Virginia."

The idea of the separate sovereign state was crushed at Appomattox, but the archaic sovereignties lived on – fifty of them now, every day losing more of their reason for being. For the past year or so, the country has been subjected to a collapsing crusade by President Ronald Reagan to pump new life into these obsolete organs of public administration under the alias of the New Federalism. The New Federalism is neither new nor federal. It is a scheme not to distribute the powers of government but to do away with them by saddling the one-time sovereign states with them. But the states are (as we say in Virginia) too po' to tote them.

In the age of high-speed technology the states have no proper function left. Banking and finance, commerce and industry, law enforcement (corporate, criminal, and investment), basic taxation, civil rights and civil liberties, welfare,

From *The Center Magazine*, March/April 1983.

employment, job training, Social Security, conservation, pollution, drug and liquor control, pornography, public health, and, of course, long-distance transportation and communication are all self-evidently interstate (or, more precisely, transstate). The truck with a half-dozen license plates is just another only-in-America phenomenon.

The state no longer has a viable existence except as an obstacle to local government on the one hand and national government on the other. It locks town and country into an utterly misbegotten union. New York City and "upstate" have no more in common than Chicago and "downstate" or Atlanta and piney-woods Georgia. Both physiographically and demographically the United States does provide the occasion for regional associations with real but limited sovereignty within the national union where such areas have common problems, such as the ecology of the Great Lakes basin or the transportation needs of the Boston-Washington corridor. But the state regulatory bodies are as often as not regulated by the private enterprises they are supposed to regulate – notoriously in the case of the public utilities and transportation commissions.

The Virginia of today is not only a political nullity but an economic racket, as James Madison of Virginia warned that it would be. Madison argued on behalf of the new Constitution that the larger the geographical unit of government, the less susceptible it would be to all the evils of what he called faction (i.e., special interest), the less anarchical, and the less readily corrupted. The loss of the representatives' familiarity with local situations would be compensated by the greater likelihood of the selection of good men to govern from the ranks of the larger electorate. Having never dreamed of the railroad and the airplane, the telephone and the telegraph, the corporation and the trade union, Madison could not foresee the total obliteration of the state's usefulness.

The great lobbyist for a strong central government had before him the reduction of the thirteen ex-colonies to a condition of national anarchy after the Revolution. Already two centuries ago the state made little sense; already the new

Americans were wandering all over the land, transferring their geographical allegiances as they went. They would soon be interrupting their sentimental rendition of "Carry Me Back to Old Virginny," to shout, "Eureka! I've found it!" when they crossed the mythical state line from the western territories into California.

Where is the Virginian today whose heart, like Lee's, bleeds for Virginia as he curses the morning traffic across the Potomac or shows his badge at the intercontinental spooks' entrance to the Central Intelligence Agency in Langley, "VA."? Where is the Idahoan (or Idahan) who knows the state motto (unless it's on his license plates), the Iowan (or Iowayan) who doesn't gag when the band at the national convention strikes up for the fiftieth time with "That's where the tall corn grows," the crazy California delegate who doesn't whoop when the band plays "California, Here I Come" (which he mistakes for the state song)?

These people are Americans first and last except, possibly, for Lone Star Texans (but never was heard a discouraging word like "secession" when, last spring, the U.S. Supreme Court compelled the outraged heirs of the Alamo to provide public education for the children of Mexican wetbacks, much to the dismay of Justice Sandra Day O'Connor, who said in her dissent, "Each state is sovereign within its own domain, governing its citizens and providing for their general welfare. While the Constitution and federal statutes define the boundaries of that domain, they do not harness state power for national purposes").

The eighteenth-century role of the federal government, apart from the national defense, was to arbitrate the disputes between or among the states. It was soon extended to jurisdiction over any interest which affected more than one state directly. By the middle of the next century – when Lee went with Virginia – the Great Emancipator was holding that it was the proper business of the nation as such to do the things for people that people could not do for themselves. Steadily, at first, and then cornucopic with the development of the steam engine and the telegraph, fewer and fewer public functions could be contained within the state. One by one almost every human action and reaction leaped across the union – VD, the gypsy moth, the fugitive criminal, the cigarette taxed high here and low there (and "imported" illegally).

Die-hard tradition alone reserved education to the states, and that began to crumble, but only after the Second World War when the illiteracy of the poor states was finally recognized as a threat to the survival of the Republic. (Forty per cent of the draftees in the three most deprived states of the South were rejected, in contrast with less than two per cent from Minnesota and Iowa.) The state was the bastion of public-school segregation until 1954, when the judicial arm of the nation held it unconstitutional. And it was only a year ago that the federal denial of tax exemption to segregated private schools was finally settled over the joint objection of the states *and* the national administration. After Pearl Harbor, the federal government (which had merely sponsored the Reserve Officers Training Corps before) as good as took over the state universities, along with the private ones, for research and training; and when the Soviet Union lofted Sputnik in 1957, President Dwight Eisenhower called for and got a stupendous appropriation for scientific and technological programs to be disbursed to the nation's high schools and colleges without regard to state lines.

The once sovereign state today provides the kind of pervasive corruption that enables Madison's "factions" to control the generality of state governments. The control is pervasive because there is so little glamour in state office, so little in the way of pay and perquisites, and, above all, so little noonday exposure to public assessment of either the candidate or the officeholder. (Local officials have much greater exposure.) However brutally it is boodled in Congress or in the agencies like the Pentagon, integrity is urged in Washington by the national spotlight; the state capital simply isn't newsworthy. Rare the congressman whose every constituent feels that he doesn't know at least a little something about the man; rare the state legislator whose every constituent feels that he does. Progressive legislation nearly all originates at the federal level, opposition to it at the state.

:

The motivation of Mr. Reagan's New Federalism, or Old Statism, was obvious as soon as it surfaced; it was obviously part and parcel of Reaganism. Our President – and his California friends, including Vice-President George Bush of Connecticut, Texas, and Connecticut again – has no consuming interest in maintaining government powers at any level, except, of course, defense so-called. They have every interest in eliminating them in favor of the trickle doctrine. The transfer of powers to the states is a transfer of costs. Those functions which cannot be got rid of altogether, when they have been dumped on the states will to that extent have got, not government, but Washington "off the people's backs." Less will be spent by the visible spender, Washington, and less will be taken (except for defense) by the visible taker, Washington. But the states will have to exercise in an ever-increasing degree the one real power remaining to them – the power of the kinds of levy, like the property, gasoline, and sales taxes, which fall most heavily on the poor because of the classic corruption of the legislatures by the special interests. Mr. Reagan's friends are content to see *that* power quietly expanded while the power of Washington (that is, the responsibility) is loudly reduced.

The worm in the vermiform apple is, of course, the Reagan depression, which has busted the states. Under the current welfare arrangement the federal government puts up ninety-three dollars and the state twenty-seven dollars for a total of one-seventh of poverty-level income for a family of four in Mississippi. "Simple logic and history," says Carl Rowan, "tell us that if the federal government walks away from welfare, through a programs 'swap' or any other means, Mississippi is not going to make up the lost ninety-three dollars." As the federal government walks away, the states have had to cut services to the counties, the counties to the municipalities. A recent survey by the National League of Cities reports that ninety percent of the seventy-nine municipalities queried say they will not be able to make up with local funds the cuts in community and urban development grants planned by the Reagan Administration for fiscal 1984. The survey showed that seventy-one percent of the cities raised municipal fees last year while thirty-eight percent introduced fees for services formerly provided free. Courtesy of Reagan & Co. public services are going through the wringer the country over. The New Federalism is dead in the womb. The powers – that is, the costs – laid on the states are fast falling into desuetude.

But the stillborn New Federalism has had a certainly unintended effect that may be of some ultimate use to the nation, and, indeed, to the world. It has thrown additional light on the hopelessness of the federal arrangement at the end of the twentieth century. With fifty sets of conflicting and overlapping statutes civil and criminal, and with fifty appellate courts handing down a tumultuous succession of conflicting and overlapping decisions, it has long been impossible to reach a national determination on crucial issues like desegregation or abortion or capital punishment. Fifty sets of lawyers have got richer and richer. The country swarms with large and small offenders against the general welfare scurrying from state to state to get the best deal they can – be it tax exemption in Connecticut, murder in Oregon, or incorporation in Delaware. With the ascension and bursting of the New Federalism balloon, the case against states' rights mounts.

:

So far has technology carried us beyond the reduction of the states to absurdities that the justification of the sovereign *nation*-state – except in the romantic terms advanced for Lee's Virginia in 1861 – comes into critical question as the red button awaits pressing to launch the intercontinental ballistic missiles with thermonuclear warheads and a ten-to-twenty-minute around-the-world delivery time. The transmission of missiles, and missives, people, and goods, is almost as instantaneous across national borders as it is across states – and in the case of electronic transmission exactly as instantaneous.

A World Without Government : *93*

True, the manners of the Andaman Islanders, if they are still eating their grandparents, are still measurably different from those of the Parisians or the Peorians – but not as different as they were a century, or even a half-century, ago. It is only a matter of time – another century? – before the Andamanders and the Peorians are as interchangeable as the Wyominganders and the Connecticutters are today. With the ever-faster proliferation of nonpolitical institutions, commercial, industrial, financial, cultural, the ancient dictum of Marx that the workingmen have no country can be much more accurately applied to Coca-Cola, Sony, Volkswagen, and IBM (and McDonald's). The great cartels, growing always greater, huckster everybody everywhere (including the Andaman Islands).

The imminent question is insistent: as the United States is to Virginia, so the world is to the United States. What is, or soon will be, left to perpetuate the nation-state is a millennium or two of custom and one people's fanatical hatred of another (or of all others). But the Swiss confederation accommodates three sets of different – even inimical – customs and three and a half different languages. The American melting pot has accommodated a stupendous variety of ethnic usages, large and small, in the process absorbing provincial consciousness into emotional attachment to the nation. In the sixty-five years since the Great War of the old nations this national attachment has, on balance, subsided very considerably and, as technology proceeds apace, seems destined to go on subsiding, without, however, a corresponding transfer to a larger conceptual unit than the nation-state. (No "national" of any of the contracting parties seems greatly disposed to attach himself to, say, the North Atlantic Treaty Organization or the Warsaw Pact.) Provincial chauvinism was intractable in the case of Robert E. Lee. It seems to be equally intractable today on the national level, when it is aroused against a national enemy. With rare exceptions – France and Germany come to mind, but not Poland and Russia – nationalist hatreds flourish today as fiercely as they ever did.

Thirty-five years ago, the atomic bomb appeared to have

illuminated the human political condition almost as brilliantly as it had Hiroshima. Not only was no man an island; no island was an island. Previously sedate people were crying, "One world or none." Was President Harry Truman sounding the death knell of the nation-state when he said, after Hiroshima and Nagasaki, "There must never be another war"? (Five years later he decided to have one more for the road.) But if there was to be no more war, what would generate or regenerate the chauvinist passion? What would hold the nation-state together?

Before the year 1945 was out, everyone everywhere in the literate world was familiar, however vaguely, with the idea of world federalism or world government. In the United States the United World Federalists spread rapidly in intellectual circles and for a couple of seasons became the "in" thing socially. The lecturers were all lecturing for it except for the handful of world-government "maximalists" who rejected the federalists' minimal surrender of sovereignty; along with the minuscule Socialist Party, doughty little organizations like the Campaign for World Government maintained that a federated world which did not disturb the worldwide economic balance between rich and poor would collapse in civil war – or, likelier, never come to be. The UWF, or minimalist, position was presented as the only realism: since the rich Americans (and a few others similarly situated) would never join a world which taxed them to feed its starving hundreds of millions, federalism would have to freeze the world's stupendous economic imbalance. A world organization without the power to levy near-confiscatory income or capital taxes on the people of the rich nations was an impossibility, with it a hallucination.

Within five years, the world organizationalists – minimalist and maximalist alike – were succumbing to the joint pressures of the cold war abroad and McCarthyism at home. Within a decade of its birth, the world government movement was somewhere between dormant and dead, and a radically shrunken UWF had given up lobbying and undertaken long-term education instead. The toothless United Nations was early made a laughingstock by the successive Security Council vetoes – first of the Soviet Union, then of the United States – and fast lost its hold on the public imagination. Naked cynicism characterized the unilateral moves of the several great powers in hot spots all over the world. When Mr. Reagan rejected the International Law of the Sea treaty he said blandly that "the 120" – the correct figure is 130 – "nations who voted for the pact represent only about 12.5 percent of the global gross national product."

Appomattox was the formal prelude to the conversion into one nation, indivisible, of the separate sovereign states dwelling together in more or less amiable anarchy until a crucial interest split them down the middle. But the substantive conversion had to wait until the adoption of the federal income tax recognized, at last, that it is not the states that constitute the nation but the people. State residence restrictions on welfare, employment, and electoral eligibility gave way, gradually, and with Lyndon Johnson's civil- and voting-rights legislation throwing the whole mantle of national protection over the politically disadvantaged blacks, it was tacitly conceded that the folly of the fifty states had to be ended.

The dismantlement (without a prior mantlement) of Mr. Reagan's New Federalism underscores the greatest single fact of the nation's political history and generates a faint spark of life in the moribund One World movement. As the anarchy of the New Federalism is intolerable in the nation, so the anarchy of the nations is intolerable in the world, intolerable among the hapless dwellers in the roofless house under the awful sky of the nuclear age. By now we ought to know what the ancients knew: that nations with no judge between them, no parliament to write the law that binds them both, and no executive to enforce that law, must fight when they cannot negotiate their differences. People talk about accidental war, but it is peace that is accidental. And there is only a modicum of hope that the accident of peace will long continue.

The swelling struggle in the European and American streets against the nuclear arms race betokens one of three alternative outcomes – the end of the world in nuclear war; a truce or cease-fire (or "freeze") doomed to go the way of every unenforceable truce before it; or the abdication of the classic and unexceptional device for rallying chauvinist passion, the sovereign national power to make war for the sole purpose of preserving the nation-state. That state, like Lee's Virginia, is indefensible theoretically, indefensible historically, and in 1983 mortally indefensible in fact.

:

Robert M. Hutchins used to say that what is necessary must be possible. Not necessarily. World government seems now to be urgently necessary to save the world. But it would not appear urgently possible to achieve. Most of the people of the world – the great preponderance of them – live as tribes ruled by chieftains or chieftainly apparatus. (Some of the tribes are vast, and many are anciently established as nation-states.) The members of these tribes have had little or no political experience or political responsibility. Their comprehension of government is limited, of self-government still more limited. A "democratic" world government would be dominated by those tribes or their chieftains and, if it did not succumb to civil war (which would leave us all where we are today), would certainly be a world tyranny. The best of the nation-states has both oppressive potentialities and oppressive tendencies. It is painful to make an argument for a still greater state than the one we know; the oppressive potentialities and tendencies of any and all states would be mightily magnified in the tribally dominated world state.

Not only would the rich members of that state be rabidly disinclined to support the poor, the civil liberties and civil rights inhering, by and large, in the rich nation-states would fall instantly in those same nation-states as the world political process supervened. As between tyranny and anarchy, on any scale, anarchy, when there is no third alternative, is the more palatable choice. But the likely tyranny of the world government, with the likely secessionist revolution against it by the one-time libertarian nation-states does not promise much more relief from the nuclear threat than the present anarchy and imposes, while it lasts, the additional inconveniences of tyranny.

The civil and political liberties of the libertarian nations are insecure. Liberty is always and everywhere insecure. But the few nations which have had the good fortune – it is nothing but fortune – to be schooled in it are much more surely attached to it than those that have not had the schooling. These latter that are long established have to go through that schooling before world government is thinkable, while the others, the newly established nations, are just beginning to have the national experience and are still delirious in their virginal chauvinism. Like our own thirteen colonies, the new nations are rebellious, not revolutionary.

Historian William H. McNeill says that "when and whether a transition will be made from a system of states to an empire of the earth is the gravest question humanity confronts." It will be a quantum leap, but some such analogous leap has been made before, long, slow, tortuous, from the tribal city to the tribal state. The race has pretty well rid itself of chattel slavery, and a fair part of it has pretty well rid itself of the profit system; these too are quantum leaps. War abides, war and the plurality of sovereign states which causes war. In five hundred years the peoples of the earth may be able to think of themselves as the people of the earth and of one world, indivisible, with liberty and justice for all. Five hundred years. Say a hundred. Say fifty. But war does not seem likely to wait five hundred years, or a hundred, or fifty (or five?). We are between the urgent necessity and the historical impossibility of world government right now; between the devil and the deep.

A Suburb of Munich

: : : *Sunset in the East* : : :

On Karmelitska Street is Prague's first baroque building, the early Seventeenth Century Church of Our Lady Victorious, housing the gorgeously dressed doll known as the Holy Infant Jesus. Having seen the Holy Infant Jesus of Prague, you go down Karmelitska to the next corner, which is Trziste, turn left, and come to a largish old structure, once a residence, now an apartment block, with a kind of sentry box in front. Did I say "kind of"? It is a sentry box, with a sentry seated inside. The sentry has a camera trained on the entrance of the palatial old building across the street. The palatial old building has a large (not largish) American flag above the arched entranceway. It is the American embassy.

You walk a couple of yards into the archway and on the right there is the entrance to the U.S. library. Thus far, and into the library, anyone may penetrate, perhaps to have his picture taken when he emerges, if, as is likely, he's a Czech student.

The library has 150 American periodicals, all certified kosher, and an assortment of similarly certified books. At noon a twenty-minute CBS news digest, containing nothing but the right stuff, is offered on closed-circuit television. The right stuff on the library wall consists of two blown-up photographs – one of Ronald Reagan, the other (I kid you not) of John Wayne. Nothing else.

You don't make the mistake, when you emerge from the library loaded with the right stuff, of proceeding further down the archway into the embassy compound. If you do make the mistake, an armed U.S. Marine, in red-striped blue, pops out of *his* sentry box and stops you. That's as far as you go unless you have an appointment within.

From *The Progressive*, February 1984.

The embassy is the hotbox of the coldest cold war in Europe. The Americans cannot forgive the Czechs (or the East Germans), "our kind of people," for their failure to throw off the Soviet yoke. After thirty-five years there is still no relaxation of the tension in Prague, no progress, for instance, in the establishment of a cultural exchange agreement such as exists between Czechoslovakia and the other Western countries. Whenever the occasion offers itself to ice up the relationship further, the *Ami* will latch on to it, refusing to half-staff their flag, for example, when a Czech president dies (not the large flag over the archway but the very large flag on top of the hill at the back of the embassy grounds, the highest point in Prague).

But the enmity has degenerated, on both sides, pretty much to the exchange of formal insults. The fire has (so to say) gone out of the cold war between the communist capitals (aside from Moscow) and Washington. And the Americans and the Russians have lost their appetite for principled antagonism; what is left is the appetite for nonprincipled antagonism between two ideologically indifferent empires, each with its one capital. Ideology is dead on both sides. Nobody in Moscow much cares any more if the Americans are good or bad capitalists, and nobody in Washington cares whether the Czechs – or the Russians – are good or bad communists or communists at all.

In the East, Marx and Lenin are read and quoted (like Jefferson and Madison here) only where they are oratorically required. If a good man is hard to find, a good communist is harder. A popular university student in Prague does not have a "Marxist-Leninist" in his whole acquaintance. A respected (and active) journalist in Budapest does not know of one true believer among his colleagues. A week-long humanities-social science conference in Dubrovnik produces no mention of communism. In the course of a dozen visits to the "socialist" countries I have never met a man or woman – public officials excepted, and by no means all of those – in whom the flaming Red fervor abides. According to the gospel of Marx (and later of Lenin), the state was going to wither away; but it is the gospel that has withered, while the state remains.

This past summer and fall, it seemed ever clearer to me in Yugoslavia, Hungary, and Czechoslovakia that communism in these three radically different countries is simply emoted out, its authenticity (like the Bible's here) evaporated. Just as they are in the West, the twin preoccupations of the Easterners are the procurement of bacon and beans and the fear of war. Nobody loves communism, but there is no more thought of a substitute for it than there is of a substitute for parliamentary capitalism here. What abides, there as here, and sustains these Reagans and Andropovs in their misgovernment, is bedrock attachment to the rally-'round-the-flag nation-state. Said Pator Josef Hromadka, that most fervent of Christians, "I love my Czechoslovakia, I love my communist Czechoslovakia."

Just as it is in the West, the prevailing sentiment is defensive chauvinism. There is a general deflation of enthusiasm for anything in a world moving relentlessly toward self-destruction, with power out of hand everywhere. In the East there is no more comprehension of the stakes in Afghanistan than there is in the West of the stakes in Beirut (or Grenada); no comprehension and no interest beyond a free-floating dread of what tomorrow (or even today) will bring.

:

There are two notable exceptions to the pervasive collapse of all passion apart from primitive patriotism. One is Poland, where, however, the prerevolutionary spirit symbolized by Solidarity is being steadily ground down by the combined pressures of the police power and the country's economic desperation. The other is the anti-American disarmament movement in West Germany, spread now to the middle-aged middle class from the best of the young people who were not even born in Hitler's time.

The polls everywhere reveal the growing opposition to the headlong course of events in the American and Russian governments, but the spirit one excavates from private and public sources, East no less than West, is resignation, the resignation of the mouse face to face with the cat and aware that he cannot get back to the hole in which he can hide. In the East, resignation is coupled with a similarly suicidal sentiment of universal cynicism that outstrips the West's by far.

It is not just that nobody in the East seems to believe in anything; nobody *believes* anything or anybody. If, say, 30 to 50 percent of the American people disbelieve what their government tells them about the South Korean jetliner, 80 to 90 percent of the people in the East disbelieve what they are told about such an event. The Easterners may be said to be in the healthier position, for they are bombarded from all sides by the Western version of events via radio channels which are impossible to jam, and the Western version has some plausibility. We Westerners, on the other hand, have no real access to contradiction or challenge of the official version we get; like our government, our press (and especially our broadcast press) habitually dismisses reports, arguments, and proposals from the East with a back-page sneer.

The Easterners live among the lies, large and small, they all know to be lies. They accept no official output on its face except the weather, the legal notices, the football scores, and the obituaries (and not always those). To live this way for thirty-five years (or, in Russia, for sixty-five) is to have one's spirit brought, and kept, terribly low; to live this way is to know that one lives under a government which cannot be trusted in any respect, and to have to rely on whispered word-of-mouth. To despise the government long enough and profoundly enough is, of course, to despise the system that perpetuates the government that reduces the citizen to a stupefied subject.

The news from Poland these last cataclysmic years is precisely the case in point. The reports from Warsaw are printed briefly in the back of the Eastern papers, invariably deprecating Solidarity as a Western-inspired movement of no consequence, and are everywhere taken as falsifications. Living around the corner from each other, Europeans have a much more acute sense of contemporary history than we have. They saw in Poland the emergence of a pattern that actually threw down the gauntlet to totalitarianism in a great nationwide uprising unlike the earlier rebellions in Poland, East Germany, and Hungary. Throughout the East bloc, every bit of the broadcast news on Warsaw was wolfed down as it came from the Western stations, from West Germany, from Austria, from the BBC foreign service, above all from the fairly reliable and extremely powerful Voice of America and from the Americans' scurrilous agit-prop Radio Free Europe. Everywhere in the East enterprising individuals tape Western programs for none-too-secret dissemination.

In East Germany and Czechoslovakia, and to a considerable extent in Poland, Hungary, and Rumania, countries which have had the experience of open or partly open systems, the people learned early in the communist era that the system they have come to despise despised them. Lenin's War Communism, which was going to last only until all vestiges of bourgeois attachment had been eradicated, persists in all its insulting rigidity in the satellite countries. In Russia – in 1917 a phenomenally backward and autocratic society – the projected short-lived dictatorship is well into its third generation. No one I know in the East expects it to ameliorate; communism (so the argument goes) is still under aggressive siege by the bourgeois world. The argument has some validity, but not enough validity to justify the treatment of whole peoples like children, and bad children at that, who are not to be trusted to hear conflicting voices.

The highly literate and socially sophisticated East Germans and Czechs, in particular, lead sullen and resentful lives (as do the Poles, who, since Solidarity, see the truth in the streets and hear the lies in that night's newscast). In the Bad Old Days before the Prague Spring of 1968 and its termination by the Russians, you could get a fair, if irregular, assortment of Western newspapers at any of the Czech hotels catering to foreigners; now you can get them nowhere, and the Westerner at the border control is asked whether he has any newspapers or magazines. Last fall, I scoured Prague in vain, finding in the bar at one luxury hotel a back issue of the French Communist *L'Humanité*. (The more recent issues had been confiscated, grabbed by guests, or never made available; the management was, of course, unable to enlighten me.)

The availability of Western newspapers is as good a crude way as any to judge the effective inflexibility of the line in the Eastern countries. In Warsaw and East Berlin, as in Prague, they are nowhere to be found. Smuggled in by an occasional visitor from the West, they are snatched up and handed around until they are tattered. In Budapest, they can be obtained easily, if spasmodically, at the "foreign" hotels. In Yugoslavia, they are for sale everywhere. True, there are few Yugoslavs or Hungarians who read a foreign language well enough to go to the trouble and expense of buying foreign publications, but plenty of East Germans would read the West German press (just as most listen to the broadcasts).

The real differences among societies are, of course, differences of degree, not of kind. Without their having to be prohibited, communist publications are scarce on American newsstands and are often stopped by the U.S. Postal Service when they enter by mail. There is the persistent suspicion that selected mail in both directions is opened here. There, of course, postal censorship is routine. (A West German customs inspector once had the post-Nazi impudence to ask me whether I was carrying any newspapers from Prague.) The Western governments may be mendacious, contemptuously asserting the incredible. But there is a press in the West to trip them up. Jefferson was never righter than when he said better an unfree government than an unfree press.

The unfree press – print and broadcast alike – in all of the communist countries is uniformly atrocious. The monopoly newspapers are simply laughable, with East Germany's *Neues Deutschland* leading them all in fatuity – the daily fare of a people at least as highly cultivated as our own. Like dirty little children, the East Europeans are careful of what they say, and where, and to whom. They still, after thirty-five years, lower their voices when they speak with Westerners and prefer private homes to public places.

:

So life is, day after day, year after year, lifetime after lifetime, no bowl of cherries for that proportion of the citizenry, varying from country to country, who are conscious of having to accept unrelenting mental and moral mistreatment as the price of physical welfare, or who engage in a lifelong conspiratorial resistance to it.

The general demoralization is abundantly and immediately experienced at the lowest level by the Western visitor, who cannot leave his hotel room – or, sometimes, stay in it – without being openly accosted by offers of crowns, dinars, forints, and East German marks at ridiculously low black-market rates in exchange for the hard currencies the denizens of these hapless lands are forbidden to have or use. If the prohibition were actually enforced (or enforceable), the "unofficial" traffic would not exist as openly as it does on the streets, the recipients of the hard currencies having no way to dispose of them. Once in a while, but too rarely to inhibit the trade, the Westerner may be police-trapped, but the money market is all but universal in the tourist neighborhoods.

The prevalence of the black market informs the inhabitants of these countries that their own currency is close to worthless and persuades them to dream of being in those lands where "real" money is the freely exchanged medium of commerce. The Eastern European governments actually stimulate the illegal market by operating special shops featuring imported and higher-class domestic goods. You can get anything from a car (without waiting) to a Swiss chocolate bar by walking into one of these special shops and paying with coupons, or "bons," obtainable only with Western money. The shops are all over the country and are always crowded with the same natives who, forbidden to have foreign currency, are permitted to have and use the bons whether they get them legally (sent by Western friends or relatives) or illegally – with no questions asked.

Tyranny, a bright Yugoslav told me, is always and everywhere inefficient. (A bright Frenchman named Montesquieu said that the slave has one liberty, the liberty to work only when he has to.) These governments cut their own throats by forbidding the possession of foreign specie and operate these special shops for their own people to attract that specie. The black money market springs up at once wherever a country blocks its own currency, and especially where other countries put pressure on it. It appeared in England when the export of the pound was forbidden after World War II. It appeared instantly last summer, when France restricted the export of the franc, doing away with holiday travel abroad except for those who had access to foreign currencies. But when it goes on into the second and third generation, it reduces common honesty and common loyalty to the vanishing point.

Thus the communist financial system staggers dispiritedly – and dispiritingly – along from year to year and from decade to decade. It doesn't work, as it never has, and, one supposes, as it never will, not against the human ingenuity that defies all central systemization and, above all, the central systemization of finance. It was thirty years ago that the wonderful old Czech communist (and Cabinet member) Vlasta Petrankova said, "It will be a long time before we have communism and a still longer time before we have communists."

By contrast, the Western nonsystem, boom or bust, carries the conviction that it is the financiers and their clients, not the system or the government, that cannot manage an unmanageably big household. In the "free world" free-for-all, financial collapse is not ascribed to the government; no one here blames the forces of marketplace hanky-panky on the White House. There being no official morale, there is no official demoralization when, for instance, the stock market plummets. A primitive Soviet primer began, "We have a plan. In America they have no plan," and that is precisely the communist problem. They have a plan. They have *a* plan.

Their one big plan falls all over itself for want of the initiative at every level that follows the competitive urge of capitalism – of cut-throat capitalism. I was in Prague more than three years ago, and found Jungmannova Square in the center of the city closed for the construction of a new subway station. More than three years later it was still closed, still under construction; the necessary materials are hard-to-impossible to come by because the central planning of the communist bloc requires the Czechs to deliver heavy equipment to the more industrially backward sister countries. They have a plan.

The controls don't control. If you want a plumber or an electrician in the West you get him pronto, at twenty to forty dollars an hour; in the East, where people moonlight illegally and nobody has the twenty or forty dollars, you wait days or weeks or months. And this, too, after thirty-five or sixty-five years. The national product at every level remains shoddy, or at least suspect. An Easterner permitted to visit a Western country returns with the maximum permissible amount of medical supplies, appliances, soap, diapers, food, towels, clothing; his bulging bundles testify to his faithlessness in the quality of domestic manufacture right down the line.

The communist governments have all been forced by foot-dragging pressure on the part of the farmers and merchants to let the private sector expand at the retail level little by little. (Half of Hungary's retail trade is now in private hands; said the liberalizing Janos Kadar, "We are going to have socialism *and* eat," and Hungary's variety of fresh foods testifies to his *non*-communist determination in a world where the distribution breakdown – this too after thirty-five years, and sixty-five – is as comical as it is chronic, and as insulting to the citizenry.)

The market functions marginally – if only marginally – better than it used to in the Eastern countries. Whoever has flown from Tashkent to Moscow in midsummer has marveled at the net bags of melons carried by passengers and crew (including the pilots) from dirt-cheap Central Asia to the sky-high capital. Midsummer, too, like as not provides cabbage as the only salad in a restaurant. "Our favorite salad," says a Czech, "is tomato and onion, but you get one in the summer and the other in the winter." On one famous occasion when trade balance or politics – probably the former – cut off the delivery of

Israeli oranges to Prague and there was no fresh fruit at all to be had, the marketplace was suddenly flooded one midwinter day with pineapples; it seemed (so the gossip went) that the Czechs had just shipped a spark-plug factory to Havana.

So the first fine careless socialist rapture dies on the vine of careful practice. All the more backward socialist countries are richer than they once were; the most advanced (Czechoslovakia and East Germany) poorer. Going up the grand staircase of the Smetana Hall in Prague, a Czech gestures at the Carrara marble and says, "Our ancestors were rich." The marble is in notoriously short supply today; the marble money goes to pay for medical care, for education, for wages, and for rent. (Item: the wage spread, apart from artistic and scientific exceptions, is of the order of ten times in a communist country, from the lowest-paid laborer to the highest-paid executive. Item: Wages are, roughly, one-tenth of ours, rents one-twentieth.)

No money for marble. No money even for the proper replacement of the anciently patterned cobblestone walks with anything more than crude cement. The patchwork shabbiness is everywhere evident in these beautiful old cities. No money for façade. There is some variety and color on the avenues of the metropolis, but out in the neighborhoods, and in the small towns, the shopping streets are universally drab, with their uniform window displays and their painted storefront designations: GROCERIES, BREAD, MEAT, PHARMACY. The One Big Store needn't be jazzed up to titillate the shopper. There are no bargains, no sales, no closeouts, no specials, and the price, along with the merchandise, is everywhere the same, proportionately at the same cost level as ours, except for quality clothing, which is very high. Hard times; perpetually hard times, if somewhat less hard than they were. But Prague's magnificent Hradcany Castle towering over the magic city is no longer illuminated except on special occasions.

:

Taken all in all, it must be said that it goes on working pretty badly – "it" being the system at every social level. And taken all in all, the nonsystem of the West goes on working pretty well, if more and more rockily. But people hunger and freeze and live illiterate and die for want of medical care in the random effervescence of the nonsystem, and nobody, but nobody, does any of those things in the dim, dismal lockstep of the communist East. "They don't care about individuals" – "they," always "they," everywhere now – "they only care about groups." Here, in the realm of economic justice, is the communist trump all over the unrich world. Modified capitalism – the modification under fire by reactionary governments and their supporters – is a fine system for the rich and for those who think they may one day be rich. It is not such a fine system for those who are poor or who think they may one day be poor.

But people are not political all their days or every day. People there no more than here assess the quality of their little lives in terms of the First Amendment. "Who," said an unreconstructed old Nazi when I pointed out that there had been no free speech under Hitler, "who wants to make a speech?"

People measure their lives by mundane considerations. And if their lives are measured by, say, the arts, they are, on the whole, much better off there than here; if by letters, even under the rod, no worse off than we are. If we measure (or are to be measured) by music, Prague has *three* philharmonics – "Every Czech a musician" – and the Budapest railway workers have a full symphony orchestra of their own, with student admission everywhere free or nominal. Their child care and schooling, besides being completely free, are far better than ours, their higher schools uninfected by drugs. They have done away with most crime and with much prostitution. They have much less alcoholism than we have, much less suicide, much less divorce and child abuse and abandonment. Are we happier than they with our little lives from day to day and night to night?

And that is not taking the comparison all in all by any means. *All* in all they have the supreme moral bulge on us, to which capitalism has no retort except the big battalions or the tragic view that man is not now, and never has been, and never will be good enough to be a communist, that he simply (and the black market shows it) isn't corrigible. The idea of capitalism is a very bad idea, permitting, as it does, one man to sit down to four meals a day while another sits down to two, or one, or none. It is charming, and its kaleidoscopic boulevards are aglitter with the competitive glut of sugarplums. It is still a bad idea – so the better it works the worse it is.

What is wrong with the bromide that it is better to fail doing the right thing than to succeed doing the wrong? Or that a nice try is better than no try at all? The idea of Christ's apostles – communism – is a good idea. True, it worked pretty badly, as witness the sad story of Ananias and Sapphira. Though the current try may want another millennium or two to accumulate decisive evidence, it too doesn't look too good after thirty-five and sixty-five years.

The capitalists did a cruel and fairly workable job of keeping the world the way it was for a couple of hundred years. The communists tried to change it. There are abundant signs that they are losing heart, but that in itself, while it may be a sin, is no crime. For all their mortal error in substituting force for voluntarism, the heirs of Christian communism still have the bulge on the professing Christians, for force is less sinful than hypocrisy (Acts 4: 34,35).

: : : *Just Like the Gentiles* : : :

To be a Jew is to be conscious of being a Jew and of being called one; conscious, too, of the world's disorder and degradation and the odds that are stacked against one in it; conscious of having to fight. And of not wanting to.

Are the Israelis Jews?

General George (Blood and Guts) Patton was not a Jew. Einstein was a Jew – like Bugsy Siegel, and Hart, Schaffner, and all three or four Marxes. (Karl was a Jew, like Groucho.)

To be a Jew is to be in trouble and/or make trouble and/ or avoid trouble. It is to maintain – that is, be stuck with – a non-low profile and to hanker after a low one plus approval. It is to be a liquor dealer or a con man or a two-pants-suit salesman or a violinist, especially a two-pants-suit salesman or a violinist. Or a professor. Or a doctor. Or a lawyer. (But not an accountant.)

In any case, an interesting (and interested) fellow, unless he's only a Gentile in drag. Gentiles, with exceptions, some of them honorable, are not at all that interesting. (Take your cold fish, now, a cheerful, incurious sort playing his cards close to the vest, and like as not you've got a Gentile on your hands.)

To be a Jew is to be a money-lender among Gentiles who don't know and don't care that the Gentiles forced the Jews to be money-lenders or lose their protection from pogrom a millennium ago. *Schutzjuden.* To be a Jew, then, is to have a little money, and, if possible, a lot more, and to spend it self-ishly and selflessly. To be a Jew is to be a big giver and to be seen giving big, putting your mouth where your money is. To be a Jew is to be a philanthropist, but not an anonymous philanthropist.

Are the Israelis Jews?

From *The Progressive*, October 1982.

To be a Jew is to fight and fight interminably but not to be a soldier and fight with carnal weapons (at which Jews are bound to lose). "I just want to bash in a few Nazi heads before I die," said Louie Gottschalk to Morris Raphael Cohen, and Morris Raphael Cohen said, "Louie, bashing in heads is for the 96 percent, not for the 4 percent."

But holocaust appears to be an acquired taste. Hitler transmitted it to the Jews of Israel, even though he was beaten and dead when he did it. That's how he won the war, recruiting the battered, tattered remnant who fled to Israel to perpetrate a racist holocaust no matter what the world says.

Are the Israelis Jews?

"I like," says a Jew who tries to stay out of trouble and maintain a low profile (and be approved), "to think of them as Israelis and not as Jews." (But the Sunday paper has a cartoon captioned, "Still Trying to Hatch," showing a dove sitting on an egg labeled "Arabs-Jews Peace.") "You know," said Otto Kahn to the hunchback, "I used to be a Jew." "I know," said the hunchback, "I used to be a hunchback."

A Gentile is something else altogether. To be a Gentile is to want to get along – not a bad thing – but to go along in any case. There's no point in a Jew's going along; there's nobody to go along with. In Chicago, some Jews put up a statue of a Jewish hero of the American Revolution, thinking that the Gentiles would admire it and be less anti-Semitic. It didn't work out. The Jews admired it, and the Gentiles went right by it. Ten years after the statue was erected there was one millimeter-to-the-nth-degree more or less anti-Semitism in Chicago (and everywhere else).

Not all they that say, "Lord, Lord," shall enter the Kingdom. Not on your tintype. Not in a pig's ear. Not all Jews fit the stereotype, but enough do to raise the question: Are the Israelis Jews?

Not all Jews are Jews, and not all Gentiles are Gentiles. Some Jews are ridiculous enough to be Gentiles, and some Gentiles are wayward enough to be Jews. You can't tell a Jew by what he says or does or calls himself (or changes his name to). Only by what he is.

Jews aren't soldiers, Masada or no Masada, Maccabees or no Maccabees. General George (Blood and Guts) Patton was a Gentile, and so was Dickie Nixon, who got his Quaker mother to take him to the Patton movie every time it came to town. A Jew is likely to be killed in any saloon brawl or lynching, so he doesn't want to kill. But he is being killed all the time, in retaliation for having sent the Jew Jesus forth to torment the Gentiles by preaching the un-Gentile preachment of redemptive love. Are the Israelis Jews?

Besides Morris Raphael Cohen, there is Philip P. Cohen, who was waiting for a rush-hour bus in Madison, Wisconsin, which he adorns, and a bus with people hanging out all the doors and windows went by without stopping. "A clear case of anti-Semitism," said Philip P. Cohen. Jews are touchy, and their best jokes, like Philip P. Cohen's, are about their touchiness. You'd be touchy, too, if you were a Jew. The Jews smile and laugh and tell jokes, but they aren't sure that the other fellow (even the other Jew) likes them at all. They want to be both assertive – they have to skate fast, the ice is so thin – and popular.

Are the Israelis Jews?

Jews are disproportionate. They are disproportionately few. They are disproportionately perfervid. They are disproportionately radical and reactionary, disproportionately redolent of the Boy Scout virtues: thoughtful, imaginative, considerate, affectionate, loyal. And disproportionately influential; in 1941 the intrepid ignoramus, racist, and innocent Colonel Charles A. Lindbergh made a speech in Des Moines attacking the disproportionate influence of the Jews in moving the country into war against Hitler, and he was run right out of American life, so disproportionately influential were the Jews.

Clout; they have clout galore. The Jewish vote may not be ignored. It may not be alienated. It has to be bought in oratorial currency by every President and candidate for President, every Senator, every Representative, every metropolitan alderman. The small Jewish vote is more important than the big black vote because the Jews have disproportionate clout. Have it and use it. When Prime Minister Begin was here at the height of the Israeli massacre of the Lebanese and the Palestinians (in that order), here to tell President Reagan that he wanted more of his guns but none of his lip, there was a luncheon for Begin by the leading Jews, that is the rich Jews (just like the Gentiles), and the luncheon raised $27 million for Israeli "development." "Never in the past," said Begin graciously, "was the great Jewish community of the United States so united around Israel."

Begin is right – and the great Jewish community of the United States is a hissing and an abomination. The American Jews are shameless when they cover themselves and say, "Nobody here but us Americans, boss," and just as shameless when they uncover themselves and hand the Israeli destroyers $27 million.

The worst thing about the great Jewish community of the United States is that it is no worse than the great Gentile community. The worst thing about the britches-busting little community of Israel is that it is no worse than the Arabs. To be no worse than the Arabs or the Americans is not to be much good. To do no worse than the Arabs did at the Munich Olympic Village or the Americans at My Lai is no good at all. The Israelis – smart Jews, eh? – did it better in Lebanon. But are they Jews?

They could be Americans, or Britons, or Huns, adjusting to the environment – the sovereign American, British, and Hun principle. But they were supposed (if they were Jews) to be different from the Americans, or the Britons, or the Huns. I will tell you how different they are, in fact, from the Americans, the Britons, and the Huns. Well along into the second month of the slaughter of the innocents in Beirut (and in sinless Sidon, and in sinless Tyre), Ronald Reagan, a Gentile Begin, deplored the Israeli use of "self-defensive" U.S. weapons for self-offense. The most frightful of those weapons – unmentioned – was, of course, the cluster bomb. But a couple of weeks later there was an obscure little leak from some sneaky corner (anti-Semitic, eh?) in Washington that "cluster bombs have not been sent to Israel in recent years. . . . Israel now manufactures its own cluster bombs" – and exports them, just like the Gentiles?

The Jews were supposed to have been chosen, perhaps for suffering, perhaps for sacrifice, perhaps for teaching the Gentiles justice, mercy, and humility. They were supposed to be different and do differently from the Gentiles. That was the Big Idea. They were supposed not to worship the work of their own hands and whore after false gods, as the Gentiles do, and abandon justice, mercy, and humility for the pursuit of money, fame, and power. In righteousness (their prophet told them) were they to be established.

Look at them in Israel now. Are these, too, these Americans, Britons, Huns – are these Jews?

"Let me tell you," said the late Robert M. Hutchins, "how I became anti-Semitic. I was already anti-Gentile, but I didn't know I was anti-Semitic until the evening of December 31, 1932. In order to stay awake past my bedtime – it was New Year's Eve – I engaged one of our University of Chicago trustees in conversation. He had money, he was generous, and, what was more to the point, he was a leader of the Jewish community – a pushover for purposes of the conversation. I told him that for $250,000 I could make the University of Chicago the greatest university in history in ninety days. He said he thought the money could be found – I always liked that 'found' – but how did I propose to bring the miracle to pass? I told him that I was a great student of modern European history and that President von Hindenburg could not avoid appointing Hitler chancellor of Germany for more than another sixty days. (I was optimistic by thirty.) All I would need, if I could get started right away, would be another thirty days after that to hire every Jewish scholar in Germany – and get them for coffee and buns. The leader of the Jewish community said, 'Oh,' and then he said, 'Bob, there is a lot of anti-Semitism in this country, and it's growing. The trouble is that there are too many Jews here now.'"

There is no adjusting to the modern world, not for the Jews. "You can change your noses," said the punster Rabbi Emil G. Hirsch during the plastic surgery boom, "but you can not change your Moses." The Israelis right now are the triumph of the modern world, swinging America (by virtue of the American Jewish clout) by the tail and hitting people at random, hitting them with only one distinction: They are Arabs. Arabs are not our kind of people; they do not bleed like the Gentile Shylock. These Israelis – a few thousand of them protested their country's atrociousness – are these Israelis Jews? Not if the protesters are.

On November 7, 1938, a young German Jewish refugee in Paris shot the third secretary of the German Embassy. The attempted assassination served the Nazis as the pretext for staging the *Kristallnacht* pogrom throughout Germany with the burning of shops and synagogues and homes and schools and the arrest and torment and deportation of thousands of Jews (and the murder of countless of them). On June 3, 1982, a young Arab in London shot the Israeli ambassador to England, and the attempted assassination served the Israelis as the pretext for staging a two-month pogrom throughout Lebanon with the burning of shops and mosques and homes and schools – and hospitals – and the murder and maiming of thousands of Arabs. These Israelis now – just like the Gentiles – are they Jews?

The Jews that Hitler left alive – the remnant – had to do something, go somewhere. The whole heartless world, including the United States, rejected them (as it subsequently rejected the Palestinians). The Israeli-Arab "crisis" began – and the statesmen all knew it began – sixty-three years ago when the British government decided it could bring worldwide Jewish influence to the side of war-torn England by saying coyly that "His Majesty's Government view with favour the establishment in Palestine of a national home for the Jewish people," adding, equally coyly, that "it [is] clearly understood that nothing shall be done which may prejudice the civil and religious rights of non-Jewish communities in Palestine. . . ." Just how this trick was ever to be turned, short of the armed establishment of multiple sovereignties, the Balfour Declaration just as coyly neglected to say.

The ancient Zionist dream of Eretz Yisrael, which inspired the Declaration, was similarly coy. Who really cared about the miserable Arabs as long as the Jews retrieved their 2,000-year-old Homeland (which was also the Arabs' 1,000-year-old Homeland)? But the world needs another Balkan ethnocracy like it needed – and was bound to get – another hole in the head. The only difficulty with the "Middle Eastern" problem is that it is insoluble (except on a bloody patchwork basis) short of great-power intervention moving the world closer to a third, and last, great war.

:

Whatever is to be done about the Jews? What ever are they to do? Where ever are they to go? Nobody wants them. (Nobody wants anybody.) They can not, it seems, help themselves very much whatever they do, wherever they go. They seem to be conditioned by ages of suffering and sacrifice imposed – the suffering and sacrifice they spurned like the tough mugs they were in the days of the prophets. What can be done for them to get them out of the mud and blood in which they wallow with the Americans, the Britons, and the Huns?

They could be prayed for, if only the Gentiles knew how to pray and the Jews themselves were not too busy wallowing to pray. The Israelis' Gentile conduct has isolated them from the only Gentile friends (dubious friends, at that) they had in the world. They stand alone, as they stood before Hitler, not in despair and mystification, but in jackbooted pride. Jewish eagles, as they were of Biblical yore, they fly high over their victims, hands hopelessly outstretched to them, dropping fire made in America. These are Jews?

A truly woebegone people with their Gentile bravura, a people who have, as their God told their prophet, "turned their back on me, and not their face" – what can be done for them? The Jewish cliché has it that the Jewish problem is really a Gentile problem. Not so. The Gentiles don't know how to solve problems; just look at them and their Gentile world. The fact of Isaiah and Jeremiah, of Amos and Hosea, is that the Gentile problem is really a Jewish problem. The Jews have got to save the world's soul and begin by saving their own. They can't do it any cheaper – least of all by being like the Gentiles.

: : : *This England* : : :

Now hear this:

England's outlay for garrisoning the Falkland Islands – apart from the cost of last year's war – is projected at a billion pounds ($1.6 billion) a year for the next ten years, enough to give every Falklandian householder an outright payment of $8 million, send him on his way a multimillionaire, and let the Argies have the bloody islands back, complete with their only natural resource, wind.

You say the British are fools.

You say it – I don't.

I say they and we and all the great warmaking peoples are fools. We are all fools because we all want butter *and* guns and we can't have both; not any more. In ages past, the great warmaking peoples were able to pay for the guns and for what little butter they consumed, partly because guns (and the men to fire them) were cheaper than they are now and partly because most of the citizens were living very low on the hog.

Furthermore, the great warmaking nations made inexpensive war on the helpless people of the Third World and annexed them as customers, servants, and slaves – and stole their resources. Winston Churchill called India "the brightest star in the Emperor's crown," and it was legendary in the business City of London that India contributed a shilling to every British pound. Belgium's Africa was fifty times the size of the mother country. With the help of their colonies, the great warmaking nations were able to maintain their guns-and-butter necessities in adequate proportions.

Every great warmaking nation contained its own Third World at home – its poor and its old and its sick. The deni-

From *The Progressive*, October 1983. Mayer published another article under the same title in the October 1968 issue of *The Progressive*.

zens of this domestic Third World were left to starve and die in the great warmaking slums urban and rural. They did not consume much butter; theirs was not what the classical economists called an effective demand. And they paid their share for the guns in exchange for crumbs of bread and continuous circuses.

But their expectations were aroused by the technological marvels of the Twentieth Century, just as the expectations of the colonial Third Worlders abroad were (much more modestly) aroused. Among the Third Worlders at home those expectations are now not rising but fully risen: The British standard of living has doubled during the thirty years of the present Elizabeth. Adam Smith's Eighteenth and Nineteenth Century "laboring poor" had had enough cap-doffing. In 1945, having flung mighty Churchill and his Tories out of office, they demanded what the Labour Party called "a land fit for heroes."

Thus the welfare state came into being in the country whose poor had been the worst off in northern Europe. (When you met an Englishman over thirty with more than three of his own teeth, you knew you were meeting a duke.) Overnight there were hundreds of thousands of publicly built houses and flats. Overnight there was universal access to free education, including Oxford and Cambridge. Overnight there was a triumphant program of universal free medical care, of which an eminent advocate of private practice admits, "The National Health Service provides extremely well for emergency patients and those who are gravely ill." (The private sector does better, he says, with its consumer orientation toward routine problems.)

Just as Ronald Reagan, if he had his druthers, would get rid of Social Security altogether, beginning with Medicare, so England's Prime Minister Margaret Thatcher would like to knock off the financially staggered NHS. But the welfare state, however these anachronists chip away at it, is not to be dismembered or dismantled. It is fully matured and untouchable in all the great warmaking countries. Economically if not politically, it is at war against the warfare state. Every welfare/ warfare state, without exception, is now engaged in the agonizing process of discovering that it can no longer afford both kinds of goody.

Nowhere is the discovery as sharply obvious as it is in the United States, the biggest warmaker of them all, where a welfare Congress halfheartedly fights a warfare President. Nowhere is it more ironically highlit than in Germany and Japan, whose warmaking expense is borne almost entirely by the United States – and whose economies therefore outdistance all the other old warmakers in investment and production (and in employment, trade balance, and inflation control). And nowhere is the welfare/warfare dilemma more pitiful and portentous than in flat-busted England.

:

England has the industrial world's highest unemployment rate. For the first time in its industrial history, England has to import more manufactured goods than it exports. Its declining economic growth rate would be more than wiped out were it not for its North Sea gas and oil extractions (which will taper off two years from now), every penny of whose proceeds is required to meet the country's social security system (which is close to the breaking point).

This flat-busted England, with a Tory government returned to office on the basis of the hollow victory in the Falklands, has announced a 13.4 percent increase in military spending for 1984.

The welfare/warfare confrontation represents a struggle to the death within each of the great warmaking countries between the poor and the rich. Welfare is the salvation of the poor, warfare of the rich. Welfare payments are everywhere too low to sustain a decisive proportion of the national economy, but warfare payments keep the economy from collapsing.

Call all the full-time jobholders the wealthy – independent as they are of public support. They have no stake in welfare – quite the contrary – and a considerable stake in war. But the poor, including the young who are jobless year after year, have no direct interest in warfare except insofar as they see that it provides them jobs; they, too, as they come gradually to the consciousness of their condition and their prospects, are among welfare's apparently irreducible legions.

But their consciousness develops slowly in England, for there is something dense about the English. In March of last year, Margaret Thatcher was by all odds the most unpopular Prime Minister in recent British history. Her Reaganesque Conservatives were losing critical by-elections one after another as unemployment surged past 13 percent and interest rates drove more and more small (and some big) businesses to the wall. Then the Argentinians, with an economy even more sorely beset than Britain's, resorted to the timeless ploy of tottering tyrants, seizing the Falkland Islands, which the British had absentmindedly seized from them a century before. This mad gambit did not save the Argentinian junta; the junta it saved was Britain's.

No sooner did the nutty Argentinians land than Prime Minister Thatcher resolutely dispatched the British Navy a hefty 8,000 miles to turn the invaders back and recover that last little vestige of the Empire. The cost to the nearly bankrupt British was horrendous – not the least in the world's respect. "Is this really the kind of nation we wish to be," asks the distinguished British historian E. P. Thompson, "and is this how we wish to be seen in the world?" But Margaret Thatcher wasn't counting the cost to Britain and its good name; she was counting the votes in the next election. Her resolve, she resolved, would sweep her jingo-starved people off their silly feet, and, as she put it in her subsequent election campaign, restore their "confidence and self-respect."

It did the trick for Thatcher & Company. The "Falklands factor" carried the Thatcher Tories back into office in a vote that cut across every age group and every economic condition. (Sixty percent of the trade unionists voted against the unions' own Labour Party.)

Margaret Thatcher spoke to the British tradition, and as good as destroyed the party of the workers who no longer want to think of themselves as workers. And in passing she turned back what a couple of years ago looked like a centrist threat in the form of the new Liberal/Social Democratic Alliance. Like Reagan, she unmistakably projects a kind of capitalist cannibalism, or Social Darwinism. She means to denationalize British Airways and the country's airports, telephone system, and steel industry; she means to establish, on an utterly insufficient island, a little America.

Why did her countrymen, including her unemployed countrymen, vote for her? They voted for her because the recklessly brutal Falklands venture aroused the brutal recklessness that underlies, and has always underlain, the genteel reserve mistakenly taken for the British character. It wasn't genteel reserve that made the scepter'd isle the ravening terror of the world a century and two ago. Among the naval and military greats, savages in uniform, to whom their victims the world around were Kipling's lesser breeds, the genteel reserve readily gave way to the bullyboy.

In the class society par excellence, the British masses always took their cue, all their cues, good and bad, from their always respected betters; the police did not have to carry guns because the policeman was respected. The masses overwhelmingly wanted, and still want, hanging restored, but their betters, in and out of Parliament, did not, and so it wasn't. If the English commoner was usually polite to strangers – not friendly, just polite – it was because his betters were.

Not any more; not really since the time between the world wars (in both of which Britain was the only country on either side to fight from the first day of hostilities to the last). The second war mingled the classes, especially on the beleaguered home front. After the war "bloody-mindedness" appeared among the commoners. Hard-nosed selfishness – "Fuck you, Jack, *Ah'm* orl raht" – gradually became the order of the day. A policeman or two a year was murdered, guns were issued to special details on the force, and crime (still minuscule compared with ours) has doubled in the past decade.

The littered streets and sidewalks of the cities, encrusted in ancient dirt, reflect the new indifference to public order. London is shockingly slovenly (not that the English at their best were ever too fastidious), a filthy city now compared, say, with Paris, whose householders and janitors turn out en masse every Saturday morning (much like Prague's "volunteer" labor brigades) to wash down their sidewalks into the gutters.

Britain's new bloody-mindedness blames the tremendous increase of public squalor on the postwar waves of "coloured" immigration from the Arab countries and the former colonies – Britishers all, coming home to the motherland to roost with their strange habiliments, their strange housekeeping, and their strange zealousness ("taking jobs away from Englishmen" – in which latter endeavor they are protected by race-relations laws). But reliable opinion hangs most of the littering on the native young Englishmen with their new craze for fast foods and fast cars and their drunken dustups after football games and their outbreaks of street violence against their dark-skinned tenement neighbors.

With unemployment as high as it is, and the unions entrenching the older workers so that half the young school-leavers are idle, and without public-works projects or conscription to absorb them, hooliganism, "Pakki-bashing" in particular, is never far below the surface. The tension between the blacks and the police is high and growing. While the East Indians are solidly established at almost every level of the British social structure, the newly arrived West Indians and African blacks are not. There is not a "coloured" member of Parliament (and almost no women).

The signs of disintegrative protest and of alienation are everywhere among the young who responded – but for how long? – to the Prime Minister's war-cry. Attire ranges from general dishevelment among the mods and the rockers and skinheads to heavily lipsticked homosexuals and orange-haired punks and their wildly attired "birds" with skirts up to here.

:

And yet . . . and yet . . . this England, this scepterless isle, let go of its colonies after the second world war with greater grace and liberality than any other colonial power has ever done before or since, and these, too, were Englishmen, and this, too, was England, and not all that long ago.

The new breed of British tradesman, the "American," is young and drives a Rolls. He uses American methods and he uses doddering members of the old nobility to front for him on his boards of directors. He has no interest in British stand-pat traditions or in British culture as it is encapsulated by the Royal Shakespeare Company and the BBC. That culture, at Eton, Harrow, and Winchester, still prepares high-collared young aristocrats for the ways of the old Empire, while the brash new elite hacks its way through, around, over, and under the British tradition of doing not very much business at the old stand. The fading class that for generations put its stamp on so much of the world grows daily less relevant and less distinct.

That fading class did not do much for the fine arts or for music; England has always been far behind France, Germany, and Italy. Nor did it do much to move the British masses, who, in contrast with the continental commonalty, are not much to be seen at the serious theater, the recitals, the opera, or the museums. But it achieved an unexampled apogee in its use of language oral and written. Its declining influence is still sufficient to maintain *The Times* against the cheapening impulses of its upstart new owner, the Australian Rupert Murdoch (who has converted *The New York Post* into a scandal sheet). England's penny-dreadful press is the world's most dreadful, but its classic national newspapers sustain a level of discussion – and vocabulary – unparalleled anywhere. (Imagine an American newspaper casually using, in one day's edition, words like "dismissive," "eponym," "psephological," and "towardliness.")

England's lettered aristocrats left England as a whole semi-literate, while imposing on the nation the characteristically British idea of undemonstrative decency and polite rejoinder, of compassion for the lost or ailing or injured stranger, of the queue formed everywhere where people are waiting, so that there is no elbowing for priority – small virtues compared with the routine repression of natives who got in the way of Empire; small virtues, too, that are failing progressively in just these years of the pedestrian's struggle to get across a street.

There has been nothing anywhere, nor is there likely to be again, like the whimsy so assiduously cultivated by "the English," that is, by, and completely restricted to, the British aristocracy. Who but an Englishman could have said, "Some say that life is the thing; I prefer books, myself," or, "The Italians were on our side in the first war, so it was only fair that the Germans should have them in the second," or, " 'My God,' said God, 'I have my work cut out for me' "? Who but an Englishman could have cooked up "O Rare Ben Jonson" for an epitaph, or produced the works of William Shakespeare or of Lewis Carroll?

What but an English newspaper could describe a season just past as "a stinking English spring" or lead off a front-page report of a storm with, "Ten people were struck by lightning yesterday . . . and a man jumped into a vat of banana custard," or conclude an elaborate exchange of Letters to the Editor on why brassieres fasten in the back with, "So you can have the fun of running around to the front and see what's happening"?

English aristocratic furnishings are splendid, like their great spectacles, but the plebs live shabbily and can neither afford nor imagine anything else. Countryside England – but not its miserable cities and its deadly towns – is more than passing beautiful and beautifully maintained, like its private little squares reserved under lock and key to the householders who abut them. But the once bloodthirsty British, bled themselves now, are not an especially beautiful people. They do not achieve the lively civilization of most of the peoples across the Channel (whither they proceed whenever they have the chance; no one ever heard of an Italian taking his holiday in England). They are by and large a pale, prosaic people, unimaginative to the point – twenty-five miles from France – of not knowing how to make a salad. And now they become a dismal people.

They are not nearly as good at the stiff-upper-lip routine as they once were; they complain now. But their complaining does not extend very far into the realm of activism. The polls confirm the common observation that the young among them – the young at Oxbridge included – are generally apathetic these days, months, and years. The only genuine sign of life on an island graced by what its weather forecasters call sunny intervals (greatly outnumbered by shady outervals) is the rugged Campaign for Nuclear Disarmament, which is getting heroically nowhere, achieving neither mass support nor mass interest.

:

Instead of puffing themselves up over the Falklands extravaganza, the British ought to be taking themselves down over their political subservience to the Americans, whom they dislike, on the whole, and what is clearly their ineluctable commercial decline to a small country of a hundred thousand charming little greengrocers, each totting up the bill in his head, in competition with the piranhas of the great buying-and-selling societies.

There is nothing revolutionary stirring among the English any more than there is among the Americans. There is nothing like Germany's Greens, a really radical party the same age as Britain's Liberal/Social Democratic Alliance but with a genuinely root-and-branch approach compared with the milk-toastish middle-ground program of the Alliance. The Labour electoral platform last June, the campaign having fallen into the hands of the not-very-far-left wing of the party, contained a plank calling for unilateral disarmament – nuclear, not nuclear and conventional. The Labour campaigners discovered early on, as the British say, that the mock-pacifist weasel wasn't catching on with the Falklands-bloated electorate and let it slide.

What impends, instead of revolution, is the steady, almost soundless disintegration into the condition of a nonpower dependency of Fortress America; incapable of sustaining itself, much less of recovering any part of its gone grandeur. "English history since the Norman Conquest," says A. J. P. Taylor, who ought to know, "falls into two chunks: first, the centuries of violence and aristocratic rule; second, the rule of the traders and capitalists which is now falling to pieces before our eyes." Anthony Sampson, probably the sharpest of England's sharp journalists, this spring published another of his Cook's Tour guides to the London establishment under the title, *The Changing Anatomy of Britain*. Great Britain, the first industrial nation, was, he says, "the first to show many ominous signs of the running down of an advanced capitalist society, and other countries were watching anxiously for their own symptoms of 'the English disease.' . . . Other countries were beginning to encounter some of Britain's difficulties. . . ."

The differences between Britain and the other late industrial states are enormous, and the differences from the United States could hardly be greater. But even the United States – as well as all the other capitalist survivors – is beginning to encounter "some of Britain's difficulties." The United States is much the greater per capita consumer of butter and much the greater producer of guns. Where Britain has spread itself comically to the Falklands, the United States has spread itself prodigally all over the world. The British go down hill perceptibly. The Americans maintain a shaky facade by means of ever more armaments and their distribution to all credentialed anticommunists.

We aren't Britain, and we never will be; we will come tumbling down not with a British whimper but with an American bang.

: : : *The Swiss* : : :

He found himself – he who was destined to be the first Swiss – on the top of a world of walls. Walls all around him. On the north walls, glaciers that never got the sun; on the south, snows that came roaring down as avalanches and then as torrents. Here and there, in the distance, a pass through the walls, open three months a year, maybe four, but no way to cross it. (Hannibal tried it with elephants.) It was the place that everybody wanted to cross (to get at the kingdoms beyond) and nobody wanted.

He who was destined to be the first Swiss found himself (and all the Swiss after him) dour. "I am," he said, "*steinreich*, rich in rocks," and he was desolate, and he prayed.

And the Lord appeared before him and said, "What can I do for you, my child?" And he said, "All I want is to survive, Lord. I came here because there was no place else to go, famine in Sweden, plague in Italy, war in Germany and France, and this was the only place that nobody wanted. If only I had a tree and an ax. . . ."

So the Lord gave him a tree and an ax and said, "Take care of them. Take very good care of them. They're all you've got." So he took very good care of them and became a careful man (and all the Swiss after him) and got firewood from the branches, boards and pegs from the limbs, and a bed from the leaves. And every night he carefully sharpened his ax (and all the Swiss after him). And he prayed.

And the Lord appeared and said, "What can I do for you, my child?" And he said, "If I had a little black dirt between the rocks, I could have something to eat besides acorns." And

Condensed from *The Progressive*, December 1974.

the Lord gave him a bushel basket of black dirt and said, "Take good care of it. It's all you've got." So he took good care of it and had some hay, and he put the hay in the barn in the evening, and he prayed, and the Lord appeared and asked him what he wanted, and he said, "I've got this hay, Lord. If I had a cow I'd have milk and I'd want for nothing." And the Lord gave him a cow and told him to take good care of it because it was all he had.

And he who was destined to be the first Swiss took good care of his cow (and all the Swiss after him) and fertilized his bushel basket of black dirt and sharpened his ax and dried his boards and built his chalet with a fence around it and saved and scraped and made do and learned (as he had to, and all the Swiss after him) to put bits and pieces together with a marvelous degree of ingenuity and precision, because they were all he had. And he prospered in a small, hard, and hardening way and never wasted and never wanted. And the walls rose all around him in the place that nobody wanted, but he never looked up. From dawn until dark – and after dark – he took care of his property because it was all he had.

And one day the Lord appeared before him and said, "My child, you have actually survived in this Godforsaken place." And he who was destined to be the first Swiss was proud, very proud, of what he had done, and said, "I've been very careful, Lord, and wasted nothing and saved every scrap and learned how to put bits and pieces together with marvelous ingenuity and precision." And the Lord said, "And how is the milk from your cow, my child? Is it good milk?" And he said proudly, "It's the best in the world, Lord. Would you like to try it?" And the Lord said, "Don't mind if I do." And he measured out a quarter litre of milk, precisely, and the Lord drank it and smacked His lips and said, "Thank you, my child." And the first Swiss said, "That will be twenty centimes, Lord."

:

And all that was before Ms. Baby Mayer and I took the 10:56 from Lucerne to Zurich one morning. At 10:55:50, precisely, the bell rang, and at 10:56 the stationmaster raised his green wand, and with never a jerk or a squeak or a rattle the train slipped ingeniously out of the station, propelled by electricity purchased (at the cheap night rate) from Germany and even from Sweden because the Swiss had learned to put bits and pieces together so marvelously that all their waterfalls did not generate enough power to power their precision industries. (This winter the Swiss will have to cut their electricity consumption 10 to 20 percent because their energy-squeezed neighbors will not sell them all the current they need.)

And the 10:56 train from Lucerne slipped noiselessly into Zurich at precisely 11:46 and Ms. Baby and I got off and went into the spotless station (which was being cleaned, even though it was spotless), and Ms. Baby remembered that she had left her cigarette lighter and cigarettes in the second-class car. So we went to the Lost and Found and the man took a chart of the train from under the counter and said, "Which car were you in, and which seats?" And we showed him on the chart (as best we could) and he said, "How many cigarettes were there?" And Ms. Baby said, "Only two." And the man said (without looking it up), "That car has gone back to Lucerne and Basel. It will be back here at 1:52 and be cleaned by 2:02. You can get your things here after that."

So we came back at 2:03 and got our things there – including the two cigarettes – in a bag marked with the train, car, and seat numbers, and the time they were found, and the number of the cleaner who found them, and the time they had been delivered to the Lost and Found, and the man said, "That will be one franc [Lord]," and I said, "How much would it be if it were a string of pearls?" and the man said, "One franc."

:

All that was before Herr Steudler, the Village Clerk of the Hasliberg, phoned me one afternoon and told me to call a number in Bern, the national capital, immediately. I didn't ask him what it was about, because he would answer, not in German, which (like all Swiss) he had learned in school, but in Swiss-German, which is a spoken, not a written, language and which all Swiss use with one another but (except for Herr Steudler) not with foreigners.

I called the number in Bern immediately and was connected with a man whose first words were, "What language do you speak?" Instead of saying, "None of your business, and who the devil are you?" I told him, and he said, "You claim to be a professor, but you leave Switzerland and return without notifying the Village Clerk." Instead of saying, "None of your business" again, and "Who the devil are you?" I explained that I'd left Switzerland the day my residence permit expired and returned to stay less than ninety days as an ordinary tourist. "You will be in this office at ten o'clock tomorrow morning," he said. Now I had to say, "What office?" "The Commandant of the Foreign Police," he said. "It is impossible to get there from here by ten," I said. "You will be here at ten," said the Commandant, "or be out of Switzerland by five P.M."

I got a lift down the mountain and rapped at the Commandant's door FREMDENPOLIZEI – at ten. It was a handsome building, like all the buildings in beautiful, slumless little Bern. The Commandant's office – and everything in it, including the two men, one at the desk, one on a chair in the corner – was strictly typecast. The room was large and dark and heavily doored and furnished. The Commandant, at a large desk with one dossier, and nothing else, on it, was thin and old with a long, lined, "sinister" face, French-Swiss or, likelier, Italian-Swiss. (His name, which I did not get from him, was something like Modriani.) The man in the chair in the corner never spoke. He was young and fleshy with (so help me) a trench coat with the collar turned up and a felt hat with the brim turned down.

"When you left Switzerland," said the Commandant, who did not introduce himself to me, "you did not inform the Village Clerk that you were going – or that you were coming back." "I informed everyone else," I said, "the postmaster, the innkeeper, the baker . . ." "Why not the Village Clerk?" "Because I cannot communicate with him," I said. "He always speaks Swiss-German instead of German, and I do not under-stand Swiss-German." The Commandant did not smile (or frown). He said, "You have been in Prague several times, Pro-fessor." (The sneer in "Professor" would be undetectable in a tape recording; you'd have had to be present to catch it.) "Yes, sir," I said. "Would you mind telling me your politics?" Instead of saying, "None of your business," like an Ameri-can, I said, shaking like a would-be American, "I am a free man." "There are all kinds of free men. You are one who has gone often to Prague." "On religious business," I said. The Commandant said, "On religious business" – tonelessly, not a question, or a contradiction, or a do-you-expect-me-to-believe-that: on a tape recording a mere repetition of my words.

I dove, unhopefully, into my briefcase. In it by (like every-thing else in it) accident was a German theological journal, *Junge Kirche*, with an article of mine on the state of the church in Czechoslovakia. He looked through it and handed it back; on or off a tape recording, nothing. "In your application for a residence permit a year ago, you said that you had to be back at your university post in America in January. This is March." "The university extended my leave." "In writing?" "Yes, sir." "I want a copy of that writing tomorrow morning."

Back up the mountain lickety-split by late afternoon, I dove, unhopefully, into my "files." I found the extension of my leave, scrawled in pencil on a half sheet of scratch paper by my department head. It read, in full, "Don't ever come back. We won't miss you. Love, Buzzy." I dove – hopelessly – into my briefcase and pulled out the official extension notice (which I had never opened), went sliding down the snow to the post office asafetida over appetite, got it into the mail as the post-master was closing the door, and never heard another word from the Commandant. The only other words I heard (that I could understand) were from the Village Clerk when he ex-tended my residence permit: "*Feef-ee-zwahnsk Frahnkeh*" for *fuenf-und-zwanzig Franken*, or twenty-five francs [Lord].

:

And all that was before my friend Peter explained it to me. "So you didn't know," said Peter, an Un-Swiss Activities type, "that we have a police state here. A very tidy police state, a very neutral police state (especially against the Communists), but a very thorough police state."

"But," I said, "one never sees a policeman on the Hasliberg – or anywhere else." "That," said Un-Swiss Peter, "is because we have a very democratic police state. Every Swiss is as much a policeman as every other."

"Informers? Spies?"

"Oh, no, nothing like that. It is just that all Swiss, or maybe I should say most Swiss, for this, too, is changing, take it upon themselves to keep order in Switzerland. This must seem strange to an American, where the only people who keep order are people hired to. We Swiss are very – very proprietary about our country. It's all we've got."

Twice in my adult life – that I can remember – a mere citizen policed me. . . . One occasion was in Tbilisi, or Tiflis, in the U.S.S.R., when I knocked my pipe dottle out into the gutter and an elderly man told me I shouldn't have done that and handed me an empty matchbox (which he put back into his pocket) to accommodate the dottle I scraped up from the gutter. The other was in Zug, in Switzerland, when an elderly woman, expensively dressed, caught up with me after I'd crossed the street against a red light to inform me angrily that what I had done was forbidden.

In the U.S.S.R., forgetting for the moment the ostentatiously threadbare civilian, you don't see a policeman except en masse at government-organized demonstrations or singly, in the crowd, and apparently off duty, listening to two truck drivers arguing (non-pugilistically) the right of way. In England you see individual policemen, unarmed, sauntering everywhere, answering tourists' questions, helping old ladies across the street, stepping out to untie traffic knots, or breaking up a fight by saying, "Now, now, gentlemen." In the ceremonial Mediterranean countries (all of them police states) they walk in pairs, sometimes with swords intended, unsuccessfully, to intimidate the crafty populace. In Germany they turn the traffic signs from green to red, fiercely. In France, a shaky police state, they are everywhere in overwhelming numbers, clubbing, gassing, and shooting. In America they, like everyone else, ride around in cars – and between cars there is always time to mug, slug, slash, slit, and run.

1. You don't need policemen to have a police state, and policemen can't keep a state policed.

2. Don't kid yourself in Switzerland.

When I reminded Peter that I had been coming back to the Hasliberg for twenty years – "They ought to know me by now, they ought to trust me" – he said, "Oh, they do, they do. But you're a foreigner, and you've been accumulating residence permits. Once you have twelve years of permitted residence you can apply for Swiss citizenship – first to the village, then, if you're accepted, to the canton, and finally to the Helvetian Confederation of Switzerland. You are suspected of wanting to be a Swiss citizen."

"Me?"

"You and every other foreigner. . . .

"We are afraid of foreigners – *all* foreigners, except tourists. Every year we have a 'xenophobe referendum' measure proposed in Parliament to limit foreigners in the country, even on a temporary basis, to 12 or even 10 percent of the population. . . ."

"Who supports the xenophobe movement?"

"Most of the farmers and villagers and some of the workers."

"To protect their jobs?"

"Not at all. They don't need their jobs protected. In 1974 we had a total of seventy-four persons unemployed."

"Here on the Hasliberg?"

"No – in the whole of Switzerland." . . .

"But I am a rich foreigner."

"But a foreigner, and therefore suspected of wanting to be a Swiss. Or at the least of wanting permanent residence, of wanting to buy, and build, and live here and 'dilute' Switzerland. In the mid-sixties rich Germans bought up much of the best land in our Italian canton, the Ticino. Germans are all crazy about Italy, but not about the lira. In the Ticino they got Italy with the Swiss franc. Then rich foreigners like you started buying up pastureland all over the country, a building lot with a magnificent view for a couple of thousand dollars, for a summer or winter chalet or a place to hide from the next war. And a couple of years ago, first in the Ticino, and now everywhere, foreigners were forbidden to buy land. That stopped it, but not all of it: For a price you can get a Swiss intermediary to buy and 'own' it. Then you're at the mercy of the intermediary – you have no title."

". . . hide from the next war." A few years back, my friend Luethi, the innkeeper, doubled the size of his inn and re-placed all his beautiful old tile stoves with central oil heating. I wanted one of the old stoves, which were now in the barn, but Luethi hemmed and hawed and finally said, "In the last war we had oil rationing in Switzerland. Now they keep talking about another war, and we may have oil rationing again. Then I'd want to put my tile stoves back." It took me a couple of years to educate Luethi on the probable character of "another war," and when he was finally persuaded that it would involve something more catastrophic than oil rationing, he let me have one of the stoves (for $35). ". . . the next war."

And ". . . the mercy of the intermediary." Corruption – in *Switzerland?* "Oh, yes," said Peter, "more all the time. Already we feel that 'the foreigners' are ruining the country, even its character. An old farmer will refuse to sell his land; he doesn't own a car or want one; his house needs restoration; his toilet is on the porch . . . but his land is 'all he has' and 'all his children will have.' Then the speculators offer him, or his children, first ten and then twenty-five thousand dollars for a corner of his land that grazes a couple of cows and brings him in a couple of hundred dollars a year. But the kind of corruption that 'Watergate' suggests . . . no . . . not yet."

I once asked my friend Dr. Schild about "the politicians," and when he realized that by "politicians" I meant public officeholders, he said that a public office was a public trust.

So I asked him about the Swiss Senate committee that controls the Swiss National Railroad. "If, say, a nephew of a member of the Senate Committee applied for a job on the Railroad, would he stand a better chance than another applicant?" "Of course not." "Your civil service examinations . . ." "Not at all. That has nothing to do with it. It simply wouldn't happen, not in Switzerland."

"Not in Switzerland." Corruption? – not in Switzerland (except as "foreigners" induce it). Crime? – not in Switzerland. . . . Accidents? – not in Switzerland. (An *Italian* tour bus ran into Lake Lucerne a few years ago. But – a Swiss postbus ran off the road a few years ago, and an American with a residence permit took some pictures of it and was called on by two Swiss gentlemen who wanted to know if he would be so kind as to give them the negatives and all the prints and sign a paper saying he had done so.) Do you want to fly safely? – Swissair. Do you want to ride the train punctually? – the *schweizerische Bundesbahn.* ("The train is eleven minutes late in Brig [Lord]; it is coming from *Italy.* But it will be on time by the time it reaches Biel.")

There are, of course, foreigners – and foreigners. The despicable "guest laborers" from the impoverished Mediterranean world are Switzerland's (and Germany's, and Scandinavia's) niggers. They do not need to be watched or guarded, only herded. They live in hidden bunkhouses. (Tenements? – not in Switzerland.) They earn almost nothing and spend nothing and go home "rich" to the families they leave fatherless for months, even years, at a time. They are exported by their countries, which have no work for them; and when the economies of Switzerland, Germany, Scandinavia slow, they are sent back home and, unemployed, live on their "riches." They make no trouble in Switzerland, Germany, etc., apart from their being "noisy," "dirty," and "disorderly."

Foreigners – and foreigners. Foreigners – "That will be twenty centimes, Lord" – bring great gouts of money to Switzerland and spend it on the precision products that, like the Swiss, the Japanese and the Germans once made. Now the

Japanese and the Germans make American junk, but "Made in Switzerland" still means precision. The foreigners make the Swiss richer and richer and heat up the economy and, in every way possible, muscle into it: Swiss workers are the world's best and most "stable," i.e., least Communist, least ideological. The Swiss fight off foreign industrial and commercial takeover with their own capital and their rigid controls. But they want that twenty centimes, Lord. . . .

Instability abroad – and there has never been any like the present – sends the speculators, the wide-boys, into the Deutschmark. (And out of it, when Volkswagen shuts down; the Swiss know better than to make cars, which are not precision products and are made by everyone else.) But the *investors* and the *depositors* – the sound men – flock to the Swiss franc, and stay there, with their numbered accounts that defy identification back home. (The world hates the Swiss for this dirty form of banking, but the Swiss don't mind being hated; and, besides, who knows better than the Swiss that all banking is dirty?) . . .

:

Xenophobia and chauvinism are more than obverse-reverse sides of the coin. People who hate their own country (or themselves) may be xenophobes. People who, like the Swiss, love their country, may also be xenophobes. There is a nonchauvinist xenophobia in Switzerland, directed, now as ever, against the Germans. "We're afraid of the Germans," said my friend Peter. "Chronologically the last segment of Hitler's Greater Germany was to be the 'German' two thirds of Switzerland. He wouldn't get it the way he got Austria and the Sudetenland of Czechoslovakia; he'd have to fight for it, and he never figured out how."

"But such a small country . . ."

"Such a small country, yes. Such a small country of nothing but mountains and passes. The passes are all mined electrically. They can all be exploded to seal us off, for ten years or a hundred. We have the world's longest military service;

the conscript has to train (at the end, a week a year) until he is forty-five, and then keep his gear in readiness all his life. 'Prussianism?' – pooh. Look at even our *new* highways – and the circular insets you see across them, wherever there is a steep rise on one side and a steep fall on the other. Tank traps, operated electrically. We can never be invaded . . ."

". . . unless somebody invents the airplane."

"I said," said Peter, "that we can never be invaded. We can only be destroyed. But we are also aware that the airplane has been invented. We have the world's best fighter force in the air. (We spend nothing for bombers, nothing for a navy, and almost nothing for a citizen army always at home.) We are a completely militarized police state, completely nationalist, completely chauvinist. Why do you think you see the Swiss flag flying everywhere here?"

Why, indeed? In France the flag means a public building, nothing else. In England it is not to be seen unless a king is being crowned or buried. The Swiss fly the flag all the time. To prove that they're Swiss – or more Swiss than the man next door – the way the Americans do? Hardly; they have been there for a thousand years, and for five hundred "melted" into their trilingual, tricultural melting pot. Every Swiss is a Swiss. Why, then? "Pure chauvinism," says Peter. " 'We' are the people who really conquered Switzerland, conquered this *land*, created this *country*."

Everywhere else, even in Germany, once a planned country with planned cities, now an arrant imitation of planless America, people build for themselves however they want to, or build to make a profit for themselves. In Switzerland people still build to build Switzerland because, building Switzerland, they build for themselves. Zurich, Bern, Geneva, Basel, Lucerne, Lausanne, and every town and village, are the only cities left that aren't hideous, that are beautiful cities right out to the rind. . . . The workmen are the world's best – but there's no hurry. In Switzerland primary building materials have to be guaranteed for 200 years; on the Hasliberg there's a handsome chalet, still occupied, with the date 1492 (yes; 1492) burned into the lintel.

:

An irrelevant land that reads us movers and shakers no lessons, neither of federalism nor of war and peace, nor of economics nor of ethnology, nor of topography. There is no land anything like it, a land wholly of mountains and rivers and waterfalls and lakes. There are no wastelands, no scrublands, no swamplands, no badlands. A singular place, this place that nobody wanted, and all other places partake of grandeur and serenity only insofar as they partake of Switzerland, or, in Europe, shade off from its borders across their own.

An irrelevant society which, if it had not been born organically, would have had to be invented, to be what it is and serve what it serves; no part of the "Europe" that fights America or itself, no part of the ruinous swagger that overtakes and, in their time, overcomes all the empires. No part of the League of Nations, the United Nations, the Nations. No part of the European Economic Community or NATO or the Grand Alliance. No *part* of any alliance – and the meticulous broker to them all. "The representatives of the Shell companies of the countries now at war today established a world clearinghouse in Geneva." "The Swiss have been asked to handle American interests in Cuba." "On Sunday the European finance ministers will gather for a crucial meeting in Zurich."

Irrelevant to the bourgeois dream of a currency that always floats and never fluctuates, never collapses, never rockets and plummets; irrelevant to the proletarian dream of a tree and an ax and a bushel basket of black dirt and a cow. Relevant only (and only perhaps) to the ultimate critique of utopianism, Marxist utopianism in particular: Here, on this mountaintop and between these walls, is the man who has what the proletarian wants, and in spades: a piece of the inaction. Here, on this mountaintop, is the man who has what the singers of the Brotherhood of Man and the Parliament of the World would all of them have (and what many of them would trade the Brotherhood of Man and the Parliament of the World for). What is it like to be this man?

Or the ultimate critique of capitalism: Here, on this mountaintop, is the Man Who Has Everything the bourgeois heart should (if not could) desire. Here, in a world where most (and more all the time) are hungry and the few fight them off (more furiously all the time) is the truly rich man. What is it like to be a Swiss, who has what the capitalist openly and the proletarian secretly, both of them forever called (or calling themselves) to the barricades, dream of, what my father and your father, and his, her, and their father dreamed of on Sunday afternoon after Sunday dinner – a little peace and quiet, neutrality?

The man who was destined to be the first Swiss – did he get to be happy after the Lord gave him twenty centimes for a quarter litre of the best milk in the world? He's a dull fellow, to be sure, producing no passion except his comical chauvinism, a dull materialist whose dullness alone enables him to live in the exaltation of his mountains without going to pieces like a Californian. As dull as that other rich materialist, the Swede – that other, and only other, neutralist. *Duller* than the Swede (whose climate drives him to drink and, via drink, arouses some passion in him). "Four hundred years of Swiss democracy have produced the cuckoo clock" – and in our time a total of a half dozen names in the arts (Duerrenmatt, Max Frisch; who else? What else?). Neutralist – neuter? Is this what the mover and shaker, the hurler of missiles and paving stones, has to hope for? "It's all you've got, my child." Is it all any of us have ever got a Chinaman's (or an American's) chance of getting?

Let him be dull, so long as he's happy, and what else does a man want for happiness? Several years ago the Swiss satirical weekly, *Nebelspalter,* the Fog-Splitter, carried a full-page cartoon in color of an agonized Swiss on his mountaintop, the great peaks around him, the great stars above him, and the caption: "I've got a house and a car, life insurance and health insurance, a job and a pension, a radio and a television – I want for nothing. I ought to be happy." This master of the masters of precision, ingenuity, survival, conquest, stability, neutrality, with no one (except his wife? his child? his neighbor? the "foreigners"?) to discharge his aggressions on – is he happy? He seems to be glum, dogged, stiff, close, tight, safe, sure, small, like Switzerland.

He ought to be put in a bottle, this lineal descendant of him who was destined to be the first Swiss, and sent to Harvard for analysis and the answer to the ancient question, "What is man, O Lord, that thou art mindful of him?" Soon, though, for Switzerland, too, is going to go the way of the world which, tearing itself to pieces, laughs at Swiss locksmiths and Swiss watchmakers and Swiss tank traps and Swiss passes ready to be blown sky-high. Ten years ago some developers from Zurich – purest Swiss – made their way up to the Hasliberg and proposed to build a ski-lift funicular. "I don't know whether I'm for it or against it," said my friend Luethi the innkeeper. "If it's built, I'll get rich – but the Hasliberg will be ruined." Now there's a network of ski lifts on the Hasliberg, and Luethi and the rest of the Hasliberger are rich.

: : : *A Suburb of Munich* : : :

All in all, Munich is probably the loveliest town in Europe. And the liveliest. ". . . In no other city in Germany are as many festivals celebrated. . . . Munich loves music. . . . Munich *Gemuetlichkeit* . . . art . . . youth . . . 40 percent of the Muenchner are under thirty. . . ." And the spick-and-span suburban line, the *S-Bahn,* runs smooth-as-silk in six different directions from the city center to "magic landscapes and quaint villages . . . recreation for the people of Munich, only minutes away. . . ."

But one of the six lines of the *S-Bahn,* the *S-2* to Petershausen, doesn't seem to have a *Muenchner* on it – or a German.

The train to Petershausen is crowded on a sunny Sunday afternoon, but the conversations are in every imaginable language but German. Fifteen minutes from Munich's Central Station, and two stops before Petershausen, the train disgorges its babel at one of those kitsch-quaint villages, a typically slumless little Bavarian town with its castle on the hill, its flower gardens everywhere, great old trees, young mothers wheeling babies in shiny baby-carriages, children on their ten-speed bikes, young folk and old enjoying the autumn sun in the garden cafes.

In a word, a suburb if ever there was (or is) one.

But why the babble, the babel, why the foreign visitors out of season? And where are the Germans?

Piling out of the train the babbling babel takes the passage under the tracks into the station and out to the street, where the town buses terminate. The crowd doesn't know how to get to wherever it is that it wants to go. In every language it asks the passersby, who point to the Number 3 bus. Num-

From *The Progressive,* February 1979.

ber 3 has a special sign in its windshield. The sign reads *K-Z Gedenkstaette*.

A few minutes from the station the crowded bus comes to the end of the line and the babbling riders all get out and walk along a pleasant broad sidewalk with manicured fields on either side, following the signs that read *K-Z Gedenkstaette*. Near the bus stop is a garden restaurant crowded not with foreigners but with Germans, their cars, many of them Mercedes and BMWs, parked in the lot behind.

Coming to the end of the sidewalk the babbling visitors stand before a wide gate, open, and their babble subsides. The gate is topped by massive barbed wire, and beyond the gate stretching out for a mile or more is an immense rectangle enclosed by a wall. The wall (topped by massive barbed wire) is broken every hundred yards by a tower with windows all around. Everything is clean. Everything, the wire included, seems to be new.

Just before the sidewalk ends – as if to beguile the visitors from the gate – there is the replica of the handsomely decorated sign they might or might not have noticed in the passage from the train to the station. The sign is attractively lettered in four languages – German, French, English, and Russian. The English version reads:

VISIT DACHAU
The 1200 year old artist's centre with its
castle and surrounding park offering a
splendid view over the country.

K-Z means *Konzentrationslager. K-Z Gedenkstaette* means Concentration Camp Memorial. Like so many German words, *Konzentration* is not a German word at all. (Nor is the *K-Z* itself a German invention, any more than conscription. It was the French Directory that devised conscription in 1789 and the British butcher Kitchener who refined the ancient horrors of the concentration camp in the Boer War.) *Konzentration* came into use on March 20, 1933, less than two months after Adolf Hitler came to power and eleven days after the country boy

"Heinie" Himmler was appointed *gemuetlich* Munich's Police Chief. The March 21 *Voelkischer Beobachter,* announcing the establishment of the first *Konzentrationslager* at Dachau, said that "all Communist Party officials and, as far as the security of the state requires, those of . . . the Social Democrats will be interned at Dachau." The *Lager's* 5,000 inmates would, of course, be *ordentlich* guarded by the *ordentlich* Bavarian State Police. (*Ordentlich* means variously properly, decently, orderly, *systematically.*)

:

In 1978, a year of so many anniversaries, the fortieth anniversary of the *Kristallnacht,* the Night of the Broken Glass, passed generally unobserved. In the course of the evening of November 8, 1938, the word went through Germany, orally, by telephone, from one SA post to the next: "*Heute gehen die Synagoguen hoch.*" "Tonight we burn down the synagogues."

The anniversary, too, of the days that followed the *Kristallnacht,* the first time the Jews of Germany were rounded up without distinction or discrimination and transported to *K-Zs* all over the country – ten thousand from the vicinity of Munich to Dachau alone.

And the bands played on, the Munich Philharmonic, the Bavarian State Orchestra, the Munich Bach Choir. Munich loved music in 1938, just as it does (so the Chamber of Commerce blurb assures us) in 1978. But in 1978 (so the blurb assures us) 40 percent of the *Muenchner* were born after 1948. Why would they visit Dachau? Why would their elders? Do we visit the scenes of our fathers' crimes – the Haymarket gallows or the graves of Sacco and Vanzetti or Sitting Bull or Scottsboro or the Birmingham Church? Or My Lai? And why should we, when we weren't even born then? Or our fathers if (as in Munich) maybe a third of them, maybe half of them, are still alive and enjoying, we hope, *Gesundheit* and *Gemuetlichkeit?*

The German fathers are thought to have repressed – Freud's word, *verdraengen* means "push aside" – the whole Nazi thing, twelve cataclysmic years of a nation's history, plus prelude and

A Suburb of Munich : *147*

aftermath, leaving its bones to be picked by the historians and the radicals and the filmmakers, all of whom, in Germany, are much more remote from the *Volk* than they are in, say, France. And the "40 percent of the *Muenchner* under thirty"? The past isn't prelude – it's *past*. Let the dying bury the dead. Who even bothers to go to the family plot in the cemetery nowadays?

The guest book at Dachau tells the story: Page after page with only here and there a recognizably German name. *And* page after page with still fewer recognizably Jewish names. Relatively few Jews passed through – or, more precisely, into – Dachau after the *Kristallnacht* roundup, and after 1939 German Jews, who were less than 1 percent of the population, were mainly "resettled," that is, gassed, in the extermination camps of the East. Since no *K-Z* inmate had any right or redress of any kind against a guard, and since Dachau's Jews were much worse treated than other inmates, very few of the relatively few Jews who went to Dachau survived. And few had surviving friends or relatives in Britain or America (whose humanitarian governments held the line on immigration and, in doing so, condemned tens, or hundreds, of thousands to death).

The American Jews are the vicarious survivors of the Great Pogrom. They do not much come to Dachau (or to Germany). Their free-lunch flagellanteism is sufficiently gratified by their infliction of college seminars and TV soap operas on their countrymen. It does not extend to the memorialization of those German gentiles who had a choice and chose to resist, nor to the systematic extermination of the Polish intelligentsia (some 10,000 transported Poles died in Dachau), nor to the Gypsies, who were generally murdered on the spot, nor to the Italians and the mentally handicapped Germans who were used for medical experimentation at Dachau and elsewhere, nor to the Russian prisoners of war sent to Dachau to be executed, of whom "5 to 10 percent arrive dead or half dead. . . . In marching from the train station to the camp a not insignificant number of war prisoners collapse on the way." (November 9, 1941, report of Gestapo Chief Mueller, who adds: "One can not prevent the German inhabitants from noticing such things." *And doing what,* in the 1200-year-old artist's centre of Dachau? Or anywhere else, in or out of Nazi Germany.)

The smart saint who said, "Nobody cares about the poor except the poor," might have said that nobody cares about the rich except the rich, or about the Gypsies or the whites or the blacks or the Jews or the gentiles except the Gypsies or the whites or the blacks or the Jews or the gentiles. Neville Chamberlain came back from Munich in 1938 – another anniversary – to assure his countrymen that the sacrifice of Czechoslovakia – "a faraway country of which we know little" – would guarantee them a hundred years of peace. Nobody cares about the Czechs except the Czechs (or about the English except the English).

The prisoners liberated at Dachau on April 29, 1945, represented thirty-odd countries. There were 30,000 of them – few of them Germans, still fewer Jews – in a penal institution designed for 5,000. Conditions in the winter of 1944–1945 had deteriorated to the point where *deutsche Ordentlichkeit* itself suffered. At the end there were 1,600 prisoners in every barracks built for 200. But even then the transcendent German virtue was tenaciously maintained: Every barracks had to be cleaned every day by the able-bodied prisoners.

The cleaning of the barracks included the infirmary barracks, which had grown from two buildings with a total capacity of seventy places (not beds) to fourteen with a capacity of 3,400. Because of the cleaning requirement the patients all had to spend the days out of doors, and Dachau has a northern winter. Medical care and food obviously – *selbstverstaendlich,* as the Germans say – had to be provided the soldiers and industrial workers on a priority basis. So the patients in (and out of) the infirmary were patients without doctors and, since their priority was even lower than that of the healthy prisoners, they were given half-rations; true, they couldn't work, so they did not have to have much energy.

And so they died and died. The immense crematorium at the back of the camp is still there, and it must be seen. (*Why must it be seen?*) It had to be built to supplement the original two-burner. (*It* is still there, too.) And at the last, too late to be used, a gas chamber, disguised, as always, as a shower room, was added to, naturally, the crematorium.

But Dachau was not an extermination camp, and in midwar its care of its inmates actually improved when it became in part a processing center for subsidiary camps and slave labor projects around Munich (the home of the Munich Bach Choir); the German State (*Germany?*) rented out the slaves to private companies which, though the rates were favorable, insisted, like the American slaver of old, on healthy stock. (And what is the German State, or the American? Is it different from Germany, or America, different from "the Germans" or "the Americans," and if so, how?)

More and more prisoners died as their number became unmanageable and supplies dwindled with the progressive German collapse; epidemic was uncontrollable, and in the last winter of the war typhus carried away as many as 200 prisoners a day in Dachau. (Prisoners were excused from work and sent to the infirmary barracks when they had a temperature of 104 degrees or more *and* were unable to stand.)

:

Enormousness diminishes enormity. Germans, as they were the world's first sociologists, are its most intrepid; they count and they measure and they measure and they count and record and compare and compare and record, and we are the better informed because so many of them could not bring themselves to destroy their records even when those records were incriminating. But the enormousness of the *K-Z* and extermination operations were too much even for German record-keeping; so we know only that *approximately* 206,000 prisoners went to Dachau between 1933 and 1945. We know that exactly 31,951 registered prisoners died there – they had been registered in, so they had to be registered out – but perhaps half again as many (or as many, or twice as many) *unregistered*, including the approximately 6,000 Russian prisoners of war transported to Dachau between October 1941 and April 1942, and shot on the SS rifle range outside the wall. *Approximately.* Approximately six million Jews, or four million, or two million, or eight million, all over Europe, unregistered, unrecorded. And yet again . . . absolute precision: The transport which left Compeigne, France, on July 2, 1944, and reached Dachau on July 6 consisted of 2,251 prisoners, 984 of whom were recorded dead on arrival.

"To determine whether the severe psychic and physical symptoms described under No. 3 are due to the formation of pulmonary embolisms, particular subjects, before they gained consciousness, but after they had recovered somewhat from this type of experiment, were placed under water until they expired." – Dachau SS Lieutenant Dr. Siegmund Rascher to SS Commandant Heinrich Himmler, May 11, 1942.

Whose words were these? A man's, we know, because man alone is syntactical; but which man? SS Lieutenant Dr. Siegmund Rascher, empirical scientist, investigator, researcher, scholar, pursuer of truth, follower of the gleam: *doctor: teacher.* But there were a thousand Raschers, ten thousand, millions, everywhere, always have been, tinkerers, curious fellows. Or simply servitors of curious fellows: mechanics, hired hands. "What we'd like you to look into is if . . . is whether . . . is how . . . is under what conditions. . . ." We know Dr. Rascher, we know him in the very shallows of his soul.

What we don't know is Dachau, and we won't know it by making a Sunday afternoon rubberneck tour of the magic landscape reached by the *S-2* suburban line from festival Munich where the bands played on, the Philharmonic, the State Orchestra, the Bach Choir, while . . . *particular subjects . . . were placed under water . . .* What was Dachau, really? What was it that happened there?

Something singularly German? Something to do with German *Ordentlichkeit* reduced to systemization and derived from being in the geographical (and therefore historical two-front, three-front, four-front) pressure-cooker, something to do with

German terror derived from black forests, with German dead-liness from Luther, with German banality derived from German deadliness? (Was there ever such banality as the words *Arbeit Macht Frei*, Work Makes You Free, inscribed over the *K-Z* gates? Was there ever a worker made freer than the *particular subject . . . placed under water?*)

Was it the Criminal State made criminal by being made God? – *Ask rather what you can do for your country.*

Was it Europe, Europe the world's slaughterer and slaver?

Was it the West, that is (*kurz und gut,* in one word) the white man who saw men not as men but as batches, black, red, yellow, brown?

Was it the impious fraud of Christianity as cover-up, of Sweet Jesus as crucified, risen, and conscripted as patron of slaughter and slavery and beatific unconcern?

Was it religion, any religion, every religion, deferring judgment and, therefore, justice?

Was it Twentieth Century Man, the first man to be arrogant not here and there in princely estate but as Man?

Was it technological man, the "savage beast" – Freud's term – of Verdun?

Or was it Man as an unsuccessful experiment of an empirical God? Botched, a monstrosity: *Homo homini lupus,* Man is to man a wolf.

Was it the "sign of the end" spoken of on the Mount of Olives, when love shall wax cold and many shall hate many?

What was Dachau? Where did it come from? Where did it go? Did it go? Is it gone? The great monument outside the museum at Dachau has the words on it – and no others – in all languages: NEVER AGAIN. Why not? What will prevent it? A Sunday afternoon chop-licking rubberneck tour to see what *somebody else* did? The Jews were Nazi Germany's niggers, after 1939 its gooks; we Americans who visit Dachau – in greater numbers than any others – must we wait a while until General Westmoreland tells us all about free-fire-zones and search-and-destroy and Ex-Director Colby of the CIA tells us all about Operation Phoenix?

What would have been done with Hitler if he had been caught? What could have? *He owes us each a death.* Or do we owe him something for dragging the skeleton out of the closet so that never again can we pretend that "separate but equal" means anything but separated out, segregated, and supremacy and subjection? Did it take Hitler and 6,000,000 Jews and 60,000,000 gentiles to produce *Brown* v. *Board of Education?* A high price to pay, but at least we got a little something for our money; for their money, rather, and the little something we got would never have been made available if it hadn't been for Hitler.

:

The stench of death at Dachau has given way to the greater stench of the dead. The gravel there is the white of dry bones, inside the preserved foundations of the barracks; the grass is green (but not picnic green) around the edges. The German order that almost broke down completely – never quite – has been restored. There seem to be no attendants; what's there to attend to? There is an odorless stench of a dead world turning in space, still turning, still turning.

We all take the Number 3 bus back to Dachau, the 1200-year-old artist's centre with its castle and surrounding park offering a splendid view over the country. On the bus I ask an Italian (in German) what he thought of the *K-Z Gedenk-staette* and he says (in English), "I couldn't get out of there fast enough."

A Suburb of Munich : *153*

The Secret of Life

: : : : : : : : : : : : :

: : : *Bed* : : :

I want to dilate on the subject of bed, and I don't know who should if I shouldn't. I have had 131,400 hours at the controls, much of it solo, under all sorts of wind and weather conditions all over the world, flying everything from the primitive sleeping bag to the pressurized four-pillow job that they built for Haile Selassie, and another 262,800 hours of ground work, most of it spent getting ready to take off.

Bed as a contribution to human welfare, and especially to sleep, can hardly be overrated, in my opinion. There is nothing that you can't do better in bed. What do you want to do? Sleep? Read? Eat? Drink? Smoke? Talk? Think? Worry? Lie down? Stretch out? Curl up? Cool off? Warm up? Rest? Relax? Twitch? Turn? Toss? Look at the ceiling? Lie on your stomach? You can do them all better in bed.

You can't do any of these things – except worry – in an automobile. But modern Americans spend more for their automobiles than they do for their beds. And this in spite of the fact that they spend almost as much time in their beds as they do in their automobiles. Nor can you do any of these things – except twitch and look at the ceiling – with a television set. Yet modern Americans who haven't got one bed to rub against another go out and buy television sets. Modern Americans don't know what they're missing.

The average modern American spends one-third of his life in bed. One-third of his whole life – you'd think he'd care. But he doesn't. He'll sleep anywhere, and then only when the last dog is hung. He thinks bed is a place to sleep and sleep a waste of time. His idea of a good bed is one near the station.

Nobody should sleep alone, in my opinion, except people

From *The Progressive*, February 1954.

who should sleep alone due to circumstances beyond their control. Such people should not make fools of themselves, not even for the sake of having someone to sleep with. People who sleep with other people get to know them better, and to know people is to love them. Love is a great thing. There is not enough of it in the United Nations and elsewhere. It is praised by all the authorities – and properly so – but very few take an active interest in it. You take love, year in and year out, and it is just about the finest thing in the world except bed. Combine the two – retaining, as they say in the newspaper mergers, the best features of each – and you have a combo that is hard to beat.

Father Zossima – one of the Russian delegates to the UN – says in *The Brothers Karamazov* that hell consists of not loving. One way to avoid hell is to sleep with somebody. It should be somebody in particular and somebody, if it is a person of the opposite sex, that you are married to. Strange bedfellows do not long remain both strange and bedfellows.

If I seem to be urging the double bed, that is just what I mean to be doing. Twin beds are just one step removed from twin bedrooms, which are one step removed from twin houses. Everything that makes the French more attractive than the Germans may be ascribed to the fact that the French sleep in double beds and the Germans in twin.

You disagree with me about the double bed. You say that people have different sleeping habits. I say, let them have them; what's that got to do with it? Sleeping is only one of the things you can do better in bed. Do they have different reading habits, too? My snoring keeps my wife awake. All right – she sleeps so quietly that I'm afraid she's dead, and that keeps me awake. If you think that the law of compensation does not operate in bed, you have a lot to learn about the law of compensation. You say that one likes to read, while the other wants them both to go to sleep. All right – let the one read and the other want them both to go to sleep. As long as they are in the same bed, things will work out all right in time, and in less time there than anywhere else.

These are parliamentary quibbles of yours. They are like saying that a million dollars is a terrible thing to have because look at the tax you have to pay on it. What's left is still better than nothing, isn't it, *estupidito?* So it is with the double bed, with all its shortcomings.

:

The advantages of the double bed being myriad, and the shortcomings being minuscule, people should sleep together in double beds. My wife likes to work very late at night scrubbing the floors and to get up at six or so to have the children's breakfast hot and the house cleaned up so that she can get to her ironing as soon as they leave for school. All right. It doesn't bother me. When she's in bed I sleep like a log. When she isn't I turn over and sleep like Mark Hopkins.

The minuscule shortcomings of the double bed can be further minusculized by the purchase and use of an oversized double bed. Our family would not be without one. The Italians all have them, and the Italians are wonderful people. The Italians are also numerous, and the king-sized oversized bed can be made up so that it can accommodate the whole family. The oversized double bed has everything, including room. If the occupants are not on speaking terms, they can occupy the outer sides of their respective halves and ignore each other. It's almost like having two tents to sulk in. And they can always make up without having to go up hill and down dale. If one wants to read, or sleep, or just be let alone while the other is sewing, doing stomach exercises, or praying, neither will bother the other in an oversized double bed.

The double bed is cheaper, too. You can make it up with an arrangement of regular-sized sheets which, if you don't slip into the bed carefully, will tie you up in a knot. Write for Auntie Jane's Over-sized Bed-Make for details. Send fifty cents in coin or stamps, and enclose the top off a boxcar. Or you can stitch regular double sheets together and get two oversizes out of three regulars. Send one dollar for Uncle Milton's Pattern Book. Forget the Pattern Book. Just send one dollar. Uncle Milton will know what to do with it.

There are those – I am, I am happy to say, not of their number – who regard the softness or hardness of beds as a matter of what the mainland Chinese call *goût*, or taste, or, as the Swedes put it, *non disputandum*. Beds should not be soft. Marshmallows should be soft. Beds should not be hard. Coconuts should be hard. A bed should have a certain amount of give, but it should have a certain amount of take, too. It should be just right. I lean to the hard, or firm side, myself, partly because of my Spartan background (my grandfather ran Joe's Fruit Stand on the corner of Fifty-first and Prairie) and partly because you can always pound a hard bed soft but not v.v. The same thing goes for abalone.

With the money you save – by buying a double bed instead of twins – you can buy pillows, lots of pillows for lots of purposes and of all kinds except foam rubber, which are terrible. (They are pestproof, but you can keep pests out by not answering the doorbell.)

The bedroom should be big, not only to accommodate the pillows, which should be thrown luxuriously on the floor at night, but also to accommodate large, many-shelved night tables with lamps (selected not for beauty but for utility), vigil lights, vacuum jugs, hot plates, keeper-warmers, snack tins, smoking articles, writing materials, extension telephones (or a pliers to tear them out of the wall), small musical instruments (recorders, jew's-harps, and so on – maybe a ukelele), sundials, chemical fire extinguishers to extinguish chemical fires, commodes, macassars, antimacassars, pest repellant (in case they get in after all), smelling-salts and mustard-plasters, salve for burns (from overheated bricks used as foot-warmers, which you should also have), disposable tissues (and a depository for them; don't throw them on the floor with your pillows), the Scriptures (any version but the Revised Standard), Proust, and other *articles de nuit,* or articles of night. The bedroom should be a home in itself. You should be able to live in it, in case of seige. I won't insult you by saying that the darkest possible shades, covered by the heaviest possible curtains, are *de rigueur.* When I am rich I am going to have a wood-burning fireplace in my bedroom and never get up.

:

Bed is wonderful. Bed is where I want to die and, until then, live. Join me in this great crusade to get everybody in bed as soon as the dishes are done. Leave the dishes until morning, but don't get up to do them. Remember – they aren't getting dirtier just standing there. Don't eat eggs, which, in addition to increasing albumen, dry on the plate and are hard to get off after two or three days.

A final word, for now. I wouldn't touch an electric blanket, especially with a fork. It isn't merely that they may short-circuit – which can be fatal if you get into bed soaking wet – but that you don't know where you stand with them. I once stayed with Keith and Martha Ellinwood in Conesus, New York, on the coldest night of my life. Martha, God love her and rest her, insisted that the electric blanket would keep me warm. I squealed like a stuck pig when she put it over me and I wouldn't switch it on. In the middle of the night I woke up freezing and switched it on. In a few minutes I was warm again and went to sleep. In the morning I learned that it hadn't been plugged into the wall. That's what I mean.

More should be said, written, thought, and done about bed. We are all preoccupied with the unspeakable indecencies of politics, none of us with the innocent splendors of bed. Count Tolstoy said that modern man had found a solution to every problem but the bedroom. The solution to the bedroom problem is to put modern man to bed. Vishinsky should be put to bed with Lodge, and both of them with Mme Pandit. Chambers should be put to bed with Hiss. Dulles should be put to bed and the wool blanket pulled over his eyes. If everyone were in bed, and no one were allowed to get up until an understanding had been reached, there would be a lot less trouble.

: : : *Like God in France* : : :

Montcuq, France

Ten, fifteen, make it twenty years ago, Ms. Baby Mayer and I went into winter quarters along the River Drave (or Drau) outside the strategic village of San Candido (or Innichen) in the impregnable province of Venezia Tridentina (or Sudtirol) at the foot of the Alpi Dolomiti (or Dolomiten Alpen), in what was once Austria-Hungary but was now (as you may by this time have concluded) Italy. The reason it was now Italy was President Voodrow Veelson, dot dope.

When the victors were taking the vanquished apart in 1919 at St. Germain, there were bits and pieces of Austria left over, among them the South Tyrol, whose inhabitants were 99^{44}/$_{100}$ percent Austrian. President Veelson, who didn't know the South Tyrol from the South Bronx, looked earnestly around the room and said, as he always did, "The question, gentlemen, is what is the *nationality* of the people there?" "Your Excellency," said the Italian Premier, Signor Orlando, whose turn it was to make a monkey out of the American rube, "it is Italian." "Very well," said the rube, "we shall award it to Italy."

There we were, then, Baby and I, in our dead-of-winter quarters, with an immense room in a big old wooden summer resort, at $3.13 a day (including a bathtub in the middle of the room and a tureen of soup at noon and a plate of cold cuts at night).

The trouble was that there was nothing to read, and San Candido (or Innichen) was three miles away, with no winter transportation. We made it there once, and went into the local cafe to negotiate some salsa, or spaghetti sauce, to take back to

From *The Progressive*, September 1982.

our room and cook illegally on our illegal hot-plate. (Do you still wonder how the Mayers got rich?) The *duchessa* of the cafe wanted 200 lire for a cupful, and I opened negotiations by saying, "What! Two hundred lire, after all we Americans did for you after the war!" And the *duchessa* said, "And what all did you Americans do for me after the war?" And I said, "Think of the Marshall Plan." And the *duchessa* said, "The Banco di Roma got the Marshall Plan. Go get your salsa from the Banco di Roma."

So there, as I say, we were, Baby and I, buried under all that Dolomiti (or Dolomiten) snow, and with nothing to read and nothing to do but play chess and hug, alternatively, the radiator and each other. But one cold-cut evening mine host served Portuguese sardines, in the can, and when we left the table we took the can with us and spent the evening reading the printing on it.

:

And now, fifteen, twenty, make it twenty-five years later, Ms. Baby and I are conducting summer maneuvers outside strategic Montcuq, in the impregnable Midi, or soft middle-belly, of France. Our nearest neighbor, half a hilly mile away, is a socialist farmer (with a National Socialist attack dog to guard his property). When he is addressed in French, he replies in Languedoc (French for "language of a duck"). Montcuq's very name (French for "my little cucumber") is unknown outside the immediate neighborhood. Rolling fields and forests, deep tangled wildwood where never is heard a discouraging, nor any other kind of, word; August, and for days on end no sight, no sound of Man the Noise-Maker.

But this time around we have something to read – the *International Herald Tribune*, an excellent daily published in France by a *New York Times-Washington Post* combine and distributed by mail to the four corners of the four-cornered globe. The headlines of the August issues of the *IHT* bring us all the latest: ARABS BOMB TEL AVIV MARKET. HOUSE, IN REVOLT, VOTES TAX-CUT MEASURE. FORD TO RECALL 1978 CARS, TRUCKS. RUSSIA CALLS FOR ARMS HALT.

Like God in France : *163*

NIAGARA FALLS FAMILIES LEAVE CONTAMINATED AREA. RUSSIA SAID TO OPPOSE U.S. MOBILE MISSILE PLAN. OPEC SAID TO WEIGH PRICE RISE.

And the current social whirl: PRINCESS MARGARET, BANKER ON HOLIDAY IN ITALY. NEWLYWED CHRISTINA FLIES ALONE TO ATHENS. IMAGE ON TORTILLA DRAWS PILGRIMS. HONEYMOON DEFINITELY OVER FOR PRINCESS CAROLINE, PHILIPPE JUNOT. SCIENTISTS IN U.S. BELIEVE MAN MAY MODIFY WEATHER. RESILIENT, HUNGRY INSECTS MAKING WORLD COMEBACK. MICKEY ROONEY MARRIES FOR EIGHTH TIME. SENATE KILLS HOSPITAL COST PLAN. WHITE HOPE IN SOUTH AFRICA: BIRTH CONTROL FOR BLACKS.

August 1982, in farthest Montcuq, and three miles farther still, and here we are with all the news from all over, every day. True, the headlines I have quoted are all from August 1978 – repeat 1978 – our Montcuq host having come to Montcuq for his holiday four years ago and bundled them up when he left. It's just as we say here in France: *Honi soit qui mal y pense.* ("The more things change, the more they remain the same.")

One or two stories, no more, from four years ago seem slightly dated: U.S. BANKS RAISE PRIME TO 8½ PERCENT. MARTIAL LAW SET IN IRANIAN CITY AFTER 4 DIE IN ANTI-SHAH RIOTS. . . . "In his press conference yesterday, the Shah promised free elections to a national parliament in 1979 despite recent violence aimed at toppling his regime. He has blamed the violence on Communist influence." And: "I'd be inclined to say" – this was Professor Robert Lekachman of City University of New York, August 5, 1978 – "that we are in the middle of a prologue to a totally unnecessary, and entirely avoidable, economic tragedy – recession next year." And a real spate of front-page headlines dealing with the peregrinations of one Vance: STALLED MIDDLE EAST TALKS AWAIT VANCE; VANCE, SAUDIS IN TALKS; ISRAELI WARN VANCE; VANCE BACK, BRIEFS CARTER; VANCE OFF TO CAIRO, etc.

Montcuq, not the city center, where a bicycle may go tearing through the street (not the streets), but the outer suburbs, is the place to discover the secret of life – "if there is one," said Baby to me and I to Baby as we set forth last spring just ten minutes before Pan-Am raised its Procrustean Special round-trip fare from California (ten or eleven hours of pretzelized hell; remember when the ads used to say that getting there was half the fun?).

Why Montcuq? Why not Tirana, the Seychelles, Pocatello? First, because a friend got us a deal on the rent. Second, because nobody would ever be able to contradict me on Montcuq, since nobody, but nobody, my dear, has ever been there. (It's next year's In place.) Third and fourth, because of the deal on the rent. And fifth, because it was, and had to be, France.

:

The best way to convey the idea of France is not the story of the American who said to his wife, "If one of us should die, I think I'll move to Paris." Neither is it the fact that every Englishman who can make it out of Maggie (Attila the Hen) Thatcher's manforsaken country retires in France instead of the Falklands. (Nobody ever heard of a Frenchman's retiring in England.) No: the best way to convey the idea of France is the quaint German expression, "*Wie Gott in Frankreich.*"

The German despises the lazy, dirty, decadent French, their houses falling down, their fields full of stones. But this same German, describing the most ecstatic adventure of his life, and running out of superlatives, bursts out with, "*Wie Gott in Frankreich,*" "It was like God in France."

If God were embodied – embellied, rather – France is where you would find Him.

But you know all about France. You know that the French no longer know how – or even why – to build Notre Dame. You know that they now know how to build cultural Disneylands of Nineteenth Century iron like the Eiffel Tower and of Twentieth Century aluminum and resin like the Centre Pompidou of Paris; supermarkets, superhighways, shopping centers, and blind skyscrapers blindly stabbing random wounds here, there, everywhere in a sky that once gazed on the grimy magnificence of Paris. You know all about the French.

You know about their meanness, their insolence, their unmannerliness, their eminently heartless, eminently mindful preoccupation with "realism" – the worst of allies, but by no means the most implacable of enemies. Their monumental splendor without and their alternatively gaudy and dingy interiors. Their uniformly dismal cafes, their dirty streets, their dirtier sidewalks. Their arrogant attachment to their – i.e., to their ancestors' – language and literature. Their sacrifice of every other value to the singular, the bizarre, the juxtapositive in the arts and sacraments; their 500,000 to cheer the Catholic Pope, their 500,000 to mourn the atheist Sartre; their madness for life *and* death, for war memorials and truffles; their banal passion for *la gloire* and their street-smart robbery of *la patrie* at tax time. *And* their scorn for common honesty – ah, the upright, or formerly upright, German – and their continuing admiration of the trickier than ever Nixon (extravagantly serialized in their most popular picture weekly).

The French? Well, I guess you know their breast-beating *Marseillaise* and their decision in 1940 to live on their knees, their exaltation of the liberty of "students" to deface walls, floors, ceilings, and the merciless crackdown of the *flics*, or *poulets*. You know their daffiness about liberty – and their realistic contempt for equality and their flat rejection of fraternity (including the fraternity of the city, of the state, the nation, the continent, the world; their apotheosis, as a people, as a person, of that singular corollary of singularity, petty-bourgeois independence displayed with a monumental flourish by the late de Gaulle and the early Bertholet. M. Bertholet's ice cream parlor on the Ile St. Louis, the best in all Paris, is closed, not May and June, not September and October, but *July and August* for M. B.'s two-month holiday).

Every man for himself and each against all; the fabled anarchy of the fabled state of Nature. They will not curb their dogs. They will not respect a queue. They will not move to let a person pass on the sidewalk. Their Boy Scouts get merit badges for knocking old ladies down on the subway steps and their Brownies get points for kicking cripples and running.

They will not interrupt their jabber with a fellow clerk to serve a customer, or install public toilets, public drinking fountains, or public telephones, or thank you if you don't leave a tip on top of the now universal 20 percent service charge, or sell you a tomato, a shoelace, or a phaeton ten seconds after closing time.

Liberty, equality, *fraternity:* Just try to cross the street in one of their white-striped pedestrian crosswalks or ask an idle kiosk operator to show you directions on your street map or get your neighbor to soft-pedal the piano. Fraternity, in a country that has 360 different kinds of cheese?

It's considerably more fraternal in the provinces, or sticks, if less libertarian and no more egalitarian. So there are none of the horrors of the big city here in Montcuq, to divert a discoverer of the secret of life from discovering it; for Montcuq, not Paris, is France, and to live in the suburbs of Montcuq is to live like God. (Only you have to be something of a linguist or, as the French say, *langouste.*)

:

Here it is – the secret of life: 1. You ply a trade, or graft, that you can carry on anywhere, on a train, plane, car, ship, mule, carousel, prie-Dieu, pool table, catafalque, saw-horse, tree-stump, strait-jacket, bed-jacket, etc. Writing is one such, mathematics another. (There's no money in meditation, only in *teaching* meditation.)

2. You have a constant companion who's a match for you – but no more than that – at chess. (It isn't at all easy to find such a companion of the opposite sex; besides the Mayers, the only couple I know of, and of them only indirectly, who go on and on playing chess are the Gromykos of Moscow.)

3. You go as far away from home as possible as often as possible and stay away as long as possible. True, as Horace, unless it was Ovid, or Aphid, said, no ship ever sails leaving sorrow behind, but you can pack up your troubles in your old

kit bag and never unpack them. It's somebody else's plaster that's cracking, somebody else's washing machine that goes awry, somebody else's roses that have powdery mildew.

4. You can go to a foreign country whose language you understand but pretend not to and whose natives are neither (a) friendly, nor (b) intelligent, nor (c) nearby.

5. You find a dwelling that has no television set and has a radio on which you can get, in English, only the BBC Overseas news for half an hour a day, with programs on "Watching the Bird Watchers," joke routines like the one about the Japanese who went to the eye doctor and was told he had a cataract and said, "No, I have a Rincon Continental," and talk shows on "How Did the One-Toed Sloth Manage to Move About?"

6. The dwelling you find is too far to walk to town, where, in any case, there are no diversions; and you acquire neither a car nor a telephone. (And what will you do if you are stricken in the middle of the night? You will stay stricken and either recover or expire. Surely you realize that the secret of life is something more than merely staying alive.)

7. You live day after day, evening after evening, night after night, without seeing or hearing anybody except the BBC on the one-toed sloth; no being dropped in on, no dropping in, no "What shall we do this evening?"

8. You come to terms with the silence of the day, and at night, the silence of the night, which you can prolong by closing the shutters tight, so that you can sleep through the day (like the factory-raised chickens whose coops are kept lighted all night so that they will stay awake and keep eating).

9. You think about saving your money, and nothing else. They laughed, in the big-dollar days, when I sat down in Belgrade, Kyoto, Teneriffe to trim the four sides of the 500 U.S. Government postcards I'd brought from home so that, having written and addressed them, I could get three of them, plus a half-sheet letter on flimsy, into an envelope addressed to the addressee of the letter at home; the whole schmier coming, as it still does, to ten grams. They don't laugh any more. That ten-gram packet, including the three ten-cent postcards, now

costs me seventy cents air mail from France; the four items, as separate five-gram intercontinental ballistic missives, would cost $2.12.

10. You carry your own luggage if it kills you – you said you wanted the secret of life, not the secret of immortality – and kill you it will if you carry every conceivable money-saving item with you: medicines and medicaments; writing materials in quantity; powdered coffee in quantity (in a plastic bag; it will lose its flavor in a month or two, but it won't have lost anything much); a transformer from 110 to 220 plus extension cords and plugs for all the electrical equipment you are carrying, above all an electric hotplate.

:

This last item is the secret locked inside the secret of life. It is what Ms. Baby in those winter-quarters days and weeks and months in San Candido (or Innichen) used to cook our pasta and heat up the salsa we were told to get from the Banco di Roma. It was what we used, oh, so long before that, when we occupied the second-floor-front room at the Hotel de Nice on the Rue des Beaux Arts in the fashionable Sixth Arondissement of Paris at $2 a day even.

One day we were cooking up some water for dried soup in our room at the Hotel de Nice – there was one electric outlet in the room, designed precisely to prevent its being used by the tenant (M. de Nice never having dreamed that he would ever have as providential a tenant as Ms. Baby). We went out, while the water heated, to get a fresh noontime *ficelle* at eight cents (now thirty-five cents), or long loaf of bread consisting entirely of crust. (No Frenchman possessed of the secret of life would eat morning-fresh bread at noon.) As we came down the Rue des Beaux Arts, unwrapped *ficelle* in unwashed hands, and gazed admiringly at our second-floor front window, we detected a curl of smoke coming through it where the putty had fallen out. We snuck up the stairs, put out the fire, and checked out instantly to attend a conference of Quakers, who never lie and never cheat and never set a hotel room on fire.

Up from Montcuq, for the day, to have a Paris dentist charge

Like God in France : *169*

us $25 for telling us that the infected gum was irritated and not infected at all, we walked past our old digs, in all of which, even in Paris, we had lived like God, and there was the old Hotel de Nice, closed. It had been closed, we learned on inquiry, for years. "They had a fire there." "Where did it start?" "In the front somewhere, in one of the rooms upstairs."

There, then, you have the secret of life as I discovered it in undiscovered Montcuq. It is just as the French say: *Partir est mourir un peu.* ("If you keep moving, they can't hit you.")

: : : *Sit Down and Shut Up* : : :

I talk too much, and so does everybody I have ever met who knows how. Yap, yap, yap; yammer, yammer, yammer. Meetings, conferences, committees, lectures; street-corners, parlors, bedrooms, and baths; playgrounds, poolrooms, love nests, and funerals. As soon as I let the fellow next to me get a word in edgewise, he will jabber his head off; and he bores me. I have never been anywhere yet where everybody wasn't trying to talk at once, and I have never heard or said anything that did me or anyone else any durable good.

I have actually wondered, on occasions when I came home inordinately hoarse, what it would be like if a lot of people, meeting as friends, just sat still and said nothing for an hour together.

Now I know.

I have been to a meeting of friends. To a Meeting, I should say, of Friends.

The other Sunday morning, while the hypocritical preachers preached hypocrisy to the hypocrites, and the honest pagans lifted themselves on one elbow and swallowed the Alka-Seltzer, I went to Meeting.

Nobody opened the Meeting. It opened with silence. Living silence, they call it. Nobody closed the Meeting. It closed with silence. When the living silence gave way to dead silence – the kind you and I know – the people got up and walked out.

When, in the course of the living silence, a Friend felt moved to talk, he got up and talked. Not like you or me, though his words were no more pretentious than ours; less so. He felt moved; not, like you or me, driven. In the course of an hour, three Friends rose and talked – the usual number is smaller – and none of them talked for more than two minutes.

From *Common Sense*, April 1945.

No Mr. Chairman. No By Your Leave. No We Are Fortunate to Have Brother Jones among Us on This Auspicious. No We Will Now Hear a Few Words from. No larruping of the Mighty Organ to rouse the House to Attention. No House. No Head Man or Hind Men. No frock coats, censers, holy water, crypts, crosses, kaddishes, or choirs. Just Friends.

The Quakers' denial of all this apparatus as indispensable equipment on the Stony Road is, I know, a horror to all the sacramental sects. The Kingdom of God is supposed to be a kingdom, not a democracy. The purple haberdashery of the Episcopalians, the cold-water dunking of the Baptists, the Wafer of the Irish, and the Tablets of the Jews are the standard targets of the incredulous moderns, who mock the faith by mocking the paraphernalia. But they can't mock the Friends; and the Friends mock neither the mockers nor the mocked.

:

One evening, long ago, I was walking down the boulevard with Ludwig Lewisohn. He paused, in the darkening daylight, in front of a great cathedral. "This," said Ludwig, "is the third we have passed in three blocks. If our civilization were to pass leaving nothing behind but archaeological evidence, the next would conclude that ours was the most religious that was ever on the earth." "Ah, yes," I replied, "and this particular spire, the tallest hereabouts, was erected by nonunion labor at the expense of the most hardened sinner of his time, who, as his arteries grew brittle, thought that he could make the Ascent by offering God a nickel out of each quarter he had stolen from his fellow men." "Ah," said Ludwig, and we hastened on.

But the Meeting I attended was held in a small, garish, sub-ballroom in a smoky hotel in Pittsburgh. If the Pittsburgh Friends paid more than $1.50 for the hire of that particular hall, they were gypped. And it could have been held, for all that went on, in the park, on a hillside, in a basement. All that went on was a living silence, a silence that made inaudible the clatter in the immediately surrounding lobbies and kitchens.

My first feeling, as the silence began, and I studied the plank platform, the plain pine chairs, and the blue-serge suits acquiring a shine on them, was, "Dear me, what a saving on overhead." Then I focused on the clatter outside and wondered how, in or out of God's name, these people could expect living silence to hold its own against living noise. Then, with proper pagan disdain, I scrutinized the ceremony of nonceremony before me. Only I was self-conscious. Only I was *looking*.

I saw, though, that some of the faces were black, and I recalled that the Quakers were the first, and perhaps to this day the only, religion formally to denounce human slavery, to oppose it, to fight it, and to have no traffic in it. Some of the faces, including mine, were, I guessed, Jewish. The man on my left told me afterward that he was a Methodist, and that the Methodists never kept quiet for more than 15 seconds. I asked myself, after the manner of Milt Gross, "Is diss a system?" Apparently it is.

All unconsciously, it must have been, I folded my arms and bent my backbone in my chair, like most of those present. And the next thing I knew, I had been considering my misspent life. The living silence had got hold of me, and the clatter outside had let go of me. What brought me to was a slight shuffling on the platform, as one of the Friends arose to his feet.

"I read in the paper this morning," he said, as if he were talking at home, "about a Negro soldier being refused a sandwich at a canteen. I thought: you can't legislate a man a sandwich. It will have no taste. I thought: what will help the Negro who is hungry for the *taste* of a sandwich? The answer seemed to me to be spiritual aid. *Certainly nothing but spiritual aid will help those who refused him the sandwich.* 'He who drinks the water at his feet shall be thirsty, but he who drinks the water I offer him will never thirst, it shall be as a living well unto him.'"

He sat down. This time I was conscious that the silence had hold of me. *I wanted to think.* But the silence, after what seemed like fifteen minutes but was only five, let loose its embrace on me. *I wanted to talk.* I was halfway off my chair when I found myself saying to myself, "Mayer, you want to talk, all right, but you have nothing to say. You just want to make your face go, shoot your cuffs, and put 'em in the aisles. You've been doing this all your life, and so has everyone else. Sit down and shut up."

The living silence embraced me again, and it was on the train that night, long after the Meeting, that I grinned and said to myself, "The boys will never believe you when you tell them that you had a couple of hundred people sitting still and ready to listen to you talk as long as you wanted and you never unbuttoned your chin."

A Friend got up on the floor and said, "I can't get it out of my head that this world organization we are all talking about is trying to make us all members one of another, and I do not see how it can succeed without the conviction that we are so created by God."

He sat down.

This time the silence slipped up on me like my mother's arms. If you asked me how I felt during this third stretch of living silence, I would say that I do not know, but I would guess that, for twenty whole and successive minutes I had realized Aristotle's definition of happiness: *I wanted for nothing.*

A man got up. "I'm not a Quaker," he said, "but it seems to me that it would be worthwhile to study the causes of war, to learn just who it is that profits by war."

The day before, or the day after, I'd have leapt to my feet and said, "You fathead, Oscar Ameringer answered that question for once and all: *The sharks and the buzzards.*" Today I said nothing.

I don't know yet how the living silence, and the Meeting, ended. I think two of the Friends on the platform made the first move by shaking hands, but I'm not sure. All I know is that at some point I found myself walking out in the crowd, neither a sadder nor a wiser, but a stiller, man.

:

What do I know about the Quakers? I know that they were persecuted, not merely as dissenters, but for many of their positive tenets, such as their denial of special priesthood; their indifference to sacrament, including their refusal to take oaths; their complete democracy of organization, down to the point of determining action on any issue by the "sense" of the Meeting and not by vote; their historic opposition to war, though in this, as in all temporal issues, they refuse to try to bind individual conscience; and their recognition, as original as their opposition to slavery, of the complete equality of women with men. I know that no one, including their own apostates, ever hates them; that Franklin was influenced by their manners and by some, if not all, of their morals; and that Jefferson, in one of his letters, wondered why men were not satisfied, as were the Quakers, to live at peace with one another. And I know that the American Friends Service Committee, unlike the Red Cross, will have nothing to do with racism or nationalism and does not, so far as I have been able to discover, understand the term *enemy*, even in wartime.

It all adds up. The only thing I know, or *think* I know, that bothers me is that Quakers have a tendency to get rich. Now industry and thrift are characteristic of all persecuted and exiled people, and the Quakers have, in their time, taken a lot of pushing around. But it is still generally, if roughly, true, as it was in the beginning, that the man who says, "That rich man's a fool, but when I get rich I won't be a fool," is a fool already. If the Quakers have got disentangled from their vestments only to get entangled in their investments, they are going to wind up with windy cathedrals and the straight Republican ticket. I will try to talk them out of their money. I feel moved already to get up in Meeting and talk for an hour and a half. And I don't want to be interrupted.

: : : *Into the Harvest* : : :

They say that Jesus saw the multitudes heavy laden and faint of heart, and they say that he sorrowed and said to his disciples: "The harvest truly is plenteous, but the laborers are few. Pray ye therefore the Lord of the Harvest, that he will send forth laborers into his harvest." That's what they say.

And the disciples prayed and prayed – that's what *I* say – and many laborers came to the employment office of the American Friends Service Committee and the Church World Service and the Catholic Worker and offered to labor in the harvest. And they were all young and their eyes shone with ardor and they went out to labor. And then they grew older and got married (or didn't get married) and got an offer at Socony Vacuum or Macy's or Time, Inc., and the ardor went out of their eyes and they saw, for the first time, the sign above the door of the employment office: Abandon all hope of getting rich and respectable, ye who enter here. And they turned away.

Pray ye therefore the Lord of the harvest, that he will send forth laborers into his harvest for keeps. For the laborers, when the young men and women grow older, are few and far between, and when you look to see whose long bent back that is, whose step that is that staggers under the sheaves, you see that it is Red Schaal's, growing old in the harvest, his eyes shining with ardor. And you say to yourself, "Now where do you suppose the Lord got Red Schaal, and where will he get more like him?"

Red was – as he is – running the Peace Section of the American Friends Service Committee for the Middle Atlantic states. One night after he and I did a stand in Baltimore, we cadged a ride in to Philadelphia and landed outside the Reading Terminal with five minutes to catch the rattler to Binghamton or

From *The Progressive*, January 1955.

somewhere. We each had a suitcase. And we had three big cases of books besides, for where Red goes his "literature" tables (on which he nets 40 percent) go with him. Red was – as he is – a sick man. I wasn't. I got the two suitcases under one arm and a case of books in the other and howled for a porter to carry the other two cases of books. The porter came hot-foot, but Red had got hold of the two cases of books and he wouldn't let go; he wouldn't pay out four-bits of the Service Committee's money. He ran tottering to the train with those cases and caught it half-dead.

That's how I see him, and that's how I'll always see him, toting those cases. I've seen kids in Europe who grew up with blood and bone because the Service Committee shoved four-bits worth of milk or medicine into them when they needed it most. The Service Committee got that four-bits out of the blood and bone of Red Schaal. I see him pinching fifty cents in Philly; another fellow sees him squandering fifty dollars in Pittsburgh, in the manager's office of a hotel. "I'd like to know," Red is saying to the manager, as he's about to sign for the Green Room for a weekend conference, "if the hotel takes Negro guests." "Not ordinarily," says the manager, "but we'll make an exception in your case." "Thanks anyway," says Red, putting the pen down, "but we'd rather you didn't make an exception in our case. We'll go somewhere else." So he signs up for the Lavender Room across the street, at fifty dollars more of the Service Committee's money. The Lavender Room takes Negroes ordinarily.

Another fellow sees him leaving the office at five o'clock with a long-distance call unmade that he ought to have made before he left the office. Now Red's a meticulous administra-tor, a clean-desk man; but he has to call Erie, and the night rate to Erie is fifty cents cheaper, so Red's going to call from home after six o'clock and save the Service Committee's money. One fellow sees him pinching fifty cents on the phone rate; another sees him squandering fifty dollars in Pittsburgh. One of Red's speakers, at a conference in Syracuse, is quoted as having in-sulted the flag. The fur is flying and Red gets a letter from a contributor to the Service Committee demanding that the speaker be disowned. So Red dictates a letter, which reads, in full: "I am sorry that you have decided to discontinue your contribution to the Committee, but there are many equally worthy agencies and I hope that you will contribute to them."

One sees him one way, one another, but everyone who has seen him, in his thirty-five years in the harvest, has been changed. Not for the better but for the greater consciousness of his own shame. Take me. Before I saw him packing those cases of books through the Reading Terminal that night, it never occurred to me that I couldn't spend fifty cents of the Service Committee's money rather than break my back. Since that night I still spend the fifty cents, but I see Red packing those cases, and I'm ashamed. It takes a long time for shame to eat its way to the bottom of a man's heart, but watch me.

I talked to three ministers about Red, three ministers of the Gospel according to Matt., Mark, Luke and John. The first one said, "He makes a man ashamed of himself," and when I said, "You, too?" the minister said: "Many years ago a 'Y' secretary got into the kind of moral disgrace that people won't tolerate. He was a good man, too; you know how those things are. I was on the committee that had to decide whether we'd keep him on. I felt we couldn't; we had to think of the organization; you know how those things are. So we decided to fire him, and as the meeting broke up, somebody said, 'I wonder what Red Schaal would say,' and somebody else said, 'I don't know what he'd *say*, but I know what he'd *do*, and it wouldn't be what we have done.' That was twenty years ago, and I can't see Red Schaal, or even hear his name, without remembering that meeting and being ashamed."

The second minister I talked to said (and I quote him verbatim), "He must have a very deep faith." "But haven't we all?" I said, meaning, "Haven't you?" "Oh, of course," said the minister, "but Red's must go down deeper, the way he stands up to things."

The third minister said, "Red? I've known him for twenty, twenty-five years. I guess I know all there is to know about him – there isn't much to know about him, really – except one thing. I don't know what he does when he gets discouraged. I wish I knew."

:

There isn't much to know about him, really, and that's what makes the question so hard: Where do you suppose the Lord got him, and where will he get more like him to send forth into his harvest? I can tell you what he looks like and how he lives. I can tell you where he was born, and to whom, and what he did after that. I can show you the finished product, the ingredients, and the process. But I can't figure out the formula, and I'm glad that that's the Lord's problem and not mine.

He looks like the man who, in college, was voted Least Likely to Succeed. A lanky, bucktoothed hayseed, with weak eyes, big shapeless features and a grin that, given his teeth, he just can't help. He's about six feet long, his feet are too big, his arms are too long (and stick out of his sleeves), and the total impression is that of his color – sandy. (They say he was first called "Red" when he was "Y" secretary at Johns Hopkins, not because of his hair but because of his radicalism. His real name is said to be Eugene; he signs himself E. A. Schaal.) That's about what the finished product looks like. In one word: ungainly. In another: unprepossessing. He could drink himself silly and they'd never hire him to pose for Calvert's. He doesn't drink. He doesn't smoke. He doesn't swear. "Doesn't he," you say, "have *any* redeeming features?" Hardly any, to tell you the truth. If integrity is a redeeming feature, he has that one, but I don't mean anything much by "integrity." I mean merely what the word used to mean before it got dressed up like a Christmas tree; I mean oneness. What he thinks he says, and what he says he does. That may be a redeeming feature, but it doesn't make friends. It influences people, though.

I've told you what he looks like. Now I'll tell you how he lives, and that won't help you answer the question, Where did the Lord get him? either. He lives with Esther Schaal – their three daughters are grown and gone – in a house in Lansdowne, Pennsylvania, Philadelphia petit bourgeois suburbia. The Schaal house looks just like all the other houses in the block and is furnished just like them, and Red thinks it's wonderful. Outside stands the car, which looks and is just like all the other cars in the block, and Red thinks *it's* wonderful too. The Schaals own the house and the car free and clear; that's Red's estate.

If the house and the car are petit bourgeois, just wait until you see the man. He is the only man I have ever known who would be caught reading *Redbook*. He reads *Redbook* every month and the *Inquirer* every evening. When he isn't reading *Redbook* or the *Inquirer*, he is looking at low comedy on television. When he isn't looking at low comedy on television, he is playing bridge, and when he isn't playing bridge, he is playing canasta. And that is the man the disciples prayed and prayed for and the Lord sent forth.

I am not kidding. That's the man: You can tell him by his necktie. It's the necktie that is absolutely identical with everybody else's.

I've told you what he looks like and I've told you how he lives. You'd die laughing if you hadn't seen him bringing in the sheaves in the harvest of the Lord. Where do you suppose the Lord got him, and where will he get more like him?

The Lord got him on a farm in Gillett, Wisconsin, the youngest of nine children. The elder Schaals were "Forty-eighters" from Germany, but they were Methodists and they never missed a Sunday. Red saw Esther Christiansen in church, where she sang in the choir. The Christiansens, whose farm was six miles from the Schaals', were Danish Lutherans, but Esther was working for a man in Gillett who was a Methodist, so she had to go to the Methodist church. Red married her and made an honest Methodist of her.

Red's father never got past the third reader, but he believed in education. When his oldest son got big enough, his father wanted him to go to high school and college, but the boy wanted to farm, so his father gave him a $2,000 farm and set aside $2,000 for each of the other children to go to high school and college. When he got old and his wife died, he sold the main farm and gave each of the children $1,000 and put the rest of the money into a perpetual trust, from which any of his descendants can draw $300 a year for two years to help them through high school or college.

That's where the Lord got Red. "Pa," says Red, "had a liberal streak here and there, and now that I think of it, he read the *Christian Century* in his late years." But Red never heard of pacifism or socialism or nonracism in Gillett or in Appleton, where he attended Lawrence College. He began hearing things when he subscribed to Bryan's *The Commoner* and *La Follette's Magazine*. He was still in high school, and he cannot, for the life of him, remember how he got started reading dangerous literature. But he overcame the danger, and after working on the farm summers and spending his senior summer in college raising money for the "Y," he went to work for the "Y" at Camp Funston, in September 1917, while he waited for his draft number to come up.

The "Y" workers wore uniforms, and one day on a train Red got talking to the man next to him. Red introduced himself and the man said, "So you're from where that damned La Follette comes from," and Red, who has never got over being tactless, tactlessly told the man what he thought. A week later Red was summoned before the camp inspector and a colonel, put under oath, and given the charges made against him by the United States Department of Justice. The charges were (1) that he had said that he thought La Follette was sincere and (2) that he had said that some people were making money out of the war. The colonel asked him if that's what he'd said, and Red said it was. The colonel said that if he'd recant he'd have the charges quashed and everything would be all right. Red, who didn't go for either cant or recant, said he wouldn't, and the camp inspector fired him and told him to turn in his monkey-suit at once. Red turned in the suit and went home. The next day he joined the Navy and came out an ensign. The Navy convinced him that you can't make a good man out of a bad system and the military system was a bad system.

But he wasn't yet against war; he wasn't a pacifist. Then he went to Northwestern University to get his master's degree in religious education and from there to American University in Washington to get his doctor's degree. It was at the student "Y" convention of 1920, at Lake Forest College, when a bunch of the delegates moved out of a dormitory where Negroes were, that the young liberals revolted under Sherwood Eddy and the man who became the greatest single influence in Red Schaal's life – Kirby Page.

In 1923 he went to Johns Hopkins as "Y" secretary, and there he remained until 1936. His student forum was the toughest in its time in this country, with speakers like Norman Thomas, Bishop McConnell, Harry Laidler, Sherwood Eddy, and, of course, Kirby Page. Tough; tough Christians; "full gospel" men. Red came out of it – his board tried to kick him out, but the students rebelled – a "full gospel" man himself. The Young Men's Christian Association couldn't – and still can't – go along with Christ on race, on war, and on the economic order, and Red thought he'd like to go along with Christ. So, when he met Ray Newton, another "full gospel" man, at the American Friends Service Committee in Philadelphia, and Ray asked him how he'd like to raise money for the Emergency Peace Campaign, Red said fine. He raised the money, but the country went roaring down the road to war, and after that Red wasn't so sure any more about emergency campaigns. It looked like a long pull, a lifetime of labor in the harvest of the Lord of the harvest. The Service Committee wanted the laborer, but it had no money. Red said he'd organize a peace education program in the Middle Atlantic states and raise his own budget. That was all right, but he couldn't go to regular contributors and take money away from relief work. That was all right with Red. He went from town to town ringing doorbells and avoiding regular contributors. His budget was $1,000. Now it's $40,000.

Some of the Quakers didn't like Red's money-raising, especially his taking an offering at meetings and especially if the meetings were in a Quaker meetinghouse. The first time I sat on a platform, having shot my cuffs on a very high level, and listened to Red tell the customers that he had to have money. I blushed myself. I don't blush any more. I rejoice to sit on the platform and see the laborer go through the people's pants for the gleanings. Red wants money, every nickel you've got. The nickels – he thinks it's good for the poor to give, because when they give it hurts – add up to $40,000 a year. He wants more.

∶

Always more. One day we were driving through the Alleghenies in the snow – we had to make four hundred miles that day to a meeting in Buffalo – and at noon Red said, "Lunchtime. We might as well make a pastoral call while we're at it." We pulled in at the coffee shop of a small college. I was going to order the blue plate, but when Red ordered a cheese sandwich, I ordered a cheese sandwich, and then the proprietor of the coffee shop came up and said, "Glad to see you, Dr. Shaw, always glad to see you. I like the Friend's Society, always glad to see you," and he hollered into the kitchen, "Two steaks for Dr. Shaw and his friend," and then he went out in the back. A few minutes later he reappeared with two checks, each for $50. "I figured the Friends' Society could use some money, Dr. Shaw. I like the Friends' Society, but I've just redecorated the place" – "It's right pretty," said Red – "and I'm a little short, so I made out one of the checks for today and one for a month from today. I haven't a pen. Is pencil all right?" "It certainly is," said Red, and off we went. "And a free lunch, too," said Red, as we got into the car. He wrote "Free lunch" down in his expense book, and I wrote "Free lunch" down in mine.

The next day we were going through Utica at lunchtime, and Red stopped and said, "Pastoral call." "Restaurant?" I said. "No," said Red, "minister." We left the parish house with $25, and Red said, "I know a good place to eat," and we went there and got the cheese sandwich. The sandwich was terrible. "I thought you said this was a good place to eat." "It is," said Red. "It has a good race policy. I didn't say the food was good."

He's not unfunny, exactly, but his humor is, like him, self-effacing, laconic, sly, and dry. With his inflexibility about things – and his sense of fairness to an audience – he begins his meetings on time and stands up behind, and then alongside, the speaker after forty-five minutes. I've seen him flag down Eleanor Roosevelt, and that takes some flagging. Once, with Gladys Walser as the speaker of the evening, Red announced, as he usually does, that the meeting would open with a few minutes of silence. Gladys, who was going through her notes on the platform, didn't hear him, and as soon as he sat down, she got up and started talking and went on until Red finally got her to quit after fifty minutes or so. "First time I ever saw a speaker run over at *both* ends," he said.

:

Inflexible as he is, rigid, and, as they say in Gillett, sot in his ways, he has a hard time seeing sense in innovations of any kind. If his associates insist on trying a new technique, Red yields with an air of mild impatience combined with the conviction that it isn't techniques but the same old labor in the same old harvest that counts. I've heard him called aggressive, but he isn't aggressive; all through the war he talked pacifism to anyone he met but without the hot fervor that annoys people. He's stubborn. He's playing for keeps, at croquet, at bridge, at the "full gospel."

I wouldn't say he speaks sweetly – never. But he speaks simply. He finds it easier to practice than to preach. He spends hours, days, with his local loyal committees in the Middle Atlantic communities. He works on them earnestly, yields to them democratically. When he knows he can't yield, he tells them so in advance. He will stand on principle anywhere, and anywhere includes the American Friends Service Committee. He loves the Service Committee; it's his life. "Imagine," I once heard him say, "being *paid* to associate with people like this." But he'll fight it on anything. His heart's on his sleeve, his resignation on the table. None of his superiors – they don't call them "superiors" at the Service Committee – would dare criticize his selection of radical speakers.

A few years ago a great foundation made noises as if it were going to give the Service Committee millions of dollars for peace work. The peace secretaries around the country were told to send their personnel needs to the AFSC central office, so that a salary budget could be presented to the great foundation. One man wanted five assistants, another ten, and so on. Red wrote, "None." The most overworked man on the staff, with no needs. When he was asked if that's what he meant, Red said, "That's what I meant. I can't find enough committed people to fill the jobs we've got now. Why create more jobs?" He wants money, but he wants men worse, and without the men he can't use the money. Commitment is all he cares about, across-the-board commitment. He's the slowest laborer in the harvest, because he doesn't want to bring in the chaff. Some of his friends – and associates – want to get a million or ten million signatures. Lots of people. Mass movement. Red says, "I'm going faster now with more people than I want to. I don't want to play God with people, get them into an institute or conference, like sheep in a gangway with only one exit, pound the doctrine into them, and turn them out converted. It doesn't work. It's waste motion. People's ideas change slowly, their lives slower still."

The harvest truly is plenteous, but it takes its time maturing. In thirty-five years Red Schaal has matured a handful of "full gospel" people in each of one hundred fifty or two hundred communities in Pennsylvania, West Virginia, Maryland, Delaware, New Jersey, and New York. A handful. In each of one hundred fifty or two hundred communities a handful of people *stay* pacifists, *stay* non-racists, *stay* social and economic radicals. Thousands and thousands *get* that way elsewhere, but the winds blow them over. Red's got his eye on the long, long harvest.

So the minister who said, "I know Red, but I don't know what he does when he gets discouraged," doesn't know Red.

Red doesn't get discouraged. "We don't have to be successful," said Red, in the only flowery thing I ever heard him say; "we have to be right." What the minister didn't realize is that Red really believes in God. The Author of history will change history when men want it changed; men won't change it. And that's the difference between Red and the reformers, and that's why his back never breaks, and that's why some of his friends (and some of his associates) criticize him for "converting the converted" and make loving fun of Red's "constituency." Laborers in the harvest because Red Schaal converted them and kept on converting them.

He used to be a lot sharper-tongued than he is. His thirty-five years with the Quakers – he's still a Methodist and a "full gospel" thorn in the side aisle of his local church – have softened him some. And have stiffened the spines of the Quakers. He's gentler now when he explains to a fellow Methodist why he can't contribute to the new War Memorial. And a lot fewer Quakers are contributing to War Memorials than were a while back, and a lot more to feeding the victims of the wars that the Memorials memorialize. "Red has learned a thing or two from the Quakers," says Kirby Page, "and he's taught them a thing or two – or three."

:

Young men who mistake age for wisdom come to see me once in a while and ask me what they should do with their lives. I say, "What do you want to do, friend?" If the young man says, "Be a writer," I say, "Write." If he says, "Be a preacher," I say, "Preach." If he says, "Be a professor," I say, "Profess." If he says, "Change the world," I say, "Change the world." But once in a while a young man turns up, bucktoothed and bucolic, long, lanky, and cross-eyed, without very much on the ball, and he says, "They voted me Least Likely to Succeed, but I don't want to succeed, I want to be right." Then I cleave to him and say, "My friend, the Lord of the harvest needs laborers like Red Schaal." If he says, "I never heard of him," I say, "You never will. He is laboring in the harvest. You can't labor in the harvest and be heard of, both."

: : : *An Extra Pair of Laces* : : :

Did I ever tell you how my Old Man made it? No matter if I
did; if Mozart's *Vesperae Solemnis* is worth hearing twice, so
is the story of my Old Man's making it.

He didn't make it good, but he made it. And so have I. And
so will you, if you do as he told me and as I tell you.

My Old Man was as honest as the working day was long in
those days. But he had his own idea of honesty. Taking a little
something from what Wendell Willkie (before he turned pious)
called "public utilities, privately owned," was the bounden
duty of an honest man. It wasn't taking a little something at
all; it was taking a little something back. For the utilities were
– as they still are – bleeding the poor.

It was a case of we or they – "them or us" were my Old
Man's words. They gave no quarter and took every nickel in
sight. If you got one back, by whatever means, you were per-
forming an act of rough rectification, or distributive justice.
And you were the same man who would walk a mile to bring
a widow a jar of hare's-foot jelly. There was no contradiction between uprightness and downright robbery of the rich,
Nottingham or no Nottingham.

The American way provided many blessings then, but one
of them, known as higgling and haggling, had already given
way to the Quaker doctrine (which had made the Quakers
rich) of O.P.O., One Price Only. A pair of shoes was a dollar-
and-a-half, take it or leave it. You could not get them for less
– or be sandbagged for more unless you were an immigrant or
a darky who could not read the price tag.

There was half a dollar's profit in a pair of shoes, and my
Old Man did not see why there shouldn't be forty-eight cents.
So, when he bought us our shoes, he would say offhandedly

From *The Progressive*, April 1969.

to the clerk, "Just put in an extra pair of laces, will you?" And the clerk, though he stood rock-ribbed, four-square, and copper-sheathed on O.P.O., was nothing loath in those happy-go-lucky days.

That extra pair of laces was the foundation of my Old Man's fortune. It was not a large fortune, but it was enough to bury him. Par for the course.

A penny here, a penny there; and thus my Old Man made it, with an occasional Pullman towel, an expired streetcar transfer, a coin in the Coin Return box, and a seven-year-old on his lap who (as he and the conductor agreed) was big for three.

I am a chip off the old block, an old chip now, curling fast and more than a little brown around the edges. But I have made it the way my Old Man did, a penny here, a penny there. A lot easier, because a penny is easier to come by. In the supraverbal society anybody who can string two words together can sell them to anybody. My Old Man had to hustle his paper-box samples on the streetcar the whole day long, including Saturday mornings, and he took in forty dollars a week. (He called them iron men.)

Me, I would not stop rocking in my rocking chair for forty dollars a day. (I call them lettuce leaves.) I'm a contemptible hack, of course. I will never write the *Ode to the West Wind*, which would take me a year and pay me five dollars and immortalize me. But I cannot afford immortality, and neither can you. These are the times that try men's bodies.

I made it by holding before me the image I commend to you.

It is the image of my Old Man, slicing it thin at the dinner table and saying, with affected amazement, "Why, there's enough left over for another meal." And if there wasn't, to Ma: "Lou, buy a pot roast tomorrow and ask Art if he has a nice soupbone he could throw in, and then go over to the grocery department and tell John that you got a nice soupbone from Art and you wondered if he had some soup greens"; a nice soupbone being one with enough meat on it for a meal.

The rest of the Armenians were starving, but the Mayers,

though they were eating low on the shish kebab, were eating. When my Old Man said, as he did, "You only live once," he, like you, was talking through his hat; but unlike you he did not mean that you should spend. He meant that you should save, a penny here, a penny there, in order to stay alive in case you only lived once.

:

Saturday afternoons the spenders were in the saloons, feeling flushed. My Old Man stayed home feeling flush. Saturday afternoon was the best time to hit him for an extra penny. Since he slipped me my weekly five on Sunday, when Mrs. Wispy's School Store was closed, I was, at the rate of a penny a day, fresh out by the following Saturday. So I would rub his back for him – those samples were plenty heavy – and he would slip me the extra penny, pretending he was joking when he said, "Don't spend it all in one place."

I would tear down the street to Mrs. Wispy's and luxuriate in front of the showcase, choosing among an embarrassment of riches – a yellow marshmallow banana, a likrish whip, a cornucopia of candy corn or peppermint hearts, a whole miniature package of Necco wafers, a whistle, a print-paper for my sun-picture slide of the Empire Express. I would then ask Mrs. Wispy what else there was, and she would say, "What do you want for a penny – the world with a little red fence around it?" And I would say, "Let's see it." Having made my choice and insisted on a striped bag, at which point Mrs. Wispy would say, "You boys are driving me to the poorhouse," I would tear back home and my Old Man would ask me what I had done with the penny. I would say, "Spent it," and my Old Man would say, "Boy, you don't know the value of a dollar," and I would say, "What's a dollar, Pop?"

My Old Man knew what a dollar was. A dollar was a conglomerate of one hundred highly productive enterprises, a holding company. Its operating subsidiaries produced all sorts of valuable commodities – a penny postcard, a newspaper, a top-string, a half-pair of shoelaces, or *two* carmels at the Greek's. You could bet a penny, lend a penny, borrow a penny, steal a penny, lag a penny, play penny ante. There wasn't anything you couldn't do with a penny, including burning a hole in your pocket. My Old Man, surveying, of a Saturday evening, the hundred operating subsidiaries of each of his forty weekly conglomerates, knew the value of a dollar.

As I do now.

And of a penny.

True, the only two things you can buy with a penny nowadays are a much thinner stick of greatly debased gum out of a slot or ten minutes in a small-town parking meter. Instead of chewing gum I chew my gums now, and if you drive around the block you'll find an empty parking place with ten minutes left on the meter by a crazy spender. You may have spent a nickel driving around the block, but that's not the point. The point is that you know the value of a penny, and unless you do you'll never make it.

Still another thing you can do with a penny is stay home and fondle it until the first of the month and then take it carefully down to the bank and put it out at interest. There is nothing more un-Christian than taking interest, but I can not afford salvation, and neither can you.

You go to the bank via the back streets, and return via the shopping streets. You don't go into the shop lest they give you credit and replevin the junk the day you can't make the last payment.

With leopard coats at $10,000 and wood-pulp tomatoes a dime apiece, you have been priced out of the market. Stay out. You won't make it otherwise. Don't repair and don't replace, unless it's a cooking-pot. A man who doesn't have a pot to cook in needs one. Buy what you need, and never anything else. And stop talking about need being relative; today Biafra, tomorrow the world, so Be Prepared.

Consider the things you think you need. Half of them you can borrow and return "some time"; books, for instance, at $6.95 for a thin one. There is no evidence that books have ever done anybody any good, but that is not the point I am making here; the point I am making here is that you can borrow books and you can most easily borrow those books about which your tasteful (but profligate) friends are most enthusiastic. The other half of the things you need not only do you no good but do you positive harm, television, for instance.

It takes time, but time is nothing; money is everything. It takes time to soak an uncanceled stamp off a letter; it takes time to squeeze every coconut in the supermarket until you have got the biggest one; it takes time to root around in the crannies for a penny you either lost or think you lost. But time is nothing; money is everything.

Once you decide that time is money, you are done for. My big brother Howard once tried to persuade me to cross the country by Pullman instead of by day coach. I would, he said, arrive refreshed instead of exhausted, having got a couple of good days' work done in my Pullman compartment; three days saved in all, "and your time is worth fifty or a hundred dollars a day." I didn't argue with him; he was right; but once I decided that time was money, I'd be done for (and never play another game of chess, besides).

It takes time to find "yesterday's" bread at half price instead of "today's" but time is what you've got and money is what you haven't.

Most of the people who get hooked on the fantasy that time is money get coronaries, and then they have time. Take it easy. The only place you can take it easy is home, once you have broken your wife's spirit. Don't go anywhere unless there's money in it. Don't play golf or tennis or Ping-Pong unless somebody else furnishes and refurnishes the equipment. You can't afford equipment. Take up sports like walking or jogging or yoga, providing you don't have to buy a sweater for them. Don't buy a book on yoga; one book leads to another. Borrow one.

It is false pride (and you can not even afford true pride) that makes people make long distance calls, leave the lights on, take taxis, go to steak joints, buy other people drinks, travel first class (or second, if there's a third), and see the plays and the concerts and the movies five or ten years before they're shown on television. It is the falsie of all falsies to keep a bowl of fruit on the table until it starts rotting and you have to throw it away. You can live without any of these indulgences. You can not live pleasurably without them, but you can not afford to live pleasurably.

You can not afford not to be a piker. You can not afford to go to a restaurant at your own expense. Go, if you must, with people who can. If you don't know people who can, stay home. Your wife will complain. Let her complain, you can not afford an uncomplaining wife. When you go to a restaurant with people who can, don't reach for the check. Say, "Let's make this dutch," but don't wound the other fellow's false pride by being a pigheaded dutchman about it. Lose the argument and don't insist next time that this one's on you. There need not be a next time. If he is the kind of small-minded person who entertains with a view to being entertained, cut him off your list. You don't want friends like that. You don't want friends who cost you money.

The principle of nonreciprocity applies with equal force to your being invited to somebody's home for dinner. Whenever people entertain you and you entertain them "back," both parties lose money; it's what A. A. Stagg used to call a viscous circle. Stay home. Stay home and look at – I didn't say "enjoy"; you can't afford enjoyment – the nice Westerns. Or save the electricity and contemplate your navel, if you have one. The life of contemplation is the highest life, and it was Aristotle who said so in the *Nichomachaean Ethics.*

If you make friends, make rich friends who do not count the cost, or poor friends who provide you with Quaker hospitality, however lumpy the bed and the mashed potatoes. You'll survive, and if you don't – well, do you want to live forever? Not if it costs money. Under present wartime conditions, with the whole world at war with you, you have got to live off the land or you won't make it. When would Sherman have got to Atlanta if he hadn't foraged, or Grant to Richmond?

On the whole, the rich should be avoided, partly because

they count the cost (how do you think they got rich?) and partly because they think that you love them for their money. (They may be right.) They want you to love them for themselves – and to prove it by spending money on them. But what you want is a free flop or a free meal. With the poor, you can lay it on the line and tell them why you want to visit them; besides, you love them. The rich will suspect that you are using them – as, indeed, you are, and as you are using the poor – and it winds up with a lot of heartbreak. You cannot afford a broken heart if it costs you money.

Stick with your own kind of people. Drink, if you must, but drink Gallo's; you can not afford wine. And don't ever drink with people who, when they get drunk, get so drunk that they say, "Let's go out and get something to eat."

Your inability to remember birthdays and anniversaries will break your wife's heart and, ultimately, her spirit. Remember, it's her spirit you've got to break. Your refusal to celebrate the Great Gouge of Christmas will take the exuberance out of your children. If the present uproar on the campus tells us anything it tells us that children should have the exuberance taken out of them when they're young.

Don't celebrate your wage raise; according to the Bureau of Labor Statistics, wages rose by 5.5 percent in 1968, but "increases in consumer prices eroded most of this gain"; plus taxes. Don't consume and don't celebrate. There isn't anything to celebrate, and the only thing you can celebrate is the Mass. Celebrate the Mass, if celebrate you must; the best things in the *next* life are free.

Enter the next life precipitately. Die, but don't get sick. If you get sick, you will find, when you get done with Blue Cross (or *v.v.*), that you were afflicted by an exotic affliction (such as a broken leg) that wasn't covered by the policy or, if it was, was covered up to a maximum of twenty cents a day when the daily cost was twenty dollars (or, more likely, up to twenty dollars a day when the daily cost was two hundred). Don't buy glasses; go blind; you've seen everything. Don't go to the

An Extra Pair of Laces : *193*

dentist; milk toast is cheaper than porterhouse. The lives these Manslaughterers in White save are outnumbered by the deaths brought on by stroke suffered by people who got their bills.

Stay out of the market. Don't buy anything. Don't buy anything pink. Don't buy anything blue. Don't buy anything borrowed. Don't buy anything new. Don't buy anything retail, and don't buy anything wholesale. Don't buy napalm, and don't buy it for the Government by paying your taxes. Don't buy anything from Dow or anybody else. Don't – but you're not *that* stupid – buy a car no matter how much it costs you to keep the old one going. My '59 Volvo is so crumpled and crummy that I'm ashamed to be seen in it even when (as is usually the case) it is standing still. I can't afford to be unashamed. And neither can you.

Like my Old Man, I've made it. I've made it by being a cheapskate and, what is more important, by being known as a cheapskate. Carlyle was right. Carlyle was right because he said that of the three great goods of life, money, health, and reputation, the one a man can easiest live without is reputation. If you start doing things for the sake of reputation, such as making money in order to help the poor, you are *tutto kaputo*. Nobody cares about the poor except the poor, and nobody is going to do anything about the poor except the poor. Comes the revolution, and the man the poor are going to go after is Mr. David Packard, who, for all I know, makes money in order to help the poor. Mr. Packard is a Merchant of Death. Upon taking up the post of Assistant Secretary of Death under Mr. Nixon, he said that he had no intention of living on his salary of $30,000 a year.

You may say that Mr. Packard is a fool; I wouldn't know. But if you think that you can go on racing down the primrose path without becoming Mr. Packard, you are already a fool. The profligate society, living it up and shooting 'em down, spends as if the bottom were going to drop out in the next ten months or the next ten minutes. It is going for broke with its increasingly nonnegotiable currency the way the kids – God bless them in general, but not in particular – are going for broke with their increasingly nonnegotiable demands.

Comes the revolution, you and Mr. Packard, unless you listen to me, are going to wish you had never been born, while I go right on making it, like my Old Man, a penny here and a penny there, a nice soupbone, an extra pair of laces.

: : : *Swing Lower, Sweet Chariot* : : :

Once in the dear dead days almost, I am glad to say, beyond recall, and before everyone wondered how soon life would end all at once, a literary con man, or fourflusher, leapt aboard the Dale Carnegie gravy train with a book called *Life Begins at 40.* Like all sweet deceits, this one sold a lot of copies. But not to me; I have never been one to be diddled by the Diddlers of the Masses; I would wait until I was forty and life began, and see for myself; meanwhile I would save my money.

Age forty came and went. I waited and waited for life to begin. It didn't. Things went on, or didn't go on, pretty much as they had. In my fortieth year I thought I was just about where I was in my thirty-ninth; I was wrong, of course, because the man who thinks he is just about where he was a year ago didn't know where he was a year ago either. I was maybe a wee bit worse in my fortieth year than I was in my thirty-ninth – just a wee; just enough to make my fortieth year a landmark.

Landmarks are hard to discern anyway. This little life flies by so fast, and a fellow has all he can do to hold on to its tail feathers. Under the circumstances he mistakes one landmark for another (or a divot for a landmark) and some, lying lower along the horizon, he does not discern at all. So flies this little life, and a fellow with it, away.

An old friend, who shall, or should, be nameless, and I were fishing up at Mud Lake once, using an empty bottle for a float. "How old are you?" said my friend, who thought he had just snagged a pike but turned out to have snagged a pikestaff and had grown pensive. "Forty," I said. My friend, who was a couple of years younger than I (and, indeed, still is), whistled. "You'd better get going," he said. "Where?" I said.

From *The Progressive*, June 1959.

"*Some*where," he said. "I've been there," I said, "and it's a sell." "You're approaching your prime," he said. "The next ten years will tell the story." "I'm retreating," I said, "and there isn't any story." "They ought," he said, "to be the best ten years of your life."

And so they have been, like every ten years before them. But nothing decisive happened, and not much even indecisive. I waited and waited for life to begin at. It never did. Things are great, even peachy, but they always were. I'm just about the same, except for my hair, or, as I am now able to say, my hairs, as I was at Mud Lake.

A couple of months ago I was in Europe saving my money and trying to drum up a little business – I'm still there, and still trying – and I got a letter from my friend. "How old are you?" he wrote. "Fifty," I wrote back, "and don't tell me I'd better get going. I'm gone." "Do you know," he wrote back, "what I want you to do? I want you to write your reflections on being fifty. You must have some. *Fifty*," and he whistled into the mail box.

I know what moves my friend to keep after me decade after decade. He is right behind me on the unlighted path of life. He looks behind him and around him, and it is dark unto ebon. He wants to know if I see anything up ahead. He wants to know when life begins. *Hélas!* my friend – never.

There is, of course, the grace of God. This, when it comes over a man, at fifty, forty, or eighty, is said to be a beginning. I wouldn't know, but I can imagine. One day, as he weeps in the garden, he hears a voice as of an angel saying: "Take up and read." And he takes up, and the book falls open, and he reads: "Let us walk honestly, as in the day; not in rioting and drunkenness, not in chambering, and wantonness, not in strife and envying. But put ye on the Lord." And he whistles a beatific whistle and sells what he has and gives it to the poor; and signing no more petitions, writing no more inspirational essays, running for no more offices in which he may serve his fellow citizens, and selling no more soul for no more money, he walks into a monastery (like the young man who bombed

Hiroshima) and escapes at last (like the young man in Stendhal who went to join Napoleon) the sorrows that are poisoning his life, especially on Sundays. Thus, it would seem, and only thus, life begins. Anything less and he is about the same this year as last – a little seedier, a little greedier, a little timider. He says, and he thinks, that he means to change; but what he really wants is *to be changed,* but he has not come to the right Party.

Fifty. I whistle up the Urals.

Where have I been all my life?

:

It's funny. The less a man has to lose, the less he is willing to risk; the worse the bargain, the tighter he hugs it. I remember the first time I heard myself saying that Socrates' choice was no mystery: by being noble, and taking death instead of dishonor, he simply traded in a couple of years of life for immortality. "He was an old man, anyway," I said. "He didn't mind dying." "Young man," said an old man in the group, "you have never been an old man."

I remember the time a vicar in the town of Wakefield was quoted as telling his son that a man must never choose the lesser evil in the hope that he might, thereby, survive to do good. "The evil he chooses, my son," said the vicar, "he must do today. The good for which he chooses it he will do tomorrow. But before tomorrow comes the book of his life may be closed, and then the evil he did will be written in it, and the good he would do ————." I remember the time I read of the man who ate, drank, and was merry, instead of building a barn for his goods, and then resolved that he would positively build the barn tomorrow, when he heard a voice saying, "Fool, this night thy soul shall be required of thee."

So fast flies this little life away. I remember a tale out of school, and what a school. I was sitting in the office of the president of the school, admiring his one hundred fifty million dollars. I had my feet on his desk. He kicked them off and told me some of his troubles. "What you need," I said, "is time off, to think." "If I had time to think," he said, "I would have to think about why I am not a socialist, a pacifist, and a Christian. Thanks just the same." Me, too. So fast flies this life, and lest we have time to think, we fly it faster.

Fifty. At fifty Jesus and Alexander had each been dead seventeen years, each having overcome the world, in his own way, at thirty-three; Mozart at thirty-five; Michelangelo had finished the Sistine ceiling fifteen years earlier, and his back still ached, and Leonardo had learned enough about Woman to paint her picture; and Napoleon had had four years on St. Helena to think about why he was not a socialist, a pacifist, and a Christian. At fifty Marshall Field II had, by pluck and luck, accumulated seventy-five million dollars; in the year 1900 Andrew Carnegie made twenty-three million dollars and paid no income tax, and his workers' wages averaged four hundred dollars a year. At fifty Hitler attacked everybody, and at fifty Alfred Krupp, who owned a hundred companies at thirty and was a war criminal at forty, owned a hundred companies again. Me – at fifty I have overcome no worlds, painted no ceilings, learned nothing about women, and accumulated between twenty-three and seventy-five million dollars worth of grocery bills. True, I have attacked everybody, I am a war criminal, and my back aches. True, too, I have managed not to have time to think about why I am not a socialist, a pacifist, and a Christian.

At fifty I'm winded. But I always was. At fifteen Coach Rosie Rosenbaum of the Englewood High School track team put me in against De Paul in the two-mile run. "But I'm a miler," I said. "You're neither a miler nor a two-miler," said Rosie, "but there are only two men entered, and if you finish, we pick up a point. You'll get your second wind at the end of the first mile. If you don't, keep going anyway." I finished late that night, and Englewood won the meet by one point and, with it, the city championship. I never got my second wind.

:

I never will. I'll keep going anyway until they repeal Newton's first law of motion. It's the end of the first mile and the beginning of the last; there's a reflection at fifty for you, friend.

Swing Lower, Sweet Chariot : *199*

The long pull, and all pull now. At twenty-five I held down three jobs and wrote nights. At fifty I hold down no jobs and write days – some days. No wind. At twenty-five Bill Benton held down three jobs and wrote nights; at fifty he held down six jobs and wrote twice as much nights; and at sixty he holds down nine jobs and writes three times as much nights. Third wind. Paul Geheeb, the greatest educator in Europe, is out mountain-climbing in the Berner Oberland at eighty-nine; when he took off, he reminded me that Sophocles hadn't hit his stride until he was ninety.

Me – I was superannuated at fifteen; never picked up a point again. The Bentons, Geheebs, and Sophocleses live forever. Me – I die forever. I feel as heavy as yonder stone.

It isn't bad. I lived long enough to hear of what the old Chassid said of the man who foreknew in his lifetime that for him there was to be no heaven: "What a unique and enviable chance that man had of doing right without fear of reward!" I lived long enough, too, to hear A. J. Muste say, "If I can't love Hitler, I can't love at all." It isn't bad, to have lived long enough to hear the Word, even on the fly.

At fifty the devil takes over, if, indeed, he has bided his time that long. He inflates a fellow's ego as a defense against being passed by by the world and the new generations indifferent to what a fellow knows and thinks and is. Kids who once wanted advice are giving it now. A fellow is ever more isolated; he has to fight now for a hearing; his gray hairs command the disre-spect of the young. It's the space age, and he hasn't found out yet how to use the space he already had.

But his friends grow old with him, and, growing old all of them together in lockstep, they are always young and fair (or fair to middling) to one another. So they maintain the hal-lucination; they go on dancing, or drinking, or walking, or whatever they always did, with one another. Ah, but then their ranks (if not they individually) begin to thin. An old friend moves away, and that's a betrayal. An old friend dies – if you haven't died at fifty nowadays, you never will – and that's a greater betrayal. They leave you there alone, with strangers, who do not care what happens to you because they themselves are beset, like you, with their responsibilities and their betrayal and (finally, when you and they are both very old) their bitterness. A very old man – I know some great men who are very old – is either a bore or suspects that he is. None of his virtues, wisdom included, offsets his one unforgivable vice of being old. "Here comes old man Mayer again. Quick, turn off the lights and we'll pretend we're in bed. I haven't got time to listen to him. I wish he'd find something to do."

You will be old and resent every thing new – plastics and light metals, calculators and computers, ranch houses, clutchless cars, frozen foods, picture windows, and turnpikes. You will know, the day it's discovered, what television is going to be and do, because you saw radio do it. Unless you're a fool clear out to the rind, you have long since discovered that there is no progress. And if you, my friend, think, you and your campaigns to change the world, that you will not leave the world and yourself a little worse than you found them, you're crazy. If you think that ontogeny does not recapitulate phylogeny – still more so, philogyny – you're out of your head.

Among the new things a fellow resents, at fifty, are his children, as his parents resented him, and with reason. What right has my Little Julie to sell a story for $350? Who taught her to write? Who's the writer in this family? Who changed her diapers and washed them and wiped her little nose and held her while she took her medicine and sat her on the toilet and wrapped her pink blanket around her to keep her warm? Confound it, I haven't seen $350 in one piece in twenty years. I don't want her $350; I don't even want her not to have it; what I want is for her not to have sold a story for $350. But she will always pretend that all that she is today she owes to her darling father; they all will, the little hypocrites.

:

It's other people's daughters who rowel me, not my own. Peaches-and-cream little girls – past their teens now; little girls who take me for their uncle, who no longer look at me on the street car or crowd over to me at parties or after lectures or receptions. To thine worst enemy, the mirror, friend! It will lie to thee and tell thee that thou hast twenty–thirty good years yet! If thou wast not handsome then, hast thou changed? Not at all, says the mirror; oh, a wee bit, but only a wee – dimples to creases and creases to ruts; a hair here and there gone, another here and there discolored, gray with the dust of life's dusty road. What right have *they* to take you for their uncle, to go out with you, unafraid, after dark?

Recollected in no tranquility the first love; rapture and agony; never anything else, and neither of them recollectable now except by analogy. Now you begin to fill up with wistfulness. Everything – a lilac bush, a sidewalk crack, an ice cream cone – bespeaks wistfulness. It will burst you unless you work or play harder to shrivel it; in which case work or play will burst you, and the wistfulness of a sprig of mignonette, of a ribbon, of a glove or a garter, will come seeping back anyway and fill you up; if you work and play by day and by evening, then by night.

But you're too tired to work and play, too tired to withstand the wistfulness. Maybe your raptures (when the dentist stops drilling) and your agonies (when he starts) will distract you. You are coming apart now. In another ten years, fifteen anyway and maybe five, you will be coming apart full-time. When you were little and you had your toy hook-and-ladder, you were doctored and dentisted and dieted all the time, and you had to leave your hook-and-ladder for them. There followed the years (when life first flew fast away and you never noticed) of no doctor, no dentist, no diet, the years you did as you pleased, the years you balanced on ladders and then the years you played with hooks. Now at fifty you must leave them and go back to being doctored, dentisted, dieted, opticianed, vitamined, and arch-supported. There are twenty–thirty years in you yet, but don't call them good years; call them good days. Not yet – but soon.

In the fall an old man's fancy turns to death. Let it turn lightly, friend; if I see darkness ahead, what see you behind except darkness? I see that the road ahead is longer than the road behind; if God exists, nothing else is important, simply because the road ahead is longer than the road behind; nothing else, then, is important except whether God exists. I don't try to tell you He does; death is wasted on the old. *Your* death – reflect at fifty, friend – means nothing except to you. Nobody will miss you; see all the relicts, a few months afterward adjusted, a few years afterward happy as birds. Let your death mean nothing to you, and it will mean nothing to anybody. Who sees the sparrow fall?

It isn't death, but dying that bothers you, is it? Ah, yes, because of all the things you intended to do. But if you were to live ten minutes less than forever, that would still be the case. The only thing you can count on doing forever is busying yourself being dust. You remember the Roman's question: "What are you busy *about?*" You remember the Carthaginian – Augie of Hippo, they called him – who despaired because children wasted their time in aimless play and then despaired the more when he considered that men wasted their time in things that were worse because they were aimed in the wrong direction. Consider how your light is not spent but thrown away. If you have an affair, put your affair in order. Fool, this night. . . .

"I will restore to you," the Lord promised me through his prophet Joel, "the years that the locust hath eaten." *That's* the kind of talk. But not yet. The locust will eat yet awhile. Now just what are the things you intend to do, friend? Cut yourself down to size and them with you, or you will be miserable when you have lived ten minutes less than forever. Reflect at fifty. If you will avoid misery, reflect. You must have a fixed hierarchy of things you intend to do and steer yourself by it, for he who will not answer to the rudder will answer to the rock. And you must establish your hierarchy in terms of two separate and co-ordinate principles; first, in terms of the things that are good in themselves, such as changing the world, and second, in terms of the things that are within your own power, such as changing yourself.

I tell you that these separate principles are not only co-ordinate but co-operative: you will change the world in so far, and only in so far, as you change yourself, for, as the men are, so will the world be, and you, though you would never know it to look at you, are a man. You insist that you would do more – maybe remake America – but America is remaking you faster than you will be able to remake it. Bite off more than you can chew – sure – but not so much that you choke on it. Hierarchy, hierarchy. It's a great life only if you weaken, and this is the Hot Gospel, the Law and the Prophets, the Medes and the Persians, and the Real Gazookus.

:

In my fiftieth year I have learned to play chess. A little child of mine led me and beat the pants off me. Then I taught the companion of my sorrows (and the cause of most of them) and now she beats the pants off me. Chess is the ultimate form of supraverbal communication. Now, as I totter around Russia and parts farther still, I need not learn the language; chess is the universal language. Brother Ziak, the vice-president of the Czechoslovakian People's Republic, beat the pants off me; I'm challenging Brother Mao. Maybe I'll change the world; if I do, it will be because I changed myself into a chess player. I have spent maybe a fourth of my fiftieth year playing chess with the companion o.m.s. (a.t.c.o.m.o.t). What a waste! But how have you spent a fourth of yours, my friend – deciding that to go to war with the Democrats is a lesser evil than going to war with the Republicans?

In my fiftieth year I have learned to sleep on straw in *youth* hostels at a dime a night. In an Italian hostel a Greek standing next to me in the washroom said, "You are the first American boy I have met in a hostel." *Boy.* In my fiftieth year I have learned, in a word, to punish myself a little, knowing that at fifty the devil's whisper is always, "Why punish yourself?" and that the masochist answer is the only right one, "Because I enjoy it." I have learned to live on a *little* less money, a *little* less fame, and a *little* less power than I lived on twenty years ago, knowing that at fifty the devil's whisper is always, "All these may be yours." I know the devil – I guess I ought to; we've been traveling companions for fifty years – and I know his name. It is Ego. Against him, at fifty, I make war. I am losing the war – winning a skirmish here and there, but losing the war – but at least I am losing the right war. Are you sure, my friend, that you are not winning the wrong one? Are you even sure you are winning it?

:

Twenty years ago I was an eagle flying high in Bombay. Money, fame, and power were a dime a dozen, but many an eye had a cinder in it. The devil took me up to the covers of the slick magazines and watched me jump off and split his sides as I screamed going down. But at least I don't have to go up there any more. I'm losing the war, but at least I don't have to go up there any more. I remember the mountain top and *its* raptures and *its* agonies and how little time it left me to think about why I wasn't a socialist, a pacifist, and a Christian, and I don't have to go up there any more.

All the breaks. Nothing but breaks. The first fifty years have been a toboggan ride, a two-mile jog. If, fool, this night my soul is required of me, my regret is that I owe the world a living and I haven't had time to pay anything on the debt. I've been intending to pay – a *little* something, anyway – but the road to good intentions, my friend, is paved with hell. I may never get it paid off, but at least I won't welsh.

Nothing but breaks. Through no virtue of my own, I'm a free enterpriser, and therefore, a free man *in posse*. Nobody can fire me; still better, nobody can pension me; best of all, nobody can retire me with a blue-plate dinner and a gold watch (which turns out to be plated) for fifty years of faithful service to – what? I was reading in the paper, and *only* the other day, that the Essex Universal Corporation, which makes missile control systems, has acquired William Gluckin & Company, makers of corsets and brassieres, and that Wilson Brothers, men's underwear and shirt makers, have absorbed the Sciafe Company, producing missile equipment. I was reading in the paper, only the other year, that sixty-five scientists who made the atomic bomb for Mr. Roosevelt petitioned Mr. Truman, on July 15, 1945, not to use it. When I go back into faithful service – if ever – I'm going to take the light yoke, and you know Whose that is, friend. Meanwhile, I am my own man and my own fool and not, like Mr. Henderson, somebody else's.

And who, did you say, is Mr. Henderson? Why, Mr. Henderson is Loy Henderson of the Dulles-Acheson-Stevenson State Department. And in Karachi a month or two ago Mr. Henderson, as head of the American observer delegation to the Bagdad Pact Ministerial Council, informed the Council, as per Dulles, Acheson, and Stevenson, that "the free nations recognize that survival requires concrete measures to meet the threat of international communism. The Bagdad Pact is playing a significant role in this effort. The American government and people have unstintingly supported the Pact. We will continue to support it and its objectives." I may squander my life at chess, but at least I don't have to tell the Ministerial Council that the American people support the Bagdad Pact – or that they know what it is.

God heard me scream when I jumped down from the mountain top. He picked me up and threw me into good company and let me see Red Schaal of the American Friends Service Committee bent in half carrying suitcases full of books through the railroad station so that the two-bit tip would go instead, into a bottle of milk for a kid somewhere far away. Then He wised me up by letting me hear the Chassid, the vicar of Wakefield, and A. J. Muste. Then He gave me the gift of prophecy, so that I knew before every brave new war began that the winners would be the buzzards and the sharks and so that I would never make an unholy chump of myself by saying, like Franklin D. Roosevelt, that the aim of the peace-loving peoples was to get rid of German militarism forever, "the cancer which for generations has produced only misery and pain for the whole world." He even saved me from saying, like the *New York Times* the day after the Nazi murderers were murdered at Nürnberg, that "mankind has entered a new era of international morality." He kept calling my attention to little items like that – always little items – like the little item from Tokyo that reported that sixty Japanese (sixty *known*) had died in the year 1958 – you heard me, 1958 – of radiation incurred in Hiroshima and Nagasaki in the year 1945.

And after doing all that for me, He crowned His free and unmerited gifts by letting me grow old without growing up. Everything is said to be easy for Him, but this was pie. All He had to do was direct my attention to the merchant prince's unbuttoned button, to the judge's cuspidor, and to the wisp of straw sticking out of the statesman's shirt. What Lucian, Cervantes, Swift, and Rabelais saw and articulated, He taught me to see and left me inarticulate lest I let the devil take me up to the mountain top again. I don't mean that He left me illiterate. He taught me to read straight, so that when I read the words, "Forgive us our trespasses, as we forgive those who trespass against us," I knew that the important word was "as," and I realized I'd better get going. He taught me that, when I read the words He spoke to the prophet Isaiah, "Cease to do evil, learn to do good," He did not mean "do good" but "learn to do good."

"Learn to do good." To your homework, friend, and I, at fifty, to mine. No use stalling around and waiting for life to begin, because it won't, not ever, not even if you live to be fifty. But maybe it won't ever end either.

Don't get excited; I only said "maybe."

The Higher Learning

: : : : : : : : : : : : : : :

: : : *Of Cawse It's Impawtant* : : :

A university president (like any other) who means to get anything done has got to get it done in his first term – five years,
say. The presidency of a great university is a great pulpit.
Charles W. Eliot of Harvard, Woodrow Wilson of Princeton, and Nicholas Murray Butler of Columbia all became
national figures as university presidents, but none of them was
anywhere nearly as widely known as young as was Robert
Maynard Hutchins of Chicago. He received a thousand speaking invitations a year and accepted a hundred – and appeared
with increasing frequency in the slick magazines as well as the
scholarly journals. There are immediate destinies for a man of
such prepossessing and precocious parts.

His classmate, Bill Benton, remembered that those attending the tenth reunion of Yale's class of '21 speculated that Bob
Hutchins would some day be the nation's president; and that
was when he had only begun to make waves as president of
the University of Chicago. Five years later the waves would
be breakers. Immediately after the Hundred Days of 1933,
Roosevelt sent Harry Hopkins to Chicago to sound Hutchins
out and kept on sending emissaries. For the better part of
eight years "Dear Mr. Roosevelt" was determined to get "Dear
Bob" on the New Deal team, and Dear Bob was the only man
he was ever determined to get that he never got. The emissaries kept coming to Chicago and going back to Washington
with the same message that the persistently inquiring reporters
got: "I am not interested in public life." Impossible: in Washington there is no such thing as a man who is not interested
in public life. Impossible, too, that a man who was moulder-
ing in a Midwest monastery couldn't be had. The emissaries

This is a chapter from *Robert Maynard Hutchins: A Memoir* by Milton
Mayer (forthcoming, University of California Press, 1991).

kept coming, among them (the Boss was given to mixing his pitches) Roosevelt's "Mr. Wall Street," otherwise known as Sidney Weinberg of Goldman Sachs.

"Damn it all, Hutchins, it's impawtant."

"Isn't education impawtant, too, Mr. Weinberg?"

"Impawtant, of cawse it's impawtant, but it's been *ovahdone.*"

Of course education is important to a university president, including one who resigns a week later to become a vicepresident of Standard Oil at twice the salary. Stand him up in front of an audience (or a donor; or a mirror) and he will say that civilization is a race between education and catastrophe. Hutchins said so too – without the banalities – and said it every time he stood up. The difficulty is to distinguish the straight men from the comics; you have to catch them off the platform, or, as Felix Frankfurter did Hutchins, on the platform of the 63rd Street Station in Chicago, where the New York Central's New England States stopped on its way out to Boston and Cambridge. It was a dreadful stormy day in December of 1932, and the States (which Frankfurter was catching after a lecture in Chicago) was running forty minutes late. The amenities of the 63rd Station being what they were, he and his host walked up and down the platform and talked.

Professor Frankfurter of the Harvard Law School was seventeen years older than Hutchins but they had been close friends since Hutchins, as the young Dean at Yale, had assisted the great man in the futile defense of Sacco and Vanzetti in 1927. Frankfurter had wanted to be invited to Chicago for a lecture precisely at that most unlikely pre-Christmas time of the academic year. What he really wanted was to talk to Hutchins about Harvard's search for a new president. He knew that Hutchins didn't want the job and he wanted Hutchins's advice. He got some of the advice in the Hutchinses' kitchen after the lecture and some more of it on the 63rd Street platform. When he got back to Cambridge he wrote his host asking him to put his advice in writing so that he could use it effectively. Hutchins did:

You gentlemen who are sitting in deep cushions in Harvard Clubs about the country have probably not heard that the condition of American education is now so critical that we are facing in the West and Middle West the practical extermination of higher learning as we have known it. Most of the higher learning in America is carried on in the state universities. The legislatures, one after another, are wrecking them. . . . at this juncture the system of public education higher and lower requires strong and vocal leadership as never before. This leadership must direct attention not merely to the financial crisis but also to the sweeping changes which must be made to adjust the educational system to the demands of the present day. This means that we must revise our methods, our organization, and our curriculum. In the good old days Harvard supplied educational ideas to the United States. There can be no doubt that the system's leadership resided in Cambridge. At the present time there is no evidence that Harvard is aware of the educational system or has anything to offer it. . . . I wish to see Harvard regain its position of leadership in educational thought and action. It should do so now when such leadership is more needed than at any period in our history. . . . The election as president of a nice Harvard man acceptable to nice Harvard men and consequently ignorant of American education and quite indifferent to its needs would be a fatal mistake for Harvard. There must be among your graduates, if you insist on electing one, a man who has knowledge of and ideas on the development of education in this country. I hope that you will satisfy yourselves that no such person exists before you become reconciled to the election of a safe, dull Bostonian, under whose leadership you will roll down the years in peace, quiet, and dishonor.

Frankfurter replied: "Your extraordinarily persuasive analysis – that happy blend that you have of impudent cajolery and venerable wisdom – came the very morning of the day that I had a chance to put in an effective lick. . . . Really, your letter not only as an astute document but as an expression of faith makes me love you more than ever with wisdom as well as with affection. . . . the dominant experience I brought back from Chicago was that out there there was a President who really was passionate about education, – and education as the pursuit, systematically, of the richest and most sensitive experience of life."

Apparently education was impawtant, and not, in Hutchins's view, overdone. He had no sooner got back to Chicago than he indicated his intention to overdo it, and less than a year after his installation, with no power other than persuasion, he had got the no-motion machinery of a great university to adopt the "Hutchins Plan." (The quotation marks here are significant.) The honeymooning Faculty Senate adopted his first proposal – presented on one side of one sheet of paper – in twelve minutes. It revived the "junior division" of the college – the freshman and sophomore years – by assigning it the responsibility for the development and administration of a program of general education. "Revived" is the word; the junior division had been the spectacular invention of William Rainey Harper, the first president of the University of Chicago, in 1892. But at Chicago, no less than everywhere else, this segment of the university had been progressively orphaned by the phenomenal increases of scholarly specialization, in whose interest the graduate schools had all but absorbed the junior and senior years. Under the combined influences of specialization and the elective system the education of a human being, without reference to his future occupation, had been nearly abandoned to the vocational interests of industry, commerce, and finance, to the whims of legislatures, parents, alumni, and benefactors, and the vagrant heart's desire of the adolescent. ("This institution," Professor Philip Schuyler Allen told a Chicago class just before Hutchins's advent, "is becoming an intellectual whorehouse – I suppose that in mixed company I should say a brothel – but I mean whorehouse. An intellectual whorehouse is a university which, like this one, permits its Home Economics Department to give a student credit for weaving a straw hat.")

It became a point of status – to avoid teaching in the first two years which were ultimately delegated to what Hutchins called a "Coxey's army of graduate teaching assistants." This practice was alone an educational atrocity, and it was to be ever more atrocious as the state universities expanded and the colleges took to pretending to be universities. But it did not, then or thereafter, arouse any appreciable scandal in or out of education. Its victims were only students, its perpetrators were the scholars to whom the graduate teaching assistants would some day have to look for jobs, and the teaching assistants themselves (with an annual turnover of 50 percent) had no other way to earn a pittance to maintain their preparation for the Ph.D.

Sentiment overt and covert was strong at Chicago (and at other great graduate schools) for getting rid of the folderol of undergraduate education altogether. Just prior to Hutchins's advent Dean Gordon Jennings Laing of Chicago's Graduate School was saying that "not even in the best university is the graduate work on the scale and quality that would be possible if the institutions were entirely free from undergraduate entanglements." But Hutchins had no sooner hung up his fedora than he announced that he – he used the polite amorphism "we" – did not intend to abandon or dismember the college but to revive it: "A college is an institution devoted to the advancement of knowledge. A college in a university is an institution devoted to discovering what an education ought to be." The discovery, he let it be understood, would be made at Chicago and the college would be the laboratory.

The Faculty Senate, composed of the full professors, was unperturbed; it didn't care all that much about the college, one way or another. What should have perturbed it, but apparently didn't, was something else it subscribed to in those twelve minutes: perceptible, if only perceptible, breaching of the walls between the departments. They would retain their myriad identities, but they would be gathered into four basic divisions – the humanities, the biological sciences, the physical sciences, and the social sciences – charged with the development and direction of the programs at the junior/senior, graduate, and professional levels. The medical school, for instance, at Chicago, as everywhere, a splendidly isolated sanctum, would now be an integral part of the biological sciences division.

A university is an aggregation of separate sovereignties "connected," as Hutchins put it, "by a common heating plant."

The sovereignties are the departments. Proliferating as specialization proliferated, the departments were and are autonomous, each and severally pitted against the *universum* of the university. There was and is nothing to unify them except the demand of their own development – demand stimulated by the use of their work in practical applications. Forced to cooperate by the prospect of application, the natural science departments, still fighting each other for research money that follows prestige, were yielding to interdisciplinary undertakings, in physics and chemistry, chemistry (and the biological sciences) and medicine, chemistry and geology, geology and physics, physics and astronomy, astronomy and meteorology, and all of them with mathematics. But where popular utility was less readily demonstrable, as in social science, or indemonstrable, as in the humanities, there was, and still is, nothing to knock departmental heads together and every parochial reason to build walls ever higher.

The argument for the department was, and is, persuasive, at least in the natural sciences. Who except a microbiologist knows enough about microbiology to say what the department of microbiology needs, or whether its work is important, or whether, at budget time, its work is more important than, say, organic chemistry's or invertebrate zoology's? The more sophisticated the university, the more exalted the unintelligibility and the higher the walls around each departmental cosa nostra. And "areas" within a department were (and would be ever more so) almost as widely separated as the disciplines themselves.

Whoever would want to bring university out of diversity would have to mount an assault against those walls. There would seem to be one way – one very slow way – to do it. The professors of the next generation, if as senior high school and college students they had acquired a common stock of learning and as graduate students and instructors continued to refine and rework that common stock, irrespective of their special fields, could perhaps have something intelligible to say to one another and a common interest in going on saying it. But then

the departments would have to be got out of collegiate education and subordinated even at the graduate level. But who was
there to try to do it? – Not an administrator with five years
at the most to try to do anything and with neither the general
power nor the special credentials to get so much as a hearing.

A university president was not supposed to be a scholar and
very rarely was; rarest of all the kind of scholar with whom
scientists might communicate even elementarily – namely a
scientist. The young president of the University of Chicago
might be acknowledged to know a little something about law.
But law was not a science, not even when it called itself "jurisprudence." And here was a non-scientist who was so impudent as to claim to have all of the competence – fortunately
he could not claim to have any of the power – to reorganize
a great university when he *prided himself* (as he himself put
it) on having a nonmathematical mind (though he would subject every student to the mastery of mathematics as the purest
form of reasoning).

The twelve-minute faculty meeting that adopted the
"Hutchins Plan" of divisional organization may be seen in
distant retrospect as the president's first sly feint at those impregnable repositories – the departments. Survivors of that
occasion say variously that there was no opposition because
the defenders of things, as they were and always would be,
were unprepared and unorganized, or believed that the president knew better than to suppose he could do anything about
the hallowed sovereignties and prerogatives. Or were they mo-
mentarily mesmerized? Besides, the divisional consolidation
made epistemological and pedagogical sense (on paper) and
was later adopted (on paper) by colleges and universities generally. (A sporadic flourish of "interdepartmental" or "interdisciplinary" courses continued to appear across the country,
even in the supposedly "soft" studies, as a supposed concession
to the imperative vagaries of the New Student of the 1960s.
The orthodox departmentalist continued to pay no attention
to them.)

The second battery of proposals, a few months later, bit

deeper into the academic bedrock, but they were adopted almost as readily as the first. The college teaching faculty was granted substantial autonomy, and the country's first faculty awards for excellence in undergraduate teaching were established by the University of Chicago in 1930, when Hutchins got the endowment for them from broker Ernest Quantrell.

In another of the second "Hutchins Plan" reforms the elective system was invaded by year-long general courses in the four divisional fields. The course-credit system was junked. A Chicago baccalaureate would no longer represent an accumulation of unrelated oddments, no sooner passed than past. Instead of being graduated on the basis of what he had known and forgotten, the candidate for a degree would take a series of comprehensive examinations on what he now knew, take them whenever he thought that he was ready to take them, and take them as often as he wanted to. The residence requirement was reduced to a year, and though most students continued to complete the undergraduate requirements in three or four years, some passed the comprehensive after two years (and in one historic case a graduate of an Italian liceo passed them immediately after his admission to the college). The examinations were to be administered by an independent board of examiners – an end to the time-dishonored system of studying the instructor instead of the subject. Compulsory class attendance was eliminated. Freshmen were to be graded Satisfactory or Unsatisfactory – the Pass/Fail "innovation" of a generation later. Some of the effects were measurable as early as the close of the Plan's first year of operation in the spring of 1932. With the elimination of compulsory class attendance at Chicago, attendance actually rose that year by 1.3 percent. Freshman failures went down from 6 percent to 5 percent and dropouts by 5 percent. Applications rose – this in the depression pit of 1932 – and went on rising. By all the tests that could be applied the entering students were markedly superior to their predecessors, and in the first year of the program thirty-nine freshmen presented themselves for examination in subjects they had studied by themselves, without the benefit of instruction. They all passed, and passed with an average higher than the general average of the class. The pursuit of knowledge had become an undergraduate activity.

All of this was revolutionary, and Hutchins wanted all of it. But it wasn't Hutchins's revolution. Bits and pieces of it had been urged – and some of them instituted – at one time or another by Eliot and then Lowell at Harvard, by Harper and Dewey at Chicago, by Wilson at Princeton. But it had never been put together in a package, and most of the bits and pieces had fallen, or been swept, away by the competitive rah-rahism, "development" programs, and fragmentation of teaching and research in the 1920s. Most of the elements of the new program at Chicago had been proposed by a faculty committee which had been sitting (and sitting on it) for two years before Hutchins got there. Everybody everywhere knew that something fundamental had to be done. What doing it had waited on was somebody to say, "Let's do it now." The something that was done was a series of fundamental changes in structure. It did no more than brush the bedeviling issues of deadly lectures and the lifeless content of traditional textbook curriculum. The "Hutchins Plan" was not the Hutchins Plan.

But it was hailed at home and abroad as the first great educational reform of the century and the young president as the century's first great educational reformer. In the midst of the general hubbub attending the reforms on the Midway* nobody paid much attention to the great reformer's ominous animadversion: "We are now in a position to teach the wrong things in the right way."

What was the matter with him? Hadn't he got everything – well, almost everything – he wanted (or should have wanted)? The faculty as a whole had overridden the traditional uneasiness which some of the leading figures in the natural sciences and the professional schools voiced with regard to the deemphasis of the specialization they wanted as preparation for

*The University of Chicago, on the Midway, often identified by its physical location.

graduate work. The thirty-year-old president had cut a great swathe in a great hurry. He could move on any time, as move he must, and cut a great swathe in another great hurry somewhere else. And on, and on.

– Provided that he was ready to move on any time without having got any of the three things he really wanted. He wanted a "new" method of education. He wanted a "new" curriculum. And he wanted a genuine consolidation of research in terms of a common set of principles which might establish an order and proportion of the goods of the mind just as there is an order and proportion of all other goods.

This last was the most scandalous of his three announced objectives (apart from his careful exacerbation of the anti-Catholicism of the academic adversaries by his use of the perfectly proper term "hierarchy" to indicate order and proportion). It was impossible for modern academics even in philosophy (or especially in philosophy) to accept his insistence that the "first principles" of "metaphysics," which would hierarchize all other disciplines, were to be determined by uncoerced consensus based on uncoerced investigation. How did he mean to investigate chimeras? *Whose* first principles? *What* metaphysics?

Hutchins said that the first business of scholarship was to recover the University from the confusion that constituted the chief glory of the higher learning. He denounced the happy anarchy that (in the name of academic freedom) held one subject-matter to be as good as another. Naturally none of the anarchists really felt that way, or really approved of a budget that allocated as much money to what they regarded as frivolous projects as they themselves got for their own fundamental projects; but the freedom doctrine, if it protected the other fellow's frivolity, protected their own fundamentalism, so they never complained outside the family. The family was the department and, little by little, it came to be widely, and correctly, suspected that Hutchins's divisional organization at the university level and his general education program for the college were backdoor tricks to perpetrate the metaphysician's absolutism.

The fact that some academics thought that his objectives were something new – and resisted them for *that* reason – simply confirmed his conviction that educators were badly educated. The things he wanted were all of them very old.

He set the scientists against him by asserting that it was philosophy, specifically that crumbled cornerstone of philosophy which went (or had gone) by the name of metaphysics and professed itself the science of being, that put all other studies in their place and sent them about *her* sovereign business. He outraged the philosophers by insisting that the philosopher's work was not to teach philosophy – or philosophies – but to teach philosophizing. In the land where every man was king, every man must be a philosopher and not an alumnus who had swallowed, regurgitated, and forgotten lectures in other men's philosophies. There was no right way to teach the things that were not matters of rote; there was only a right way to learn, in which the teacher was an auxiliary to the process, the classic "midwife" of ideas that the student himself must bring to birth.

In coming to that position – by whatever magic one comes to a position in such matters – Hutchins had enrolled himself in the everlasting dispute over cognition. How do we learn, and how, if at all, is what we learn imparted by others? "Man learns," said Erasmus, "at the school of example, and will attend no other." Augustine wept: "The unlearned arise and take heaven by force, and here are we with all our learning, stuck fast in flesh and blood"; and then weeping, heard the voice of an angel saying, "Take up and read, take and read," and the Book fell open to Romans 13:13, and he had no need to read further. "They are wise to do evil," said the Prophet, "but to do good they have no knowledge." "The triumph of my art," Socrates told Theatetus, "is in thoroughly examining whether the thought which the mind of the young man is bringing to birth is a false idol or a noble and true spirit. Like the midwife, I myself am barren, and the reproach which is often made against me, that I ask questions of others and have not the wit to answer them myself, is very just; the reason is that the gods compel me to be a midwife but forbid me to bring forth. And therefore I am not myself at all wise, nor have I anything to show which is the invention or birth of my own soul, but those who converse with me profit. . . . It is quite clear that they never learned anything from me. The many fine discoveries to which they cling are of their own making." The twentieth-century progressives, with John Dewey at their head, maintained that we learn by doing and argued that the school should somehow prefigure the experience of "real life."

But Hutchins could not get the right way of teaching – even teaching the wrong things – introduced at Chicago. Nor would he ever until a race of teachers would arise in the spirit of Socrates, asking pertinent questions in persistent dialogue instead of reciting answers, forcing disputation instead of information on their students, converting education from a process of absorbing to a process of challenge and counter-challenge. Some young instructors, marvelously uncorrupted by their own experience as students, could employ the Socratic method; some always had. But not often the old hats whose attitudes dominated the colleges and the universities. Socrates was, of course, born, not made, and until the schools, at whatever level, would recognize that there is no other true teacher and hunt out this one and hire him away from taxi-driving, or half-soling, or a bench in the park, or a jail cell, or even a schoolhouse, even the wrong things would never be taught in the right way.

The things the misnamed "Hutchins Plan" went on teaching in the wrong (not the right) way were the wrong things. These courses could not be taught via the textbooks that went on dominating, or trying to dominate, education, books written (or pasted together) by academic hacks. The textbook publishers, corruptionists of school superintendents, school boards, state boards of education, were as rich as the school-marms (of both sexes) were poor. They could give a $5,000-a-year professor $5,000 for a month's cut-and-paste job. His rank, on the title page, was secondary; what was primary was the name (by implication, the imprimatur) of the institution he was connected with.

With the rise of the one-semester or one-term "survey" courses for freshmen in the 1920s the publishers had turned their attention to the assembly of teams to produce survey texts which were just as pedantic. The most (and in some respect the only) impressive exception to this output was a series of Chicago faculty lectures in the University's one survey course "The Nature of the World and Man," inaugurated in 1924. This introduction to natural science became so popular that the University published it as a book which colleges across the country had adopted long before Hutchins became president.

But the right things that Hutchins wanted taught the right way were neither lectures nor surveys. He wanted the Socratic method of discussion to draw the young into the great debates of the ages conducted by the great minds of the ages on the great issues of the ages. The great books would constitute the heart of a fixed curriculum to be taught to "everybody who can learn from books" in a four-year institution beginning with the junior year of high school, an institution open at public expense to every member of the rising generation, whether or not he meant to go on to university work. That curriculum would consist of the greatest books of the Western world and the arts of reading, writing, thinking, and speaking, together with mathematics, the best exemplar of the process of human reason. "If our hope has been to frame a curriculum which educes the elements of our common human nature, this program should realize our hope. If we wish to prepare the young for intelligent action, this course of study should assist us; for they will have learned what has been done in the past, and what the greatest men have thought. They will have learned how to think for themselves. If we wish to lay a basis for advanced study, that basis is provided. If we wish to secure true universities, we may look forward to them, because students and professors may acquire through this course

Of Cawse It's Impawtant : 223

of study a common stock of ideas and common methods of dealing with them."

The reason that these objectives – and the curriculum that served them – were unlikely to be pursued at Chicago or anywhere else was that they were profoundly un-American. *And* un-German. But the German university was a scholarly institution concerned entirely with investigation and the training of investigators. It did not prepare its students for the practice of the professions but for the advancement of the professions, both in science and the humanities. Vocationalism (in every vocation but scholarship) was beneath it, beneath it, too, everything that the American thought of as college life. The German (and European) elementary school was six years, after which the sheep, rigorously separated from the goats, went on to the four-year *Gymnasium* or – this was a twentieth-century development – to the science-oriented *Realgymnasium*. There they got their general education, which, after a total of ten years of schooling, was regarded as terminal. Most of them went into white-collar work, a relatively small minority to the technical institutes which produced professional practitioners, and a very few to the university. There was no institution comparable to the American college on top of which, little by little, the Ph.D.'s from Leipzig superimposed little Leipzigs.

The result was the melange of the American university. From the start it did not know what it was – a collegiate extension of general education, a center for research and scholarly training, a gaggle of professional schools. And it never found out. The time came, with a rush, when American affluence sent a hundred (or a thousand) young people to "college" where European austerity sent one to the University.

The American founding fathers wanted to establish a popular form of government. Such government, even with a restricted franchise, had as its first requirement an educated citizenship. The American fervor for popular schooling, unknown anywhere else in the world, was such that by the turn of the twentieth century, education appeared to have become the state religion. But what was worshiped was not education.

What was worshiped was the schoolhouse, which ultimately displaced the church as the national ground cover. What went on in the schoolhouse depended on what the public wanted, for (as Hutchins never wearied of quoting from Plato) what is honored in a country will be cultivated there. What was honored in modern America was the "practical" – the realizable return on the investment. Americans were the most practical people in history, and with good reason. They'd had to be. But their preoccupation with the practical – a national motto, "Do it," was coined by the Yippies a half century later – diminished their interest in the theoretical to the vanishing point. Their founding fathers had been spectacularly practical theorists. But their latter-day heroes, right out of Horatio Alger, were nontheoretical, even anti-theoretical, men. The only defensible object of schooling was not thinking for oneself but doing for oneself (and always for oneself).

Reality meant improving oneself, and improving oneself was a measurable matter of money. The disparagement of hereditary aristocracy in the euphoric name of egalitarianism disparaged only one kind of aristocracy; in a society where being born ahead was treason the only way to be ahead was to get ahead. The privileged few who, in the 1930s, went to college were expected to get rich. Parents scraped and borrowed to send their children to college, not so that they would be better than they themselves were but so that they would be better off. For the poor, education meant a better job – or, in times like the '30s, any kind of job – and was appraised accordingly. Job training, once the province of apprenticeship, with the rise of technology became vocational training in the schools, and vocational training, to gratify both its democratic practitioners and its democratic beneficiaries, became "vocational education" (and, a generation of gobbledegook later, "career education").

This wasn't education, but it was what the country honored and, in its schools, its colleges, and its professions, cultivated. What Hutchins wanted had once been called education – the preparation of the few to whom it was open for independent participation in the common life and the development of the individual's highest powers. It was now called liberal education, generally disparaged as at best useless and at worst élitist. Hutchins called it education for democracy, on the ground that the best education of the few, where the few governed, was the best education for all where all governed. It was the education he fought for for twenty years at Chicago and for twenty-five years afterward; fought for unsuccessfully, and ever more unsuccessfully as the national plunge to illiteracy proceeded and the American "kid" entered college with 30,000 hours behind him of staring at 30,000 electronically projected dots on a glass screen. Still, the end of Hutchins's tenure at Chicago saw the great books occupying as much as 25 percent of the syllabi of the general courses of the College and the College faculty preponderantly staffed by men (preponderantly younger men) who used the method of instruction-by-inquiry in which the teacher was only the midwife.

It is one thing (and no presidential thing) for a university president to think he knows what education ought to be. It is another and still less presidential thing to try to foist it on the great faculty of a great university. But the unpresidentialest thing of all is to show them how it is done. And this, in his honors course for (of all things) freshmen, Hutchins had the effrontery to do as soon as he became president and to go on doing year after year. In "The History of Ideas," 4 to 6 P.M. every Tuesday, with another impudent young pup co-badgering the forty honors students ranged around an immense seminar table, the president of the University of Chicago went ahead and taught in the way he said the professors ought to teach. And if that wasn't effrontery enough, his co-badgerer was the same Professor Adler who, on an April day in 1937, came into his office behind me to tell him (as Hutchins put it) what to think about Aristotle's *Metaphysics*.

: : : *The Ivory Tower of Babel* : : :

I recently slipped away from my enchanted bower in California to visit the scene of my second childhood at the University of Massachusetts at Amherst. The scene was a little dejecting. The professor emeritus was confronted with the premonitory spectacle of the university emeritus. There were massive indications that education was to be retired in favor of vocational training – the same vocational training which John Dewey long ago denounced as élitism pure and simple. The young man or woman who emerged from the lower depths of the Commonwealth in earnest search of a little learning would be able to get it at Harvard, if only they had the money. For the rest, they would have access to programs designed to prepare them for jobs. The design is historically undemocratic. It is also historically unrealistic and impractical; the majority of vocationally trained young people do not enter – nor have they ever entered – the occupations for which they have been trained. And the overwhelming majority of those who do, do not remain in those occupations.

We are told that the hard fact is that these are hard times and that luxuries must be dispensed with. Marx himself seems to have written the scenario for the current and recurrent condition of the capitalist economy deprived simultaneously of war and colonial markets. Hard times in this Commonwealth, and in others like it; and the first of the luxuries to go is the kind of education which Jefferson (in his classic letter to Peter Carr) set forth as the keystone of the democratic arch.

I make bold to recall my beleaguered colleagues, in Amherst and elsewhere, to the grand abstractions on which their realistic and practical struggle to save education is grounded.

The university represents the cultivation of rationality or it

From *The Massachusetts Review*, Summer 1978.

represents nothing. It does not represent government or the state or industry or business. It does not represent the passions of the public or the public's passing interest. It does not represent the vagaries of the adolescent palate, the enhancement of the GNP, or the kaleidoscopic demands of the labor market. It does not represent progress or peace. Least of all does it represent war. The achievement of the self-sustaining nuclear chain reaction was a triumph of rationality; Hiroshima was the apotheosis of irrationality. The university is the only institution in the society that represents rationality and nothing else.

It may operate dormitories and dining facilities. It may operate psychiatric counseling and job placement services. It may operate pinball machines and parking lots and swimming pools and billiard halls. It may subsidize athletic teams and student publications. I am sure that these amenities are all salubrious and ornamental. But they are all incidental to – and dispensable from – a university's unique reason for being. The University of Paris has managed to stumble along for eight hundred years without any of them.

These are, as I say, hard times, and they are growing harder. We are told that we are running out of the raw materials of a mechanized society. We are ridden by disillusion and mistrust. Our reaction to all this is pervasive panic, to which rationality and its cultivation fall early victim. Our young people, like our old, understandably see their sudden situation in stark materialistic terms. We have never really seen it otherwise. Confronted by unexampled material challenge and opportunity, we and our ancestors here have tirelessly met that challenge and pursued that opportunity and left the ideals of the Declaration of Independence to take care of themselves and us. We care about thinking provided the thinking butters parsnips at home or abroad. Our national motto – unearthed by the Yippies in 1968 – is, "Do It!"

What is honored in a country is cultivated there. As a whole people we do not cultivate rationality. The reality by which we have lived is, on the whole, a bigger bang and a better job. Education in our culture has always been associated with vocation. A high school diploma once, and then a college degree, was taken to be the first milestone on the highroad to riches. If it wasn't, what was it for? The fact that the men who traveled that highroad farthest, Rockefeller, Carnegie, Ford, did not have diplomas or degrees did not disturb the myth. My father wanted me to go to college so that I would be better off than he was; not better, but better off.

The fact is that Rockefeller, Carnegie, and Ford got to be better off by learning the job on the job, just as the great lawyers and doctors of yore were prepared by being articled to a Blackstone or a Lister. Truly vocational education – apart from the mere tricks of the trade – begins with apprenticeship. I'm a newspaperman by trade, and the last thing that is wanted by a good newspaper is a journalism school degree. What is wanted in a journalist is an irrepressible aptitude and a bowing acquaintance with the native tongue. The native tongue in these parts is English. Thus the separation of Communication Arts (*né* Journalism) from the English Department of a college or a university is nothing worse than a crime against nature. Outside of preprofessional study, job-training (call it career education or what you will) is preparation for the most humdrum of occupations. Strictly speaking, animals are trained – human beings are educated.

Education in this country, including higher education, has always been, if not altogether illiberal in content, largely illiberal in intent. Truly liberal education with a liberal intent was the province of Spiro Agnew's effete snobs who were so snobbish that it was not supposed that they would have to earn a living and so effete that it was not supposed that they could. It was not all that much different in England, as witness the case of the impoverished Cantabrigian who asked a don why he should study Greek and the don replied, "First, because it is the language of the Holy Ghost, and second, because it leads to great emoluments and preferments in the Church."

Our early American universities, except for Clark and Johns Hopkins, and later Chicago and Stanford, arose from colleges privately established for the vocational training of ministers. Most of the state colleges were established, in the words of the Morrill Act of 1862, "to teach such branches of learning as are related to agriculture and the mechanic arts" – the function to which it was now proposed that the University of Massachusetts (and how many others similarly established) be reduced in principle.

The true university was conceived – on the German, not the British, model – as a seat of scholarly investigation and the preparation of scholarly investigators. But its historical genesis here confused its purposes. The professional schools which clustered around it were visibly utilitarian and ever more narrowly vocational, and their requirements pressed an increasingly preprofessional character on the university's work as a whole and on the curriculum at the collegiate level.

But the truly liberal college curriculum fell into desuetude at the turn of the century for two independent reasons. It was taught by deadly rote by men and women who had got their jobs through scholarly, not pedagogical, achievement and who did not want to teach but had to in order to do what they wanted to do, namely, scholarly work. The second reason for the deliquescence of the liberal curriculum was its increasing irrelevance to the condition of the undergraduate institutions which a hundred years ago accommodated less than 1 percent of the college-age population and now accommodate close to 45 percent in an economy which in peacetime can not think of any other way to keep the rising generation off the streets.

The democratic society, in which, as Aristotle says, we rule and are ruled in turn, elevates its every member to its highest and only permanent public office – the office of citizen. The citizen has the society at his mercy, and it is the recognition of this portentous fact that moves the citizens of enlightened Massachusetts to provide tax support for the schools of benighted Georgia, against the event, however unlikely, that a Georgian might one day be presiding over their destinies in the White House.

The democratic society is the universally élite society. If it is to advance and endure, the ancient prerogative of the few – liberal education – will have to be the education of every man and woman in it. The difference between democracy and mobocracy is the insertion of the word "intelligent" before the word "man" and again before the word "vote," in the doctrine of "one man, one vote." The democratic society can not be uneducated and survive democratic.

This is not to say that sovereign citizenship, the vocation of every adult, is the end purpose of the liberal arts – as if they would be of no service to a subject or a slave. On the contrary; their objective, though they make a better American of a man, is to make of him not a better American, or a better working-man, but a better man; richer not in his purse, his politics, or his patriotism, richer, rather, in his person. John Stuart Mill took issue with the hit song of Gilbert and Sullivan's *Pinafore* when he said, "I am a man before I am an Englishman."

If we reject Karl Marx, it has got to be because Marx took man first and last for an economic animal, moved to every other end by his economic condition and his economic considerations. A Calvin Coolidge who says, "The business of this country is business," has no quarrel with Marx except on the technical nicety of the management of the enterprise. The business of this country, and of every country, is liberation, liberation from political and economic servitude and from the subtler but more devastating servitudes of ignorance, bigotry, and boredom. Man is a thinking as well as a feeling animal whose self-realization, unlike that of the barnyard critters, requires the lifelong activity of a persistently inquiring intellect and a persistently discriminating taste. These are the objectives that the liberal arts serve, and liberal education is nothing but the beginning of their habituation. It is a platitude (but none the less valid for that) that the masterpieces of the liberal arts do not teach us what to think and feel, but how. There abides the great Latin pun – *Facio liberos ex liberis libras libraque* – "I make free men out of boys by means of books and balances."

A playful Englishman once said, "Some people say that life is the thing, but I prefer books myself." The great works of the

The Ivory Tower of Babel : *231*

mind and imagination all disagree with one another. But their disagreements are the important disagreements, no different now from what they were two thousand years ago or five. As long as man remains man the great questions remain the same. The cumulative wisdom of the race changes the face of the world and unveils the ancient mysteries of the universe, but the great questions abide, noncumulative, confronting us each and severally precisely as they confronted every one of our first forebears. Stringfellow Barr reminds us that the Greeks could not televise Oedipus Rex – but they could write it. So Scott Buchanan used to say that the questions that can be answered are not worth asking; and he said it at the same time that Gertrude Stein was saying, "Anything for which there is a solution is not interesting . . . the things that can be taught, not learnt but taught, are not interesting."

The masterpieces of the liberal arts are the timeless environment in which we learn to ponder the things that are interesting; the environment in which we practice ourselves in thinking clearly and coherently about those things, and in thinking for ourselves; the environment in which we practice ourselves in disagreeing coherently and comprehensibly with our fellows. And the great works of the imagination and the fine arts similarly provide an environment in which we habituate ourselves to the discrimination of the beautiful. This is the environment that we call collectively the humanities, the congeries of disciplines that deal with man *qua* man.

There isn't a second-semester freshman who does not realize, vaguely or sharply, that the disorders of the day, public and private, are first and last moral disorders. The political disorder is moral. The economic disorder is moral. The racial disorder is moral. The issue of human rights is a moral issue. The environmental issue is a moral (and in part an aesthetic) issue, as is the so-called "quality of life." Moral and aesthetic enlightenment is the domain of the humanities. The humanities – and they alone in the secular order – together represent the implacable effort of the human race to preserve its humanity, an effort which the race relaxes at its mortal peril. But the vestiges of this effort are far to find in the higher learning these parlous days.

The decline and fall of the humanistic studies has been loosely ascribed to the rise of the empirical sciences after the fifteenth century and their phenomenal triumphs since the eighteenth. But the sciences, though their marvels inadvertently depreciated the arts, left the fundamental distinction in the great areas of learning undisturbed. Science was the study of the measurable, nonhumanistic aspects of the world (including the nonhumanistic aspects of human beings). It was the rise of the social sciences, in this century, that, again inadvertently, muddied the distinction, perhaps irretrievably. The social sciences made themselves respectable by using measurement – the prime symbol of natural science; by asserting that they too had a laboratory, in the form of the world of people in the mass; and by boasting that they, like the "hard" disciplines, were value-free, without principles or predispositions (except, of course, as to method). Like the natural sciences, they followed the gleam wherever it led and suspended judgment in the manner of the respectable men in white.

Meanwhile men in and out of white had to make moral and political and aesthetic judgments every day – unsuspended judgments based on values in which the humanities, and the humanities alone, had credentials. The humanities, and the humanities alone, examining the axioms of science, could assert a competence to establish the order and hierarchy of all the other studies and their application in the learned professions.

The end is the first principle of human action. The purpose determines the procedure, the instruments, and the materials. But value-free science has no purpose of its own. It is human beings, scientific, nonscientific, or anti-scientific, who have purposes, and (as Robert M. Hutchins said long ago) they do not get their purposes from science. The sociologist can tell us what the social situation is, but not whether it should or shouldn't be that way; the medical man can tell us how, but not why, to perpetuate a comatose life; the engineer can tell us how, but not if, we should build a freeway rather than, say, a hospital to accommodate its victims. A recent dispatch from darkest New Jersey informs us that "scientists at Princeton University have urged the school to begin genetic research which they say could either lead to a cure for cancer or produce a 'doomsday organism' that could destroy mankind." So much for the gleam. In July of 1945, sixty-five of the great physicists and chemists who made the atomic bomb went to the President to ask him not to use it. They could not get in to see the President, or anybody who could get them in. They were finally informed that the decision was a political, not a scientific, decision. So much for the gleam.

But science, and its application, satisfied the ruling passion reflected in the national motto, "Do It!" It produced sure cures at home and sure kills abroad. It had something to *show* for its arcane exertions. It was not necessary that its beneficiaries know how it was done, but only that it was.

It had two other things going for it which the humanities hadn't. As specialization proceeded apace, and fields became subjects, and subjects became fragments of subjects, and vocabularies became mutually exclusive, a Spenser man meeting a Milton man could talk about the weather and nothing else, and neither of them could talk to a James man, and none of them could talk to a Beowulf man. As the humanities disintegrated into snippets, the sciences had the solidarity of a common vocabulary of mathematics, and the solidarity of a common method. Even the oldest of them, astronomy, has in the past fifty years advanced from observation to empiricism.

But the most exemplary triumph of the scientists has been their realization, going back five hundred years, that everything in all their fields is related to everything else. Interdisciplinary study is no curricular game with them, no pretense of cooperation on a lip-service basis. It is of the essence of all their work. In terms of humanistic knowledge the natural scientists may be uneducated specialists, more grievously uneducated all the time as their mastery of all their related fields increasingly commands their energies; but in terms of their own vocabulary and their own method, they are the only men of general education left in the academic world.

One of the many disintegrative horrors perpetrated at the University of Massachusetts since my departure, and, doubtless, because of my departure, has been the separation of the sciences from the College of Arts and Sciences, now, *horribile dictu!* the College of Humanities and Fine Arts. I dare say the scientists, those uneducated specialists, were glad to go; what use had they for reading and writing? – and the Humanities were, I suppose, too enervated to resist the dissolution. Only the university could have been expected to save the unity in the diversity. Where was the university? Where is it?

I do not mean to suggest that there is villainy or even malfeasance in connection with the balkanization of the university into a pluribus without an unum. The innocent misfeasance was perpetrated a century ago when the most influential man in the history of American education reintroduced the elective system at Harvard College and fastened it on the country. President Eliot was reacting, and rightly reacting, against the sterility of the fixed curriculum of Greek, Latin, and mathematics, "the education of a gentleman" who would have no use for it. But like all reactors, including John Dewey, the next most influential American educator, Eliot overreacted by throwing the educational baby out with the dishwater – if I may mix the metaphor to a fare-thee-well. In principle Dewey was right, of course, as Eliot was. Education had to be meaningful to the educatee, and it would not be meaningful unless it was interesting to him. But the most meaningful education is that which serves a person his whole life and tackles the problems which life brings down upon us all like a ton of bricks. Of course the problems interest the students, and will interest them more profoundly as they grow older. The problems are, in their most elementary form, What is the good? What is the good for man? What is the good for society?

By 1886, seventeen years after Eliot was inaugurated, Harvard had only one required course in the College, freshman composition. I suppose that there is not a college in the country today any more repugnant to education than Harvard was ninety years ago. But there was at least one college, a decade ago, that was better than Eliot's Harvard, and that was the University of Massachusetts at Amherst. A year-long course in the great works of the human mind and imagination was required of every second-year student in the then College of Arts and Sciences. Sophomore English was the vermiform vestige of liberal education in America. But everybody outside the humanities was after its vermiform scalp – and no wonder. It taught everything – or, rather, students and instructors knocked their heads together under the tutelage of the greatest teachers who have ever lived. With our students we read and argued ethics, politics, philosophy, psychology, economics, theology, speech, drama, rhetoric, composition, and, yes-m'am, comparative literature and linguistics and sociology and jurisprudence and history and art. We talked about getting some of our colleagues in the natural sciences and mathematics in to teach us – us and our students – something about method in terms of the great theories and the classic experiments. We met each week – the instructors – to argue the ideas we were arguing with our students.

Don't misunderstand me. Sophomore English wasn't a very good saloon, but it was the only saloon in town. It was the only general education that most of our students – and most of us – had ever got or would ever get. It reprobated the compartmentalization of life and the life of the mind and the spirit. It asserted that all humanistic subjects were inseparably related, all inseparably relevant to every human life. It was a standing insolence in the proud and jealous shambles of the modern university. We fought for it in vain. We were bucking the dismemberment of the higher learning. Sophomore English was vermiformed out of the university and its place was taken (in terms of enrollment) by electives with course titles like "The Gangster in Film." *Sic transit* – as I learned to say in required Latin – *gloria aeternitatis.*

The curse of the elective system is simply its denial that

236 : *The Higher Learning*

there is such a thing as the education of a human being, that there is something that every schoolboy and every schoolgirl ought to know, that there is a way to construct a curriculum and a competence to construct it, a qualification to judge a student's progress, a distinction between the learned and the unlearned, and a utility of the former to the latter. In the end electivism had to place the teacher and the student on an equal footing and make a mockery of schooling altogether – on a worse than equal footing, for the time came when the teacher was terrified of judging the student lest the student burn the place down and the student judged the teacher by means of the atrocity of evaluation – one student, one vote. Thus knowledge and ignorance, preparation and improvidence, industry and ecstasy, experience and inexperience, were equated, and this and almost every other college stood on its head in the circus of the permissiveness which Brother Agnew both denominated and exemplified. Thus Eliot, thus Dewey, and thus, in the end, their gung-ho successors running amok until, in the 1960s, their sorcerer's apprentices ran amok with them. The student demands reflected their contempt of us. They recognized that we didn't believe in what we were doing, that we didn't *know* what we were doing. Any group of them who asserted a special interest furiously enough – "furious" was the operative term – got what they wanted, whatever it was they wanted. They had only to rush into the great vacuum. We could not resist them because we had nothing to resist them with. We had no common body of professional principles: We had no philosophy of education.

Why aren't the perennial challenges of every human life – the subject matter of the humanities – more challenging than nonhumanistic matters? The supposition that they aren't, that young people are not interested in love and hate, in ambition, frustration, failure, treachery, jealousy, betrayal, pride, liberty, tyranny, slavery, greed, anger, lust, fear, sorrow, repentance, reform, redemption, justice, competition, cooperation, benevolence, wealth and poverty, fame and infamy, happiness, tragedy, death, immortality – the supposition is untenable on its face. Their case-hardened elders may be too stuffy to argue these issues; not the young. It is patently absurd to say that Socrates, Sophocles, Dante and Machiavelli, Dostoevski, Goethe, Sterne, Fielding, Melville, Emerson, Thoreau, T. S. Eliot, Marx, Freud, Joyce are uninteresting or can not be interestingly taught. What is not absurd is that they can be made uninteresting, even stultifying, by teachers who are not themselves fired by teaching and who pour their hard-won and harder-wrought store of dead information over the nodding heads of students held ransom for a passing grade. The agonies of Othello, Macbeth, and Lear never die; but the precise dimensions of the Elizabethan stage and the conflicting accounts of Shakespeare's ancestry are stillborn.

The humanistic studies had a modest resurgence after the Second World War to save the World for Democracy. The bestialities of Dachau and Hiroshima, the empty-handedness of victory and the hypocrisy of victors' justice at Nuremberg, the idiocies of chauvinism and its monstrous spawn in McCarthyism, were beginning to come home to us. We were beginning to understand what the Greeks meant when they said that the ingenuities of man undirected by the moral virtues made him lower than the lowest brute. At the end of the 1940s college after college hurried to introduce more or less (usually less) adequately designed general courses emphasizing the liberal arts and the relation of science to society. Specialization was deferred or reduced. Interdisciplinary programs were everywhere projected. If there was to be a new world – as there had to be – it would have to be erected by a new generation schooled in human values and the comprehension of social processes and personal development. A date can be put to the end of that modest resurgence of the humanities: December 30, 1957, two months after the first space ship had been launched by the Soviet Union. On that date President Eisenhower summoned up enough elementary school grammar to ask Congress for what would now be a pittance but what was then the astronomical amount of one billion eight hundred million dollars "to expand scientific education." This – not television – was the beginning of the educational catastrophe that is now upon us – the catastrophe, unique in history, in which a people have plunged overnight from literacy into illiteracy. Out went the humanities (or the superficial survey courses that passed for humanities), in went the superficial survey courses that passed for science, and up went the pre-professional preparation of technologists and technicians. We were a backward country; we had to catch up with the Russians, who did not pretend to teach the liberal arts and couldn't care less about teaching students to disagree intelligently or unintelligently.

And along came government grantsmanship and government control. The colleges and universities were put on notice by President Johnson that unless they reinstituted university course credits for the anti-intellectual shenanigans of ROTC, their federal grants would be jeopardized – and the faculties rolled over. And along came the legion of administrators, supposed to be mere ministers to the faculty, mere custodians of the plant, men who were not, and did not need to be, learned, men appointed because they knew their way around corporate practice and the government agencies that had the money. The faculties abdicated their sovereignty; they were glad to be let alone to do their work and get their wages. Their wages rose to baronial heights at the senior level, and the wages of the administrators were positively Byzantine; they had to be, to be competitive with the rest of big business. In no time at all the administrators – and their system analysts and their management engineers – took over the governance of an institution whose peculiar character they were peculiarly unequipped to understand. I am told that their ratio to faculty and their share of the instructional budget has doubled at Massachusetts since 1970.

They were not bad men, these quantitativists and operationalists, not in the least. What they were was value-free men, like the television executives who have only a few hours of prime time in which to do anything at all and find themselves compelled to fill those few hours with whatever the market demands. The educational marketeers, with only four years of a human being's prime time at their disposal, would like to see everything taught – the more important with the less important, the durable with the transient, the serious with the trivial – but they are under the tyranny of the market. The ratings determine the programs. Like the television executives, the educational administrators are managing a service institution. They have no other master than clamor. They are value-free men. Nowhere, except in television, has the managerial revolution moved so far so fast as it has in the university.

And nobody cared – until the money stopped. Then the faculties came back to life, not to recapture their professional responsibilities and prerogatives but to organize – these faculties, mind you, who were meant to *be* the bosses – against the bosses – and fight it out in the usual adversary relationship of the corporate world on the issues of wages, hours, and working conditions. Whatever else it has done or will do, unionization will not restore the unity of the university or recapture the shattered concept of education.

The end of education, says Carlyle, is not a mind but a man. It's a big order – too big an order. It is the city that educates the man. So education, including humanistic education, has reason to be humble and restrain its claims. Most of what the student will ever be he brings to school, certainly to college, with him. Humanistic education will not humanize him except to the extent that it can nourish his consideration of the good and the bad, the honorable and the shady, the decent and the callous, and the harmonious and the cacophonic. I submit that this country would not be much worse off today if, somewhere down the line, somebody had tried to direct Mr. Nixon's attention to the difference between right and wrong, and in case you think that somebody did, I give you the recent words of Mr. John Ehrlichman, a graduate of an expensive college and a still more expensive law school: "I lived fifty years of my life without ever really coming to grips with a very basic question of what is and is not important to me, what is and is not right and wrong, what is and is not valuable and worthwhile. . . ."

The man or woman we want does not need to know the discreet content of particular sciences. He will be no better or worse a man for knowing how an internal combustion engine works; he will not even be a better driver for it. It is enough – if it is a better man that is wanted – that his technician in white knows whether the blood goes around the heart or the heart goes around the blood and his technician in blue knows how to take his refrigerator apart and perhaps put it together some day. The formula for measuring the hypotenuse on a right-angle triangle will no more make a man just, courageous, and temperate, than his mastery of the eccentricities of the aorist optative middle in the minor poems of Menander. The virtues he might fortify in such studies, the virtues of application, pre-cision, and persistence, are the virtues of a competent scientist, a competent philosopher, and a competent bank robber.

What our humanistically educated man or woman wants is the comprehension of the procedures of science, the estima-tion of its possibilities and its limits, and the heady analysis of the "givens" it employs unexamined – the principles of being and becoming, essence and accident, change and motion, con-tinuity and discontinuity, gradation and classification, sim-plicity and complexity, and the levels of causation, so that he can distinguish nonhumanistic from humanistic materials, methods, and uses. He will be a sharper and more discrimi-nating mind (if not a better and more discriminating man) for his work in the basic fields of mathematics, the most im-placably logical of all learnings. But there is no behavioristic evidence that he will be able to transfer his training, in mathe-matics or any other discipline, to the achievement of the great desideratum – a better man.

To hold before him what Livingstone called the habitual vision of greatness, in the great works of the intellect and the imagination, may (I say only may) focus his attention on his and all men's perennial problems. For the rest, the liberal arts, like all arts, are acquired by their practice, and practice is active, not passive. Our student will no more learn to think for himself by being lectured to than he will be reformed by being preached to. He will learn by challenge, and by meeting challenge – or he won't learn at all. He will learn, in a word, by what the Middle Ages called dialectic, or reasoned disputation. I give you the words of Rabanus, *primus praeceptor Germania,* written before the Middle Ages, before there was any higher learning except in natural and dogmatic theology, and before the laboratory was ever dreamed of: "*Dialectic* . . . is the *disciplina* of rational investigation, of defining and discussing, and distinguishing the true from the false. It is therefore the *disciplina disciplinarum.* It teaches how to teach and how to learn; in this same study, reason itself demonstrates what it is and what it wills. This art alone knows how to know, and is willing and able to make knowers. Reasoning in it, we learn what we are, and whence, and also to know Creator and creature; through it we trace truth and detect falsity, we argue and discover what is consequent and what inconsequent, what is contrary to the nature of things, what is true, what is probable, and what is intrinsically false in disputations." That was the Ninth Century.

I bring you exactly one thousand years forward to Mill: ". . . He who knows only his own side of the case, knows little of that. His reasons may be good, and no one may have been able to refute them. But if he is equally unable to refute the reasons on the opposite side; if he does not so much as know what they are, he has no ground for preferring either opinion. Nor is it enough that he should hear the arguments of adversaries from his own teachers, presented as they state them, and accompanied by what they offer as refutations. He must be able to hear them from persons who actually believe them; who defend them in earnest, and do their very utmost for them. He must know them in their most plausible and persuasive form; he must feel the whole force of the difficulty; else he will never really possess himself of the portion of truth which meets and removes that difficulty."

I put it to you: Is it possible, after all these aeons, that we have no least glimmering of what every one of us as human beings most needs to know in this life and to know how to do? – no order and importance of the myriad kinds of knowledge spread out before us? – no body of experience that informs us of the most effective methods of teaching and learning? – of transmitting the wisdom of the race from generation to generation and describing and prescribing a course of study for doing so? – in a word, that we do not know what education is? The legend, apocryphal or not, rearises to taunt us, of the little boy who came home from the progressive school and said to his mother, "I'm tired of doing what I want to do. I want to learn how to read and write."

Amid the fantasies of high pressure recruitment, of burgeoning athleticism and tasty courses in baton-twirling, cosmetology, and wine-tasting, and food science – of pressure-group programs and the service institution concept of doing anything that enough people want right here and right now; amid the cost-cutting alarums of larger and larger teaching loads, audio-visual substitutes, and auditorium lecture courses, there are some small signs of revulsion, some small indication of an answer to the old hymn-book prayer, "Reclothe Us in Our Rightful Mind." Recently *The Chronicle of Higher Education* carried this headline and subhead across the top of its front page: "Many Colleges Re-Appraising Their Undergraduate Curricula – Movement to reinstate required courses gains; institutions trying to define a 'common core' of knowledge they would deem essential for all students." Equally recently the *New York Times* reported that Worcester Polytechnic Institute now requires a humanities minor of all its students, to prepare what it calls "technological humanists." The Institute admits – hear this now – that most job offers in commerce and industry are indifferent to the applicants' humanistic background – but it is, nevertheless, determined to graduate students who have some comprehension of the relationship of science to society and the common life.

If they can do it at a polytechnic institute in Worcester,

why can't they do it at a university in Amherst? A union – a professional union professionally motivated – may bring a faculty together at last. If it brings them together to decide what a university is and what a college in a university has got to be, their demands upon the managerial usurpers may bear the most glorious educational fruit. But the issue before the house is not educational alone. The social issue has been thrust upon it. The faculty of the American university is called to the struggle against a retrogressive social doctrine that would restrict humanistic education to the children of the rich and condemn the children of the poor to the undemocratic – undemocratic and fraudulent – training for the treadmill.

: : : *Commencement Address* : : :

As you are now, so I once was; as I am now, so you will
be. You will be tempted to smile when I tell you that I am
middle-aged and corrupt. You should resist the temptation.
Twenty-five years from now you will be ineluctably middle-
aged and, unless you hear and heed what I say today, just as
ineluctably corrupt. You will not believe me, and you should
not, because what I say at my age should be unbelievable at
yours. But you should hear me out because I know more than
you do in one respect: you know only what it is to be young,
while I know what it is to be both young and old. In any case,
I will not lie to you in order to make you feel good. You will
be old much longer than you are young, and I would rather
that you believed me the longer time than the shorter.

I tell you today that instantly is not a moment too soon if
you are going to escape the fate I predict for you and embody
myself. For what was said long ago is still true, that corrup-
tion·runs faster than death and the faster runner overtakes the
slower. It may indeed be too late already, unless you mend
your ways this least of all likely moments. I once heard Robert
Hutchins tell a graduating class that they were closer to the
truth that day than they would ever be again. I did not believe
him. But I have seen most of the members of that class since,
and I regret to inform you that Hutchins was right. Mind you,
he did not say that they were close to the truth; he only said
that they would never be so close again. They had been taught
what right and wrong were and had not yet had a chance to
do what e. e. cummings calls "up grow and down forget." If
my own history and the history of the race is instructive, this
commencement is for nearly every last one of you the com-

From *Christian Century,* May 14, 1958, © 1958 by the Christian
Century Foundation.

mencement of disintegration. A cynic once said that he would not give a hang for a man who wasn't a socialist before he was twenty or who was one after that. I do not know if socialism is a good ideal, but I know that it is an ideal and I know that the cynic was confident that you would lose your ideals. You may even have trifled, in your springtime, with such radical aberrations as pacifism. But you will soon stop trifling; and when, at thirty, you have already begun to molder, your friends will tell you that you have mellowed.

All societies are deplorable, and history indicates that they always will be. You have lived twenty years in a deplorable society. You have lived sheltered lives, but you have had no one to shelter you from your parents and teachers. Your parents have done what they could to adjust you to the deplorable society to which they, as their advanced age testifies, have successfully adjusted themselves. When they said you were improving, they meant that you were getting to be like them. When they said they hoped you would keep out of trouble, they meant that you should not do anything that they wouldn't do. But some of the things that they wouldn't do should have been done. The condition of the society to which they have accommodated their lives is the proof of their criminal negligence. Your teachers have been no better, and no better an influence on you, than your parents. They may have had higher ideals; it takes higher ideals to teach children than to have them. But your teachers' survival (like your parents') testifies to their adjustability. They have done as they were told, and in a deplorable society there are some things that men are told to do that no man should do. A high-school teacher in California told me that not one of his colleagues wanted to take the anti-Communist oath required of teachers in that state, and neither did he; but every one of them took it in order to hold his job and escape the national blacklist. As they are now, so you will be.

Like your teachers and your parents before you, you will be told to do bad things in order to hold your job. In college you may have quit the campus daily or defied the old fraternity on principle. It will be harder to quit the metropolitan daily or defy the old country on principle; it will be easier to forget the principle. And if, in addition to holding your job, you want to be promoted, you will think of bad things to do on your own. And you will have good reasons for doing them. You will have wives (at least one apiece) and children to maintain. You will have a home and mortgage to enlarge. And life insurance, purchased against the certainty of death, dread of which in turn adds preciousness to staying alive at any price. And neighbors who are having their children's teeth straightened. Your dentists' bills alone will corrupt you. You will have doctors' bills to pay, and they will increase as you grow older, becoming extremely heavy when you are moribund and powerless to earn money. You will have lusts, as you have now, to gratify, but the lusts you have now are relatively inexpensive and they will give way to more expensive if less gratifying lusts. You will have worthy philanthropies to support and the respect of people whose respect depends on your supporting those philanthropies. You will have an automobile (if you are so wretched as to be a one-car family), and you might as well turn it in every year because the new model will be so revolutionary that it will depreciate the old one to the point where there's no point in keeping it.

Some of the things you will be expected to do (or will expect yourself to do) for the sake of your wife and children, your community, your health, or your burial are bad things. You will have to have good reasons for doing them; and, thanks to your education, you will have them. The trouble with education is that it teaches you rhetoric while you are young. When, for rhetorical purposes, you embrace the doctrine of the lesser evil, you ignore its fatal flaw of present certainty and future contingency; being young, you think you will live forever, so that you may do bad things today in order to do good things tomorrow. But today is certain, tomorrow contingent; and this night an old man's soul may be required of him. When you are old, and too tired to embrace doctrines for rhetorical purposes, you will find that the doctrine of the lesser evil has embraced you and destroyed you. You protest my melancholy prediction, but the Great Actuarial Table is against you. Twenty-five years from now nine out of ten of you (or all ten) will tolerate an existence which, if you could foresee it now, you would call intolerable. If such an existence has any virtue at all, it has only one: it will give you a wistful old age. You will look back to your springtime, fifty years gone, and say, "Those were the days." And you will be right.

:

The only thing that will save you from wistfulness is the one talent whose lack now redeems you – the talent for self-deception. You won't even know that you are corrupt. You will be no worse than your neighbors, and you will be sure to have some that you won't be as bad as. You will have friends who praise in you the characteristics you have in common with them. They will persuade you that there is nothing wrong with either hoarding or squandering as much money as you can get legally. And if, some sudden night, you go berserk and bawl out that life is a sell, they will put you to bed with the assurance that you will be all right in the morning. And you will be. Worse than being corrupt, you will be contented in your corruption.

Twenty-five years from now you will celebrate your twentieth wedding anniversary. Because you love your wife – still more if you don't – you will want to celebrate it in style. You will reserve a window table for two at the choicest restaurant in town, and the champagne bucket will be at the table when you arrive. You will not be the cynosure of all eyes, but you will think you are. The head waiter (or maître de, as he is known here) will address you by name. As your eye travels down the menu it will be distracted by something outside the window, which will prove to be a hungry man. What will you do? Do you know what you will do then, twenty-five years from now? You will call the maître de and tell him to have the drapes pulled, and he will tell the waiter, and he will tell the bus boy, who will do it.

Your table, even before you have ordered, will be laden with rolls and crackers (of several sorts) and butter pats on butter plates. Hungry, and a little nervous, as you should be, you will break up a roll and butter it and eat it as you wait for your wife to make up her confounded mind. The waiter will ask you if you want the champagne poured, and you will say yes; and he will open it with a pop which, beneath the dinner din, will be unheard by the rest of the diners (but you won't know that). Thirsty, and a little nervous still, you will sip your glass, forgetting to toast your wife, and resume your study of the menu. And then, for the first time, you will see, in fine italic print at the bottom, the words "The Management reserves the right to refuse service to anyone." And then you will know (for you will be an educated man) that you are sitting in a Jim Crow restaurant – that being the meaning of the words "The Management, etc."

Now the country in which you were raised calls itself a Christian country, and the parents who raised you up called themselves Christian people, and the church whose vestry has just elected you calls itself a Christian church, and you call yourself a Christian. Jim Crowism is un-Christian. It is also un-American, and you call yourself an American. What will you do? What will you do then, twenty-five years from now?

The champagne is open and sipped. The roll is buttered, half-eaten. Will you get up from the table and tell your wife to get up and tell her why, and tell the waiter and the maître de, and maybe the management, that you are leaving the restaurant and why, and pay for the champagne and the rolls and the butter pats and, if necessary, for the dinner, but refuse to eat there? Or will you pretend, as the management (by printing the notice in fine italic type) intended you to pretend, that you did not see the notice. You will stay at the table and order your dinner and eat it.

You will have been measured for corruption and found to fit. You may be the man who raised the flag on Iwo Jima – a hero abroad but not at home, where it's harder to be a hero. At Iwo Jima you had either to raise the flag or drop it. It was publicly shameful to drop it. But the night of your anniversary dinner it would have been publicly shameful to *raise* the flag by leaving the restaurant. And public shame was what you could not bear, either at Iwo Jima or in the restaurant.

There are a lot of involuntary, non-voluntary or reflexive heroes. I am one myself. I do not doubt that I would have raised the flag at Iwo Jima rather than let it drop in public. But I was the man who took his wife to dinner at the Jim Crow restaurant. Believe me, there is no contradiction between the corruption which will consume you, day by day, in the face of unpopularity or public shame and the heroism of the moment accompanied by public praise. And when you have been measured often enough and long enough for corruption, you will like what you see in the mirror. I don't mean that you won't continue to have good impulses. You will. But you will have persuasive reasons for suppressing them. From time to time, as the vestige of your springtime idealism stirs you, you will want to do the right thing. But you will have to put off doing it until you have buried your father, and then your mother, your brother, your children, and your grandchildren. You may live to be very old, but you will not outlive the last descendant for whose sake you will suppress your good impulses.

:

What life did to me, because there was no one to tell me what I am telling you now, it will do to you if you do not at once adopt *Principiis obsta* as your motto and spurn every other. "Resist the beginnings." At twenty I was what you are; I had had all the middle-class care that a middle-class society and a middle-class home could provide. My parents wanted me to have what they took to be advantages, and I had them. But my advantages were of no use to me at all when life came down on me, as it will upon you, like a ton of bricks. I had studied morality, just as you have, but it was the easy morality designed to sustain my character in an easy world. I would not steal another man's watch unless my children were starving, and my children would never be starving. Nor will yours if, with what your parents call your advantages, you do as you are told and get to the top. The reason your children will not be starving is that you will have been corrupted. Your corruption will save you from having to decide whether to steal another man's watch. I was prepared, like you, to be a hero the instant heroism was required of me. I saw myself at Iwo Jima, at Gettysburg, at Concord. But I did not see myself at home, so weakened by the corrosive years ahead that I would not be able to stand up on my hind legs and say no when I had to do it alone. Never knowing – as you do not know – that my needs would be limitless, I never imagined that my surrender would be complete.

My education prepared me to say no to my enemies. It did not prepare me to say no to my friends, still less to myself, to my own limitless need for a little more status, a little more security, and a little more of the immediate pleasure that status and security provide. Corruption is accompanied by immediate pleasure. When you feel good, you are probably, if not necessarily, doing bad. But happiness is activity in accordance with virtue, and the practice of virtue is painful. The pursuit of happiness requires a man to undertake suffering. Your intelligence, or your psychiatrist's, will tell you whether you are suffering for the right reason. But it will not move you to undertake the suffering.

:

God is said to come to us in little things. The Devil is no fool: he comes that way too. The Devil has only one objective, and if he can persuade you to justify your derelictions by saying "I'm only human," he has achieved it. He will have got you to deny the Christ within you, and that is all he wants. If you are only human you are his. The Devil will keep you quiet when you ought to talk by reminding you that nobody asked you to say anything. He will keep you in your chair when you ought to get up and out by reminding you that you love your wife and it's your twentieth anniversary. He will give you the oath to take and say, "As long as you're loyal, why not say so?" He will tell you that the beggar outside the restaurant would only spend the money on whiskey. The Devil has come to me in little things for twenty-five years – and now I say and do

Commencement Address : *251*

the things in which, when he first began coming, he had to instruct me.

I tell you that you are in mortal jeopardy today, and anyone who tells you differently is selling you to the Devil. It is written on Plato's ring that it is easier to form good habits than to break bad ones. Your habits are not yet fully formed. You are, in some measure still, only potentially corrupt. Life will actualize and habitualize every bit of your corruptibility. If you do not begin to cultivate the habit of heroism today – and habits are formed by acts – you never will. You may delude yourselves, as I did, by setting about to change the world. But for all that you do or do not do, you will leave the world, as I do, no better than you found it and yourselves considerably worse. For the world will change you faster, more easily, and more durably than you will change it. If you undertake only to keep the world from changing you – not to lick 'em but to avoid j'ining 'em – you will have your hands full.

Other, more agreeable commencement orators have warned you of life's pitfalls. I tell you that you are marked for them. I believe you will not escape them because I see nothing in your environment that has prepared you even to recognize them. Your elders tell you to compare yourselves with the Russians and see how much worse the Russians are; this is not the way to prepare you to recognize pitfalls. Your elders tell you to be technologists because the Russians are technologists and your country is technologically backward; this is no way to prepare you to recognize pitfalls. You are marked for the pit. The Great Actuarial Table is against you.

What you need (and the Russians with you) is neither pharisaism nor technology. What you need is what the psalmist knew he needed – a heart, not a head, of wisdom. What you need is what Bismarck said was the only thing the Germans needed – civilian courage. I do not know where you will get it. If I did, I would get it myself. You were divinely endowed to know right and to do right, and you have before you, in the tradition of your country and of human history, the vision to help you if you will turn to it. But no one will compel you to turn to it, and no one can. The dictates of your society, of any society, will not serve you. They are the dictates that corrupted your parents and your teachers. If Socrates did not know where virtue came from – and he didn't – neither do I. He pursued it earlier and harder than anyone else and concluded that it was the gift of God. In despair of your parents and your society, of your teachers and your studies, of your neighbors and your friends, and above all of your fallen nature and the Old Adam in you, I bespeak for you the gift of God.

: : : *Teacher's Pet* : : :

I was in fourth-year Latin at Englewood High School. Virgil. *Arma virumque cano, qui primus* – and that was fifty years ago. My big brother had been in fourth-year Latin four years before, and now he had a front-page by-line, 12-point bold, in the Chicago *American* on an exclusive interview with his friend Dickie Loeb at the 63rd Street police station. (Dickie was being held on suspicion of the murder of Bobby Franks.) I brought the newspaper to class and showed it to Mrs. Manley. Mrs. Manley looked at it and said, "Mayer, I don't think it's especially noble to capitalize on the troubles of one's friends."

I had never heard the word "capitalize" used that way, and I scurried down the hall to the library after class to look it up in the unabridged dictionary. And that was fifty years ago.

Twenty years later I was scurrying through the lobby of the Palmer House, late for an appointment in the bar, when I heard a low whistle behind me. It was the whistle of a superior to an inferior. Recognizing no superior here below – I had yet to learn that I was the world's oyster – I paid no attention to the whistle. At least I thought I didn't, but I recalled afterward that I had slackened my pace a little in response to a forgotten reflex. Then I scurried on to my appointment.

A few minutes later the headwaiter was going from table to table saying, "Is Milton Mayer here?" Not "Mr. Mayer," mind you, but "Milton Mayer." He told me that a lady would like to see me in the lobby. Now I half remembered (but only half) the imperious whistle and I jumped to my feet and followed the headwaiter out into the lobby.

There, in an overstuffed chair, sat an overstuffed woman, haunchy, paunchy, jowly, and withal as imperial as Victoria Imperatrix, her Struwwelpeter hair, gray now, but black when

From *The Center Magazine*, September/October 1976.

I had last seen it, flying all over around her big head as it had flown around when I had last seen it in Virgil. It was she who had whistled at me. It was my superior here below. It was Mrs. Manley.

She held out her hand and said, "I'll only keep you a minute, Milton. I wanted to tell you that you're doing all right." I tried to say something, even "Yes, ma'am," but I didn't. She had called me Milton, she who for four pitiless years in Latin had called me Mayer. She had called me Milton and said I was doing all right.

Twenty years earlier, in Virgil, I knew that I would come when she whistled twenty years later and stand tongue-tied, a mute inglorious Milton Mayer come to judgment, and then go scurrying down the hall as I had scurried to the library that day in Virgil, in search of an unabridged something that would tell me the meaning of "capitalize" or something harder than that to discover the meaning of. But twenty years earlier, in Virgil, I didn't dare to imagine that she would some day call me Milton and give me a grade, even an F, in life. (F was for Fair at Englewood High School, and P was for Poor.) (S was Superior, E was Excellent, and G was Good.) You stood at her desk, a small desk, a Victoria Imperatrix she, and watched her put the heavy square letter on your report card and initial it F.B.M. for Florence Ball Manley.

I had no reason to suppose that I'd see her, or she me, twenty years after Virgil in that hotel lobby or that she'd whistle to me if she saw me. And I had no reason in the hotel lobby that day, thirty years ago, to suppose that I'd ever look at her again. And I never did. But I don't have to look at her. I see her. The Teachers Pension Office of the Chicago Board of Education says that she died April 4, 1950. Not bloody likely.

:

You have to find your hero at just the right time and in just the right place. The heroism of Ma and Pa is too close, Pa hustling his paper-box samples on the streetcars until he can't make those streetcar steps any more, Ma scrubbing the clothes on the scrub board in the basement until her wrists and knuckles give out. The heroism of a public figure is too far, of a big brother too oscillate, of a doctor or a preacher too fearsome, of a candy-store lady or a milkman too busy, of a professor in college too remote, too remote and too late.

A professor might change your career or your life but not you; you-changers materialize when you're in high school and you sit in front of them fifty minutes a day five days a week for four years in something heroic like Latin (and an hour at night when you're doing your homework). Not your grade-school teacher: your grade-school teacher made you spit your gum out, made you ask to be excused, made you stay after school, sent you to the principal. Your likelihood of finding a hero is circumscribed and scant.

When she whistled to me in the lobby, thirty years ago, Mrs. Manley was finishing her fortieth and last year of teaching at Englewood. After that the generations of darkening children would come along and come undone in a darkening world – the children who would never have Mrs. Manley in Latin.

I took Latin because my big brother had taken Latin. He'd taken it because he wanted to write, and somebody told him that Latin taught you to write. It didn't, but it taught you how. You took Spanish – you had to take two years of a foreign language then – because it was easy. You took French because you were a girl with pretensions. (German hadn't come back yet, though hamburger was no longer liberty steak.) You took an unemployable language like Latin to learn about language – something you'd never be able to do with an employable language, above all your own. You took a classical language to learn how the bones of language hang together and articulate, how the synapses and membranes route and reroute and resist the impulses, and how nouns and verbs (and not adverbs and adjectives) do the trick. If anything would teach you how to write – nothing would, of course, if you were born a non-writer – it was Latin.

Mrs. Manley didn't teach Latin for forty years, only for

thirty. In her thirtieth year of Latin, Ed Manley died, and Mrs. Manley did as much dying as she ever would: she quit teaching Latin and taught economics, which Ed Manley had taught for thirty years at Englewood while she was teaching Latin. She was, among other things, but only among them, a woman of liberal learning. (Was it his learning that immortalized Socrates or he who immortalized his learning?)

She had got the liberal learning as Florence Ball at the wonderful new University of Chicago, where Ed Manley had been a lineman on the faculty-student team that played football for, ah, wilderness, the fun of it. There weren't many future high-school teachers who got the kind of education Chicago offered (though most of them had a respectable state university degree). The sidewinder grade-school biddies, with their Normal School diplomas, were generally the sisters, cousins, and aunts of parish priests and precinct captains.

If Ed Manley and Florence Ball were made for each other, they were both made for their old Model T. Few teachers had autos then, but most teachers were spinsters and the Manleys had two jobs and no children. He occupied the front seat and she occupied the back. They were both very big and she was big and shapeless. (He still looked like a giant lineman.) They lived near the university in an apartment which none of us ever saw, and spent their summers at a cottage on the White Pigeon River in Michigan. If we stayed late enough after school for play rehearsal, or practice, or the student paper – I wrote the Vertebral Column, the Backbone of the Paper – we saw the Manleys sputtering off in their Model T, he in front, she in back.

They were known, both of them, as tough teachers; I never knew anybody except my big brother who had the hardihood to take Latin and economics at the same time. They were forbidding, as of girth, so of mien, and cool of demeanor, both of them; not cold or curt, only short. In my four years at Englewood, Ed Manley never more than nodded to me and Mrs. Manley didn't do much more. Neither of them, childless though they were, was under any need to be meddlesome, cuddlesome, or reprobatory. They were formal, and formality was something that an ex-grade-school pupil had to learn.

:

One day in my second semester as a freshman, just turned thirteen, I learned the difference between a pupil and a student. A hard lesson. I had got S's in my other courses and a big square E in Latin grammar. When we compared grades after class I learned that there had been two S's. Carolyn, the Woman I Loved, had got one of them, and that was all right because she was a girl and the Woman I Loved. But Louis Johnson got the other, and that wasn't right at all. He was a boy, and he was slow.

Like the crybaby I was, I mustered my vertical row of S's and showed them to Mrs. Manley. She looked at them and said, "Well?" and I stammered and stuttered like a desperate pupil and said, "I thought I deserved an S if Johnson deserved one." She stared at me and I shook, my desperation drained, and she said, "Mayer" – I still winced at being called by my last name, the rite of passage – "you got what you deserved and Johnson got what he deserved, though you and I may have different ideas of desert" (another word I hadn't heard used that way). I said, "Yes, ma'am," but she didn't say, "You may go now." She said, and it was the longest speech she ever made to me, "When you have had as far to go as Johnson and you've gone as far as he has, you'll get an S. You'll get it for the kind of work I expect you to do" (without explanatory emphasis on the "you"). "Do I make myself clear?"

I said she did – what I said was, "Yes, ma'am" – but she didn't. She didn't make herself clear because I wouldn't let her. I wouldn't let her tell me that she had given Johnson an S because he was a nig – Negro. The only one in the class then. (Long afterward, Englewood began filling up with poor whites and poorer Negroes and I heard the rumors that she and Ed Manley had been offered fancy schools and turned them down.) So Mrs. Manley taught me the difference between students and pupils and poverty and whiteness and blackness and the consequential situations of consequential persons. (She was still to teach me about nobility, when I showed her the Chicago *American* by-line three years later.) She was supposed to be trying to teach me Latin.

Since she was supposed to be trying to teach me Latin, she didn't say anything to me about Carolyn, all through Caesar, Cicero, and Virgil. Carolyn and I were in love, through Caesar, Cicero, and Virgil, and some of the teachers at Englewood, spinsters of both sexes, had been doing some of the damnedest things to break it up, even unto taking the initiative to talk to the mothers of both *pupils*. They tried to break it up because Carolyn was a Gentile, and I was a Jew, though I never felt, nor do I now, that anti-Semitism was involved; it was simply the quaint notion of *mésalliance*.

On the last day of the last class in Virgil, the last day I should ever expect to see Mrs. Manley, she put a square S on my report card and looked at me (without smiling). Then she asked me to stay after class. After class she said, "Mayer" – I no longer winced; I had passed the rite of puberty – "I hope you won't ever pay any attention to anybody's being a Jew or a Gentile. You may go now."

So I went now.

I went out into the world of Jews and Gentiles and niggers and Negroes and ignobility and nobility and from there, twenty years later, into the overstuffed lobby where I heard the low imperious whistle that I still hear. "Milton," she said, twenty years after she had told me I could go, "I wanted to tell you that you're doing all right," and I tried to say something, even if it was, "Yes, ma'am," and didn't. "Your stuff is good," she went on. "You're saying some things that need saying." And I girded my arrogant loins and said, "Yes, ma'am." "Your articles in the *Post* about the war and the Jews – I hope you weren't bothered by the stupid things people said about them." "No, ma'am," I said. "That's all," she said, "you may go now."

And I went, back out into the world and held up a shaking finger and ordered a double brandy and drank it facing the wall. She was gone, but I drank it facing the wall. She was as gone as she ever would be, but it wasn't far enough. Or close enough; I never really knew her, or whether she was all that heroic or heroic at all. But she knew me.

So, *Say I'm weary / Say I'm sad // Say that health and wealth have missed me / Say I'm growing old, but add* – Mrs. Manley called me Milton.

A Long, Long Talk

: : : : : : : : : : : : : :

Went down to Terre Haute the other day to see Gene Debs. It was his hundredth birthday and I figured there'd be quite a turnout. But the street was quiet and the home place was quiet – needed a coat of paint bad, but, then, it always did – and Gene was sitting in his rocker on the porch. The day was un- seasonally warm and sunny, but the old fellow was bundled up pretty tight. Not much flesh and blood on him, but come to think of it, there never was.

Doesn't smoke any more, but he still chews that long che- root, and he hasn't a tooth in his head. Never took care of his teeth. Still wearing his silver-rimmed specs, and his eyes are as bright as ever, but I don't believe he sees very much any more, or maybe he doesn't try. I guess when you get to be a hundred, things are a lot of work.

Otherwise he hadn't changed, hardly, but those long bony fellows never do. He was pretty bent, but he was that as far back as I could remember him. He tried to get up, and I took his hand and pushed him back. His first words, then, were "Who d'you think you are, son, George M. Pullman?" Frisky old dog. "Nope," I said, "Justice Oliver Wendell Holmes." He grinned up at me wickedly. "You know," he said, "I'd forgotten all about the 'great dissenter.' Didn't dissent about me, though," and he cackled and went on. "Yes, sir, I was a clear and present danger. Obstructing the war. Never did get it obstructed, though," and he cackled again. "That's what I should've told 'em in Cleveland. 'Gentlemen, you have con- victed me of obstructing the war. That's what I was trying to do, but I didn't know I had succeeded.'" We both cackled, and then I sat down.

I handed him a box of cheroots and said, "Happy birthday,

From *The Progressive*, November 1955.

Gene." "Happy birthday?" he said. "Why, I'd clean forgotten this was the day. I shouldn't have, either. I've been hearing from a lot of people."

"Socialists?" I said.

"Yep, socialists," he said. "Asian and African socialists."

"And American?" I said.

Gene seemed to peer at me the way a foreigner does who isn't sure he understands you. Then he said, "Are there any American socialists?"

"Lots," I said. "Young people" – "I reckon they think I'm dead," said Gene, "it's been so long since they've heard a peep out of me" – "and," I went on, "a few old socialists, too." "Old socialists," said Gene, with some spirit, "that's what I'd like to see, *old* socialists. Seems to be easy when you're young; natural, like. Harder when you're old and dreaming of death instead of life."

"Gene," I said, "what happened to socialism in America?"

He sighed a long sigh and said, "Well, the old socialists died, the old Germans and Irish and Swedes – ."

"And new ones were born," I said.

"No," said Gene. "That's where you're wrong. Socialists stopped being born and that's what happened to socialism. Socialists are born, not made, and when Socialists stopped being born, there were no more socialists."

"There's one," I said.

"More than one," said Gene.

" 'There are today,' " I said, " 'upwards of sixty million socialists, loyal, devoted adherents to this cause, regardless of nationality, race, creed, color, or sex. They are waiting, watching, working through all the weary hours of the day and night. They feel – they know, indeed – that the time is coming – .' "

I stopped. His head was bent, and a tear had fallen on his hand in his lap. "I'm sorry," I said.

"Oh," he said, looking up and blinking and forcing a smile, "that's all right. I'm just thinking of the day I said those words."

"There were twelve in the crowd," I said, "and there wasn't

a socialist among them." Gene cackled, softly. "Twelve honest American farmers," he said, "good men, good men. I watched them while they were being impaneled. Good men, good men. But they could no more help convicting me than I could help 'obstructing' the war."

"Were Wilson and Holmes good men, too?" I said.

"History says so," said Gene, closing his eyes, "and I guess I agree with history. I scared 'em, I guess. They didn't believe in revolution. I do." I noticed the difference of tenses.

"Still?" I said.

"Still," said Gene. "After Russia and Italy and Germany, I still believe in revolution. While you're quoting what I said in court, you ought to remember what I said in Canton three months before. I said, 'The I.W.W. in its career has never committed as much violence against the ruling class as the ruling class has committed against the people.' That's the statement that the District Attorney told the Attorney General was 'the kind of criticism of the government of the United States which I believe Congress intended to forbid by its enactment of the Espionage Act.' That's what they really indicted me on – though they never said so in court – and that's what really convicted me."

"Why that," I said, "when you said in court, 'I have been accused of having obstructed the war. I admit it. Gentlemen, I abhor war. I would oppose the war if I stood alone.' That, my friend, is what I should suppose convicted you. It was wartime, and you stood in a United States courtroom and said, 'war is the trade of savages and barbarians.' Isn't that what convicted you?"

:

"No," said Gene, "I think not. I think that every man in that courtroom, including the prosecutor, the judge, and the jury, agreed with me. They wouldn't say it themselves, of course, but they wouldn't convict another man for saying what they all knew was true, and what every man knows is true. No, it was what I said in praise of the Bolsheviki – even though I added that they might fail in the end – and the I.W.W. It wasn't war or peace that worried them, it was revolution. And it wasn't their lives that they thought they might lose, but their money that they knew they would lose. The I.W.W. was as red a flag in 1918 as Communism is in 1955 – and, in America, as much of a straw man."

"So you're not an anti-Communist, even now?" I said.

"Even now," said Gene. "I leave anti-Communism to my successors in the 'Socialist movement,' formerly the Socialist Party. Anti-Communism means exactly what anti-I.W.W.-ism meant. It means an excuse for conscripting half the world's workers to kill the other half. I know you've got to be anti-Communist to be effective in politics, but I'm not a politician and the Socialist Party wasn't a political party back in those days."

"You did pretty well in the 1920 campaign," I said. "You got a million votes" – "Nine hundred fifteen thousand, three hundred and two, to be exact," said Gene, smiling – "and that's an awful lot more than any of your 'effective' predecessors or successors ever got."

"That," added Gene, and his wrinkled old eyes were flashing behind his specs, "was because we stood somewhere."

"You stood in Atlanta Penitentiary," I said.

"That helped, too," said Gene. "The fact that I was in prison when even the *New York Times* – even A. Mitchell Palmer – decided I wasn't a criminal meant that we stood somewhere. We weren't 'constructive critics.' We weren't popular-fronters, recruiting young idealists for the wars of the New Freedom or the New Deal or the New Look. We said 'No' – in those days – and a million people wanted somebody to say 'No.' A hundred million, maybe, but only a million were up to going all the way."

"Times have changed," I said.

"Yes," said Gene.

"What changed them?" I said.

"The Russian revolution," said Gene. "It doesn't matter how it came out; what matters is that it happened. It proved that the revolution *could* happen. It was the death-knell of capitalism. In its death-throes capitalism will electrocute anybody who gives away the secret of the atomic bomb, because the atomic bomb is (or was) the only secret capitalism has left. Now the revolution is everywhere; misguided, perverted, yes, but everywhere, and you're either a revolutionary, whether or not you know it, or a counterrevolutionary, and the counterrevolutionaries include all – well, almost all – the 'socialists' and all of the 'former socialists.' They're the best advertisement the counterrevolution has."

"And the pacifists?" I said.

"I don't know," said Gene, and he seemed to be thinking hard. Leastwise all the heat went out of his voice all at once, and when the heat goes out of Gene Debs's voice, even on his hundredth birthday, you know he's thinking hard. "I don't know," he repeated.

"But you're a pacifist," I said. "Always were."

"I don't know," said Gene. "You know," he raised his head, "I'm darned if I'm *good* enough to be a pacifist."

"Neither am I," I said.

"But you are one," said Gene.

"I didn't say I wasn't one," I said, "only that I'm darned if I'm *good* enough to be one."

Gene really laughed hearty at that one. "I guess," he said, "that that's about the size of it, as far as I'm concerned. Whatever they did to me, they couldn't make me mad. So they thought I was a pacifist. But, comrade, when I saw what they were doing to other people, the state militia murdering women and children in the Colorado mines – I remember saying, that time, that 'every district of the miners' union should purchase and equip and man enough Gatling and machine guns to match the equipment of Rockefeller's private army of assassins.' You wouldn't call that pacifism, would you?" And all the dried-prune wrinkles of his face grinned at once.

"Sometimes," said Gene, taking the cheroot out of his mouth, and turning it around in his fingers, as he always did,

"I wish I'd had a chance to get an education. There are things I don't understand. I don't understand about God and immortality. Always believed in 'em. Still do," and he cackled again and said, "I still believe in everything I always believed in. There's a fool for you, comrade."

"You mean," I said, "that you 'stood somewhere.'"

He looked at me quizzically. "Yep," he said, "I guess that's it, all right. I'm a standpatter. Some of these other fellows, they learn something new and they switch around. They don't hardly any of them say what they said twenty, thirty years ago. Most of 'em say the opposite, when you boil 'em down. They must have learned a lot. I never had time to. Work, work, work. And now I'm too old to learn."

"You always were," I said.

"What's that?" said Gene, pretending that he hadn't heard me. "'Socialists are born, not made,'" I said.

:

Gene cackled, very softly. Then he turned his long skull up to the sun, and the sun flashed on his specs and glittered on that great bald dome. His eyes closed, and he began to breathe heavily. His mouth opened, and I got quietly up and took the half-chewed cheroot out of his mouth and put it into the battered old one-cigar case that lay on the floor beside him. I stood there a while. He was sleeping. A flight of jet planes went screaming by. He didn't wake up, but I thought he smiled a little. But it's hard to tell when a very old man is smiling.

I tiptoed down the stairs. They creaked, but Gene slept on. I started down the street, and, to my surprise, I found myself whistling "The St. James Infirmary." I stopped, and wondered why, of all things, "The St. James Infirmary." And then I started whistling it again and let the words go through my head as I whistled. When I got to the last two lines, I knew why:

> Put a twenty-dollar gold-piece on my watch-chain
> So the boys will know I died standing pat.

Then I stopped and said out loud:

While there is a lower class, I am in it;
while there is a criminal element, I am of it;
while there is a soul in prison, I am not free.

Then I cackled and said, "That must have gone over big with those twelve farmers."

Then I said out loud:

I have no country to fight for; my country is the earth, and I am a citizen of the world.

And I said, "Holmes delivered the unanimous opinion of the Court and said, 'We are of the opinion that the verdict on the fourth count, for obstructing and attempting to obstruct the recruiting service of the United States, must be sustained.' Wilson said, 'I will never consent to the pardon of this man. This man was a traitor to his country.' Harding ordered him – still a prisoner – to come to the White House from Atlanta, alone, and the warden drove him to the train in his car and Gene got on the train and went into the diner and ordered fried chicken. And Harding held out his hand and said, 'Mr. Debs. . . .' and released him from prison. But he never was pardoned and he never had his citizenship restored, and now he's a hundred years old."

Then I went on down the street and met James Whitcomb Riley. "Where you been?" said Riley. "Down to see Gene Debs," I said. "Where *you* been?" "Up to see God," said Riley, "and we was reminiscing, and I asked Him how He come to make Gene Debs, and He says, 'Let Me see, that was just a hundred years ago today. I remember I was feeling mighty good, and I didn't have anything else to do all day.'"

:   :   :   *November 22, 1963*   :   :   :

Neither [Kennedy nor Nixon] seems to be a man at whose funeral
strangers would cry.
Murray Kempton, *The Progressive*, 1960

When we saw him drinking the poison, we wept. "What is this
strange outcry?" he said.
Plato, *Phaedo*

The discussion had just resumed after lunch – this was Eastern Standard Time – when a secretary came in and put a
note in front of the chairman, Professor Samuel Cummings
Carter. Carter looked at the note and said to his eleven fellow
philosophers around the table, "President Kennedy has just
been assassinated in Dallas," and went on with the discussion.

"He should have adjourned the meeting then and there,"
said one of the eleven philosophers a week later. The same
group (plus a visitor) were around the table. Carter was absent.

"But," said the visitor, "the discussion was important,
wasn't it?"

"As important as the assassination of a President?" said
another of the philosophers.

"I should have supposed so," said the visitor, "to a company
of philosophers."

"Nonsense," said a third philosopher.

"His behavior was unspeakable," said a fourth.

"Did you all find it unspeakable?" said the visitor. (He knew
that three of the eleven had, because they had got up and
walked out of the room immediately after Carter's announce-
ment, and one of them had been crying before he reached the
door.)

From *The Progressive*, December 1964.

: *270* :

There was an unencouraging silence after the visitor's question, and then one of the philosophers, a youngish man, said, "I suppose he did the right thing. But it seemed somehow – incongruous. It still does. Maybe it won't a year from now."

"So," said the visitor, "he was guilty of incongruity rather than unspeakableness?" Silence, and the cross-grained visitor went on: "You chide Carter for not having adjourned the meeting. Do you chide television for not having gone off the air?"

"Television's business is to inform," said another of the philosophers.

"And yours?" said the visitor. Silence again. "Why shouldn't you have stayed 'on the air'? And why shouldn't television have shut down like the department stores? Its business is no more to inform than theirs is to close. Its business is to make a profit. Isn't yours more important?"

The silence was angry now, and the visitor did not trust himself to go on.

One of the philosophers got up and studied his watch and said, "Back to work." Others got up, and the group dissolved. The visitor was left with an elderly philosopher, who had said nothing. The two were old friends. "It's the bathos," said the visitor, "everywhere. Even here."

"I know," said the elderly philosopher, "but you're in the wrong. So is Carter. You fellows think that ritual is infantile. You want society to be above it, to be 'adult.' But it isn't adult to be above ritual. It's angelic, but it isn't adult. Ritual and ritual alone holds society together."

"Primitive society," said the visitor.

"All societies are primitive," said the elderly philosopher.

:

I've run into individuals since who think that this detail or that was overwrought, but none who thinks (or in any case says) that the whole weekend of November 22–24, 1963, was a manifestation of the deepest social disorder. A minister finds the eternal flame at the grave "inappropriate." A commentator wonders why the widow had to have exactly ten Secret Service men to protect her for exactly two years. A town meeting in New England declines to erect a statue on the common. A geographer is worried about the precedent of changing ancient place names like Canaveral.

A detail here, a detail there. But no one seems to believe, now any more than then, that the whole thing was a manifestation of the deepest social disorder.

I'm not thinking of the Unseen Millions whose Giant Screen diet of mawk and mummery and mayhem (and assassination?) keeps them buying the cigaret than which no other brand has been proved to be less baneful. I am thinking of the hep – the non-bowlers and non-barbecuers and non-bucket-seaters. I am thinking of the philosophers, heirs of Socrates, who fell apart that weekend and were still fallen apart a week later. I am thinking of the theologian who wrote me, "I'm sick inside and drawn like a chicken over Kennedy's death. But we pick up and start all over again."

Why should a man have been sick inside (or any sicker than he had been) or drawn like a chicken? What were we to pick up? What had we been carrying? Whither were we to start all over again? Where had we been going?

Of course we were shaken, every last one of us – and we should have been; but shaken like men and citizens, not drawn like chickens. Why in John F. Kennedy's fall fell we all? Who, and what, was he that his sudden death unstrung us as it did? Who and what were we that it touched off a riot of grief across the land?

(There was, to be sure, the classic catharsis of the true tragic spectacle, which always involves a ruler: if *he* is vulnerable, how vulnerable *we* must be; and the equally classic – and repressed – exultation: *He* is dead, and *I* am alive.) Mr. Kennedy (having closed the nonexistent missile gap) probably had more power to do violence than any man in history, and here he was powerless. He could deter the Russians but not the Americans. The Soviet tyrant goes through the streets of Moscow alone, and the American People's Choice is ineffectively surrounded by bodyguards. In the *Redbook* for November 1963, published before the assassination, European children were asked what Americans were like, and one of them said: "The average American is, of course, a Texan. . . . If he doesn't like who is his President, he usually shoots him."

Why? Who, and what, were we and are we, we shooters of Presidents, we freedom-lovers who indulge our freedom in 45,000 highway deaths every year and call for still more horse-power (and get it from freedom-loving free enterprisers)? Is there at the center of our freedom fixation a cataclysmic tension that provides the Oswalds to provide the cataclysm that releases the tension?

:

There has never been a people at once so fortunate and so unhappy. Witness Barry Goldwater, champion not of the dis-possessed but of the possessed, of those who "never had it so good" and can't bear it. For the possessed are dispossessed of their confidence, and their anxiety drives them to refuge in a past that never was. Before Dallas we were (as of course we are again) pent up with no way to break, like a woman unable to expel at birth. Ours was, and is, the same hopelessness to cope that invites the relief of war in which, for four years (or three days) a people can smash the insolubles and let go, giving themselves over to whoop and holler and death and then tears.

We are a murderous people who love all kinds of freedom, and our disorder is deep. We are rich and fat and strong, and we will let no tyrant provide *us* with bread and circuses; we will each of us, in fine freedom, provide his own. In our singular historical and geographical accident, we are weaned on the inalienable right to euphoria, on the pursuit of kicks. We are the most lawless – and nonrevolutionary – people in the world. And becoming more so.

The Southwest was the ironical place for the author of the New Frontier to meet his end by the lynch law of the Old Frontier; ironical, too, that it provided the two slicked-up cowboys in ten-gallon hats, Johnson and Goldwater, to con-test his succession.

The Old Frontier, kept fresh, South, West, East, and North,

November 22, 1963 : 273

by the free enterprise of the movies and television, is a crude (and, in happier times, comic) counterfeit of freedom. The shame and the shock and the hurt of last November 22 – how could this happen here, in America the Beautiful? – has its instant parallel in the old aftermath sagas of the cattle-thief posses. But it happens here every day, in the streets, in the suburbs, even in the countryside, and in our shallow romanticism we work it out in a carnival of weeping and wailing and high resolve that, at its end, leaves us where we were, only a little worse disordered.

The loss of the President could not, in 1963, have been a national calamity, as, indeed, we have since seen that it wasn't. The very strength of our society is that the chief of state neither provides the society's strength nor takes it with him when, in a few years, he goes his way. The American Presidency is now a stupendous, self-sustaining apparatus, and on November 22, 1963, the office itself would be filled by a thoroughly knowledgeable and masterful *apparatchik*. That much we knew about Mr. Johnson.

And one of the weekend's infinite reruns on TV might have told us more: In 1960 the Democratic nominee for Vice-President was being interviewed by Walter Cronkite of CBS. "Of course, Senator Johnson," said Cronkite at one point, "you're first of all a Democrat," and the Senator said sharply, "Just a moment there. First of all I'm a free man – secondly an American, third a Senator, and fourth a Democrat."

"First of all I'm a free man, secondly an American" – hardly the words of a Texas pol *or* of a Massachusetts pol. But the country was overwhelmed, then and since, by the words of the fallen President, "Ask not what your country can do for you . . . ," words which could have been addressed just as appropriately by a Stalin to the Russians.

:

Three glassy-eyed days and nights we stared at a flag-covered coffin. Three days and nights we stared dewy-eyed at an heroically demeanored widow denied a private occasion. Three days and nights we conjured up a Euripidean voice that whispered, "What will become of you now? What will become of you now?"

A jag-prone people is fearsome to behold. Overnight, that weekend, John F. Kennedy Place and Street and Bridge burgeoned in Germany, just as Adolph Hitler Avenue and then Karl Marx Boulevard burgeoned overnight in Beethoven Alley. (Burgeoned with massed torches that some of us had trembled to see there a generation ago.) Would West Virginia and Indiana both be renamed before the weekend was over? Would every airport in America be Kennedy Airport? A newspaperman carefully covered his irony by reporting a nameless proposal to rename the Lincoln Memorial.

The placards in Dallas that read Hail Caesar! that Friday morning disappeared in a hurry. The fallen flag was hung everywhere – or almost everywhere: At the Santa Barbara Republican Women's Club it flew at full mast. The Birchers – children and fathers of fear – were afraid. There were anti-Catholics, too, and they galore, who had their fun (or was it fun?) with the "Irish Mafia," plunged now into the guilty gloom their fun had excavated to receive them when the man they wanted gone was gone. The few who said they were glad he was gone only underscored the general pathology, for Mr. Kennedy was no more ardently hated than he was ardently loved.

Ninety days after a million Negroes wept unabashed for Father Abraham in 1865, the "Illinois ape" was fair game again North and South. So, too, at the death of That Man, in 1945 (for whom one weepy acquaintance of mine wept abashed). And these were wartime chieftains and warm men. But in 1963 all the strangers cried and cried at the funeral – how marvelously wrong Murray Kempton had been, and how much more marvelously right – and there was none to say to them, as the dying Socrates said to his friends, "What is this strange outcry?"

What was this strange outcry? What is this mute lament that persists, to be broken so raucously by the Democrats in Atlantic City who roared their mechanized delirium at every mention of the dead man's (or any other live or dead Democrat's) name? Even in Barry Goldwater's cheapshow "the Kennedy failures" were instantly translated into "the Democratic failures" and then "the Johnson failures." Goldwater, in his mad campaign, made every political mistake but one: He did not invade the sanctum.

:

What was it that happened, that day in Dallas? What was this wound that bled torrents of tears? An able man died violently and untimely; a man, moreover, rich and famous and powerful who had savored richly of all his gifts. Too bad, too terribly bad, truly, that he died; but are most of our lives any more satisfactory or better (if later) rounded?

Of course he had had to sacrifice the pleasant blessings of men more inconspicuously situated. But the measure of their sacrifice is the value he himself put upon them, and many men have eagerly forgone them for less than a mighty place. As for the burden of his office, he had panted for it as breathlessly as he ever panted under it. And he had his reward of it each kaleidoscopic day.

Who was he, that his assassination unstrung us all?

Hard to say so soon, and it may not be easier when the market for the hurrying memoirs has been wrung dry of the last maudlin dime.

He was above everything else a sinner (like the rest of us). We should never have known it – certainly not that weekend or since – had it not been for the Requiem Mass in which the Cardinal Archbishop of Boston prayed for the forgiveness of his sins above everything else. But the Cardinal Archbishop's testimony, though it is unsupported by any other public authority, and though it still stands alone in violation of the injunction, *nil nisi bonum*, may be taken to be authoritative enough.

The petrifactive fiction of history doesn't assess such men as Mr. Kennedy; it fixes them, Caligula in his place, Cato in his. Who today or tomorrow would hear (or expect to hear) that the sainted Lincoln bought convention delegates, that the devilish Hitler provided free milk for every hungry child at school? History written is already history rewritten, and the book is closed.

John F. Kennedy did possess the brightest virtue in the modern American lexicon: bright youth. The vigor (no longer called "vigah") of youth has always been our hallmark. But youth is not a father figure, and since August 6, 1945, we have been afraid of the dark that we ourselves hung between man and the sun that day. We have groped – having shucked a venerable God – for a venerable man.

But venerability wants a settled preoccupation with grand purposes, purposes that evoke commitment, contagion, and passion from the depths. Four years ago the editor of *The Progressive* found (as did everyone else) "an absence of the kind of contagious passion and deep commitment. . . . Most Americans see both [Kennedy and Nixon] as men who are cool and calculating. Men of measured merriment . . . and of measured tears."

Tears again . . . and who would supply them when they were wanting in a man in whom "what we miss most" (I am quoting the editor again) "is a militant dedication to something greater than the single-minded pursuit of power"? Who would supply the tears? The other 180 million of us, four years later.

:

A newspaperman traveling with Hubert Humphrey in West Virginia in 1960 asked him what kind of man his opponent in the primary was, "in one word." "In one word," said Humphrey, "cold"; and it was clear that, had he been allowed a second word, it would have been "ice."

No *charisma* in this cool and calculating man at whose death a whole people cried and cried and cried. No identification with what we were and are. No adoration, no madly-for-Adlai following. No magic and no mystique beyond the mystique of competent power. Here was the Boss with his hand on the tiller, and the methodologist with his eye on the computer he used to be elected.

"In my family," he once told *Time,* supererogatorily, "we

were interested not so much in the ideas of politics as in the mechanics of the whole thing." "A Kennedy-Humphrey ticket," said Walter Reuther before the 1960 nomination, "would be a liberal ticket, and a Kennedy-Symington ticket would be a conservative ticket." John F. Kennedy once said he wanted the Presidency because "that's where the power is." "A man of his age," the eulogists called him (and who, apart from the Cardinal Archbishop, wasn't a eulogist?). But the age is not the age of obstinate principle. It is the age of adjustment to reality, the age of fast footwork, of the streamline and the hot line, of the hard sell and the soft, of the adman and the admass, of the "people machine" and the polling of polls and motivational research. "A man of his age."

I see a brown photograph of Woodrow Wilson at his obstinate typewriter, an Oliver, if I remember, a real photograph of a real man writing a real speech on a real typewriter. A still photograph. Now the speeches are written by many and rewritten by still more and put on a moving prompter and read by the man whose name is given them. And they are not such speeches as that given at Gettysburg by a man in whom there predominated the mysterious dread (as Lowell said) of praise, not blame. The words and the phrases ring on the counter all right; they're pretested; but you who have teeth to try them bite into the lead: "Ask not what your country. . . ."

:

For three years the editor of *The Progressive*, and everyone else, waited for the emergence of "what we miss most"; and it never emerged. Three years' time is too short, surely; but not too short for a man to make himself, and not his image, clear. Not too short to define a slogan. But the first two men escorted across the New Frontier were J. Edgar Hoover and Allen Dulles, and the last was Adlai Stevenson; and Mr. Kennedy was shoved and hauled across it by four little Negro Sunday School girls in Birmingham. The test ban was irresistibly pressed by the Russians and the English and the howl here at home. The country didn't "get moving again." There was no war on poverty or on wealth (including Bobby Baker's). And there was never a mumbling word, in three years, on the un-Americanism of the Un-American Activities Committee.

The country, and with it the world, was not much better and not much worse after three years of vigor. In the December 1963 issue of *The Progressive* – gone to press just before Dallas – the editor said what the other independent editors around the country were saying: "There is more than one mess in Washington. . . . The President's lame response [in the Korth case] falls far short of measuring up to his campaign concept that the White House 'must be the center of moral leadership.' . . . Nor was it civil rights opponents who shot substantial holes in the Subcommittee's bills, but the President himself. . . . He preferred to put politics above principle."

His tenure was impeccably stylish: Chiang Kai-shek's was "the only rightful government of China," and the people of Cuba would "have their freedom restored." (Whose China? What freedom?) He spent a couple of billion a year more for war, like all the Old Frontiersmen before him, and on October 22, 1962, he took the step to the brink from which Dulles himself had recoiled: No more freedom of the seas (for which we had gone to war every time out), and the Russian missiles ninety miles from Florida would have to go (and the American missiles ninety kilometers from Russia stay) or we would burn up the world. He united a dumbfounded country; politics ends at the water's edge, and the grave's.

But the Kennedy computer, like all computers, was not infallible. It had failed him when he turned his courageous profile to the wall of a Boston hospital instead of casting an absentee vote in the Senate censure of McCarthy. (The censure was already acceptable, even in Massachusetts.) A premonitory failure, for as President he was unable, for all his computations, to carry his own Congress with him. And the crude and clumsy aggression he ordered at the Bay of Pigs in 1961 turned out to be a – quick! the right word for the image! – "fiasco." The fiasco went into the computer and the "missile

November 22, 1963 : 279

crisis" of 1962 came out. (But Barry Goldwater could have plunged the country into both the fiasco and the crisis without a computer.)

The computer is a capricious as well as a ruthless master. Forty-eight hours after he found himself at American University, urging coexistence, Mr. Kennedy found himself urging a perfectly rabid anti-Communism at the Berlin Wall (rejoicing an audience that had learned its anti-Communism under Goebbels). He found himself alternately *for* humanity and *for* the starvation of Cuban humanity; *for* the Bay of Pigs and the Caribbean blockade and *for* international law and "our solemn agreements"; *for* peace in London and *for* "*Guerra! Guerra!*" in Miami.

Of course he had to be pragmatic – is this what pragmatism is? – because he was President by the skin of his teeth. More people actually voted against him than for him in 1960; and he squeaked through to victory over a man known by the two epithets "tricky" and "slippery." It was the first American election in which the candidates had been fully exposed to the electorate; in our spectator society we look men over and size them up; and we found these two to be of a size. There were even bumper stickers that read, Vote No.

What kept us all sitting on our hands in 1960 and for three years thereafter – until the day we all began wringing them? We had reason aplenty, after Ike, to admire Jack Kennedy's at-homeness as manager of the national enterprise. But we didn't cotton to him. Why not? We didn't know precisely. He didn't remind people – as Ike and Harry always did – of somebody they knew. He reminded people of an actor, on stage. (And at his side, on stage, Jackie.)

The family itself – the whole proliferation, including hidden "old Joe" – seemed to have a fine corporate flair that seemed to be busied with arranging the multi-million-dollar set for the leading man. The Lincoln rocker was a real help to his bad back, and ineluctably a stage prop (never more so than the night it was taken away from the White House under the klieg lights). The "Lincoln-Douglas" debates of the campaign were real – and a prop whose ham falsification on Cuba and Quemoy and Matsu seems to have been made for the medium whose forte is ham falsification. Robert Frost – the idea of using him was not Mr. Kennedy's at all, but Stewart Udall's – was splendidly real and an incomparable prop.

Was something going to be played out here, on both sides of the lights, to the very end? How right it was, after Ike, to bring culture into the White House, and how right the Housekeeper (and her stylists and designers). Was Jacqueline Kennedy hanging lace curtains? Well, aren't we all, these days? Not all of us: There was once a White Housekeeper, and not so long since, who was ridiculed because she went into the factories and the mines and the fields and let the lace curtains take care of themselves; Eleanor Roosevelt.

:

To the end, and beyond. Under the headline, "The Kennedy Sense of History," the *New York Times,* in one of its two accounts of the incident (one placing it on the plane itself), reported that immediately upon landing from Dallas, Mrs. Kennedy summoned the Chief of Protocol and said, "Find out how Lincoln was buried," and the Chief of Protocol summoned a team of seven researchers who did "ten hours of fast and furious work" in the Library of Congress and had the report ready for the former First Lady before dawn. And so the ritual was staged, under the direction of those masters of grand illusion, the military.

Dallas, too, was on stage in the most amazing of all TV spectaculars, to the end and beyond. "Grandma," said a lady I know, "is not quite right in the head any more, and she's always phoning us to turn on the TV. Usually it's Martians or Nazis. When she called and said that President Kennedy had been assassinated, we paid no attention to her. A couple of days later she called and said that the assassin had been assassinated, and we paid no attention to her. She lives in a dream world." To the end, and beyond: "The assassin," *Life* called the suspect; in the midst of Death we are in Life.

:

John F. Kennedy's death and burial were possessed, like his life, of a formal magnificence. "Ritual alone holds society together." Everything he did and suffered – including the loss of his baby – seemed to be transcendentally timed. He was the player, but he played a script that might have been written on Olympus; a script that carried us all with it, that weekend, in its elegant, almost Roman, rightness. The Greeks had a word for it – a word that means both necessity and destiny.

We may be sure that this was a good man, as men go. He appeared to have great qualities that other men do not appear to have. He was, for instance, a man of apparent captaincy, unlike the man who said to his friends in 1864, "I claim not to have controlled events, but confess plainly that events have controlled me." He was a man of apparent unambivalence, unlike the man who said to his enemies in 1864, "If God now wills the removal of a great wrong, and wills that we of the North, as well as you of the South, shall pay fairly for our complicity in that wrong, impartial history will find therein new cause to attest and revere the justice and goodness of God." He was a man of apparent aplomb, unlike the man of unmeasured tears who was more of a myth a hundred years after his assassination than he was a year after it.

President Kennedy was nonetheless a martyr, and nonetheless did the most that a man can do for his country. His death was – as Chief Justice Warren said at the bier – an awful lesson to the purveyance of hatred and distrust among us. But the lesson went unread; hatred and distrust rolled on.

For fifteen years we have not known what to do but keep our finger on the trigger. We put our faith in the Big Bang – we invented it – to purge us of the troubles with which wealth and fat and strength have paid us out. In Dallas something went bang. In Dallas we did what great power enables a great people to do: Destroy, and then weep like a little girl in a pet who has torn her doll to pieces.

: : : *An American Banality* : : :

There was a mortgage banking house in Chicago – this was September of 1929 – that advertised "One Hundred Years Without a Loss to a Single Investor." In its one hundred and first year all the investors (single and married) lost everything, and so many were the millionaires who leaped – or fell – from the windows above LaSalle Street that it was variously urged that the passing pedestrian carry an open umbrella and that the street be repaved with rubber. Suicide was still indemnified by the insurance companies – which in *their* turn went out the window – and the policyholder figured (so it appeared) that his widow and orphans would more comfortably survive the loss of pater than the loss of their patrimony. Sam Insull caught the rattler to Greece under cover of darkness; a midget climbed up into J. P. Morgan's lap in front of a Senate committee; and Franklin D. Roosevelt turned out to be a Traitor to His Class.

We grew gaunt, and some of us grew ghostly. But we didn't die, most of us. Had we, I think we'd have died laughing. I do not remember the word tragedy ever, in that time, applied to the American situation, to the American people, or to Herbert Hoover or the indemnified suicides. The language had not yet been debased to its present nadir. President Ford speaks of Watergate as an American tragedy. Others (if not President Ford) speak of the Nixon tragedy. A punctured tire en route to a cocktail party is a tragedy, and so is a hostess' discovery that she has run out of olives for the cocktails.

As a Nixon-watcher (at a self-defensive distance) from the beginning of his career, I have watched him with the flaring nostril of a newspaperman for so much as a whiff of the tragic in him, in his place, or in his time. I do not detect it. True, he

From *The Center Magazine*, May/June 1975.

rose (as Sam Goldwyn should have said) like a plummet and fell like a rocket.

I like to think that I watched him closely, the more closely to watch the country that raises such men up and pulls them down, the country that adheres so fanatically to the cult of personality that it responds with equal fervor to the antimagnetic (as it did in 1972) as it does (and did in 1932) to the magnetic. Mr. Nixon was the all-American boy, risen from tatters to tiaras, from inconsequence to stupefying power, least likely, in his origins, to succeed, and successful beyond the dreams of Tamerlane. His was, and is, a characteristically American epic that may say something portentous about our country's condition. How could this morally disoriented man – his disorientation a matter of public record – have been anything but the product, and, in November 1972, the unabashed triumph of a morally disoriented society? What other intelligible explanation of his career is there?

He has suffered, I am sure, having been born of woman (and a Quaker woman at that). But I am not sure how Mr. Ford, and especially Mr. Ford, knows that he has suffered enough – or, indeed, whether suffering is a bad thing. The Greeks thought that suffering was edifying. The edification, in the instant case, is a little slow in making its appearance. For all I know, this marvelous man has suffered enough; and for all I know, and for all the evidence I have to the contrary, he lies among his silks and satins saying with a chuckle, "You can't win them all."

I am not sure, in a word, that he has suffered enough or that we have. As I ponder his marvelous history and our own, gorged as he and we are on the blood and bone of the poor at home and abroad, I am tempted to believe that Christ may have suffered enough at Mr. Nixon's hands and ours; and that we have not yet begun.

On its face, but only on its face, there ought to be a tragedy here. But I cannot fathom where it actually lies or whether there actually is one. In crepuscular despair I have consulted the most distinguished clinical psychologist of our time, a man who, moreover, in his investigation of tragedy has so stead-fastly refused to use any methodology but the empirical that his procedures would rejoice the heart of William James (were James alive today). I refer to Aristotle of Athens. Having studied all the spectacles of modern times, Aristotle has come to the heady conclusion that tragedy can never be accidental. It has to be the ineluctable consequence of an inexorable pattern of behavior. But Mr. Nixon seems to have been the archtypical accidental man, in his going out as in his coming in. He seems to have risen and fallen on the wings of American chance.

Still, as Aristotle warns us, we should not be misled by the mere appearance of accident, and he cites the case in which the statue of Mitys of Argos falls upon his assassin and crushes him. Aristotle wonders about Mr. Nixon's insistence on build-ing a more commodious press room at the White House and filling in the swimming pool to do it. Had he taken a daily swim, it is unlikely that he would have been stricken with phlebitis – and it was the denizens of that more commodious press room who (in Mr. Nixon's view) destroyed him. Even more suggestive, of course, was his determination, in his genu-ine innocence of banality, to record all his conversations on the ground that what he said would be historic – as, of course, it proved to be. Without the accident of the tapes it is probable that the stone wall would still be standing.

The debasement of the language has affected emotional and emotive terms with special severity. Sternly resisting the de-basement, Aristotle warns us against taking for tragic those incidents which are only lamentable. Tragedy is first of all a certain sort, and a singular sort, of magnificence. The death of an octogenarian or an infant is not tragic. An automobile acci-dent is not tragic, nor is Socrates' subjection to the hemlock; nor the assassination of a good or bad ruler. (Lincoln's death was the capstone of his life. John F. Kennedy died in the full exercise of his powers, his status, and his riches, at a peak from which he even then appeared to be beginning his premature descent; and his martyrdom instantly installed his vacuous injunction "Ask not," etc., in the national hagiography.)

Events of this sort, however emotive, are no more Aristotelian tragedy than, say, My Lai. Perpetrators and victims alike are simply involved in a simple set of circumstances. The incident has no integral relationship to character or its development, or even to antecedent action. It is a kind of accident, inherent in this man's having found himself in this situation at this time and place. It reads us no lesson. It tells us nothing.

But tragedy is above all else meaningful. Its magnificence is that of culmination. It is something foreshadowed – as Mr. Nixon's fate was not – by the unfolding of every action that has gone before. It is something that, given this kind of man, and this man, as he moves (or fails to move) from decision to decision, had to happen. It is the inescapable consequence of willful choices leading, in the end, to two alternative courses of action both of which are fatal. In the end it is always too late for the actor to do (and now, we see, to have done) otherwise.

We have all heard it argued that Mr. Nixon's legendary compulsion to crisis was his undoing. I am not persuaded on this point. So far was he from having brought it on himself, plunging implacably forward (and always more visibly so) to his ruin, he would appear to have done all that he could, and some things that he couldn't, retreating from prepared position to prepared position, to avoid the denouement. He made very careful choices, and they were on the whole good choices for a man on the run to have made. But his earlier crises were all of them crises he himself provoked. They were canny crises, low-risk adventures with a high-risk facade. He was the Evel Knievel of statesmanship, riding a motorbike which wasn't a motorbike at all but a rocket with a motorbike fuselage. Watergate was an *un*canny crisis. There were just too many bodies to be buried too fast, and too many gravediggers digging each other's graves. It was the imperfect crime par excellence.

Aristotle's clinical analysis of tragedy convinces him that the power of the genre consists essentially of the pity and terror it arouses in the spectator. We pity the tragic hero not because he is a bad man who has got his just deserts – such a man's catastrophe is closer to the comic than it is to the tragic. Neither is tragic pity aroused by the calamity of an ordinary, or even an extraordinary, man felled by an affliction wholly outside his power; pathetic, yes, tragic, no. It is too commonplace, too much like accident, to shake us to the marrow.

Tragic pity requires the hero to be an ordinarily good man destroyed by some failing. It is not an intellectual failing – though the psychologist at one point speaks loosely (in accurate translation, however) of "some error of judgment" – the very phrase Mr. Nixon uses to exculpate himself. The failing has got to be a failing of character.

The psychologist takes *Oedipus* to be the perfect tragedy. Oedipus is made the king of plague-stricken Thebes because, having solved the riddle of the Sphinx, he may be wise enough to save the city. But he has a headstrong disposition which, in his arrogant situation, turns on anyone who presumes to criticize or even to counsel him. His angriness finally goads the blind prophet Tiresias to tell him that he himself is the curse of the city; and his fury moves him to pursue his own destruction.

It may be a bit difficult to cast the buttoned-down figure of John Dean as the blind prophet; still, there is some small trace of analogy here. The real difficulty is the analogue of the Washingtonian and the Theban heroes. Mr. Nixon was elevated because he already knew the nature of the curse upon the city. He had fought it all his life. The curse was, of course, Communism. And then, when once he was elevated, he made peace, not with the bogeyman at home, but with the real Communists in Russia and China.

Shall we strain at analogy and say that in 1972 Mr. Nixon solved the riddle of the modern Sphinx by answering, "Communism," to the question, "What is the ravening monster with which we can live in harmony?" A strain indeed. Détente was an incongruity which flaws the flawed figure of tragedy. Mr. Nixon may yet prove to have saved his country from destruction from without even while he was consummating its destruction from within. But his reversal – could this be the stuff of comedy? – fits neither his bad character nor his good one. Still less does it fit the inexorability of the tragic spectacle.

It may be that (with the Occidental penchant for saving face) he thought simply to take the heat off the lost war in Indochina; or that détente was another political stratagem whose time had come. Just prior to the beginning of the Ping-Pong diplomacy one prescient journalist said, "Nixon would go to Peking for the Chinese laundrymen's vote," and after his fall another journalist, without benefit of prescience, said, "If the American people had demanded moral leadership, Richard Nixon would have given them even that." A man, it would seem, of less than tragic mold, unlikely to encompass his own ruin by an Oedipean insistence on discovering the truth that the plague of the city was not after all what (in Mr. Nixon's case) he had always known it was.

Tragedy has got to evoke not only the spectator's pity (which it can hardly be said to have done here, except for the spectator he chose as his successor). It has got to evoke terror in us. The question has often been asked, "How can this be? The great tragedies are unexceptionably about kings and queens, not about ordinary people like you and me. Why should *their* calamity terrify *us*?" Aristotle doesn't bother to answer the question. Should he, I can imagine that he would say, "The bigger they are, the harder they fall." Here am I, a person of no worldly consequence, unguarded, unarmed, and unprovided for. "If it can happen to *him,* up there on top, how much easier can it happen to *me*?"

The spectacle proceeds from the outset with a premonition – as Mr. Nixon's did not (not, at least, after he got away with the Checkers speech in 1952). The premonition is that of discovery (as Aristotle calls it). The discovery in a tragedy is not made by a Senate committee or a special prosecutor in an investigatory or adversary proceeding. It is made by the tragic hero himself. It is his discovery of what he is and what he, and he alone, has done. The perfect discovery turns on irony, and it is irony that marks the ultimate distinction between the devastation of the tragic and the entertainment of the epic. Oedipus mocks the blindness of the prophet Tiresias, who cannot even see where he is going. But when the great king's world comes crashing down upon him, he discovers that it was he who could not see. The awful grandeur sweeps him away as the curtain falls, and sweeps our passions with it. The retribution is so majestic as to be divine. Oedipus is never more truly godlike – now from his empty sockets he sees everything – than when he totters away to self-imposed exile in that San Clemente called Colonus.

There was never anything palpably godlike about Mr. Nixon. Certainly the most memorable thing he ever said was, "I am not a crook." Probably the most memorable thing he ever did was to select Spiro Agnew as his running mate, not in 1968 but in 1972. The plastic flag in his buttonhole was his measure. Such men, common politicians, battening on the infirmities of democracy, are not great to do good or evil but only to catch at its crumbs. They are not the stuff of which heroes are made. If they are tragic at all, they are tragic midgets.

Nor do they act alone and alone achieve their comeuppance, but in constant concert. Mr. Nixon was certainly, if in a still uncertain degree, a creature of a succession of retinues. And his German Mafia consisted, except for Mr. Mitchell surely, and possibly Mr. Colson, of lusterless men like himself, interchangeable men without eccentricity. Their concert was engaged complicitly not in glorious enterprise but in larceny, the larceny of money, fame, and power. They were bound not to devotion to their country, or even to its dismemberment – they liked it here. They were bound to one another; bound, rather, as we now know, by the cohesive ties of public plunder which ruptured when the plunder ended. Little men – as the late Senator Taft said of Mr. Nixon himself – in a big hurry. Little men, indeed; it is not so much the four-letter words of their private conversations that astonish us but the fact that they appear to have known no others. And these, most of them, were officers of our country's courts, and all of them the product of the higher learning in America. Shame, perhaps. Tragedy, hardly.

As Mr. Nixon flies at public expense from the stage of history, still blind, though the most credulous of spectators has been compelled to see, whining and squirming and scrabbling still for the crumbs, our eyes are pried open and we see that our country, and not through its helplessness, had come into the hands of a primitive spirit in caricature of its founding. Open-eyed we cannot now tell ourselves that we are the last best hope of earth. We cannot now suppose that our very existence is the terror of tyrants everywhere.

An American tragedy? Or an epic comedy, which the clinician tells us embodies the merely ugly? We may discount the preoccupation with credibility that men like Mr. Kissinger display. By credibility they mean image, which is a species of show biz. We lost our credibility not by leaving Vietnam but by going there. An American tragedy? Aristotle makes bold to take issue with Gerald Ford on the point. An American tragedy is impossible; the essence of the tragic spectacle is one man's effect on one spectator. Collective tragedy is an unmanageable concept.

Besides, Mr. Nixon's exile did not purge the city. He may have been a carrier of the plague; the plague, so recently endemic, becomes epidemic. Pity gives way to every-man-for-himself. And the mounting terror of the spectators has nothing to do really with the antics of the past few years on the highroad between Washington and Southern California.

There seem to be elements of epic comedy – Aristotle points tentatively to *Don Quixote* – in our situation. The non-ideological non-system we call politics precludes our discovery of what we are and of what we have done. It forecloses self-governance and governance alike. A good man is hard to find, and hardly to be looked for in the places of public power. The salary of a United States senator is a fraction of what it costs him to get the office. But ours is a representative government. My father said, "They're all crooks" – and went down to the corner to exercise his plenipotentiary representative power to vote the straight Republican ticket.

High comedy? We have delighted to see the highbinders fleece the yokels and to pay for the spectacle. We are most of us highbinders ourselves in our feckless way, unconcerned, as we move on, and move on again, with the salvation of the city or the welfare of the yokels here or elsewhere. Mr. Nixon may have been the highest binder of them all, as highbinders go in Yorba Linda, but whether he had won it all or lost it all our impulse was to slap our thighs in amiable observance of the outcome and say, "Darned if he didn't get away with it," or, "Darned if he didn't almost get away with it."

As tragedy is the tragedy of the powerful, so comedy is the comedy of the rich, reflected in the low comedy of the silk-hatted fat man slipping on a banana peel. He doesn't have to have stolen the hat; he has only to be wearing it. Our country is history's unexampled instance of general profligacy. For a solid century now we have worn the hat.. What could we do, six per cent of the world's people consuming forty per cent of its product? What could we do but strangle the poor everywhere? What could we do but tell them, "You buy at our prices or you starve"? And now, of a sudden, a new strangler appears and says, "You buy at our prices or you freeze." And the silk-hatted man slips on the oil slick and falls on his face in amazement.

Comedy, says Aristotle, is not just the ugly, but a certain species of the ugly, namely, the ridiculous. But he adds that its purpose is amusement and that no one is injured by it. We are not amused these days, though we clamor so avidly for amusement that we find it even in Mr. Nixon. And injury abounds, and malevolence laughs at locksmiths. Ours may not be an Aristotelian comedy or an Aristotelian tragedy. It may be that what we are rehearsing for is a comic epic worthy of an American Homer as yet unborn, as yet unenrolled in remedial English.

: : : *Robert M. Hutchins, 1899–1977* : : :

The Fellows were ranged around the conference table, pondering the limits of liberty and law. A secretary came in and put a note in front of the Chairman. He looked at it and said, "President Kennedy has been assassinated in Dallas." The conference – and the conferees – fell apart. All except the Chairman. He tapped his water glass with a pencil and said, "Can the discussion go on?"

He was a notoriously precise man: If he'd meant "may," he'd have said "may." What he said was "can."

Can the discussion go on? This was Bob Hutchins's question the whole of his long life. This was why he fought for liberal education in the universal elitism of democracy. This is why he fought for unity in the modern shambles of the university. This is why he fought for academic freedom. This was why he opposed his country's entrance into World War II. This was why he established the Fund for the Republic to try to save the First Amendment. This was why he established the Center for the Study of Democratic Institutions to ponder the basic issues of society. It was all of a piece.

It was thought, mistakenly, that he tried to revolutionize education. He didn't try to revolutionize it; he tried to revive it. Rabanus Germanicus in the Ninth Century: "Dialectic is the *disciplina disciplinarum* . . . through it we argue and discover what is consequent and inconsequent, what is contrary to the nature of things, what is true, what is probable, and what is intrisically false in disputations." Or J. S. Mill one thousand years later: "He who knows only his own side of the case knows little of that. His reasons may have been good, and no one may have been able to refute them. But if he is equally

From *The Progressive*, July 1977.

unable to refute the reasons on the opposite side . . . he has no ground for preferring either opinion."

He was a lover of inquiry, inquiry unfettered by the fear that it might corrupt the young or overturn the state or scandalize the neighbors. This Ninth-Century–Nineteenth-Century Man was that Ancient Man of Athens who said (just before his countrymen killed him), "The unexamined life is not worth living."

Can the discussion go on? "The American people must decide whether they will longer tolerate the search for truth." – This in the pre-McCarthy days of the Dies Committee – "If they will not, we can blow out the light and shoot it out in the dark."

It might take a hundred years or a thousand to make the world safe for rationality – "all the more reason to get started this afternoon." It might never come to be – but "it isn't necessary to hope in order to undertake, nor to succeed in order to persevere."

Most of what he did at the University of Chicago went down the drain. ("I was the plug in the bathtub.") Liberal education everywhere declined and the production of uneducated specialists flourished. The dismemberment of the modern university proceeded. Academic freedom became the freedom to moonlight for the CIA and fight for higher wages and lower hours. The blue-collar McCarthy from Wisconsin gave way to the white-collar McCarthy from San Clemente. The civilization of the dialogue didn't radiate from the Center in Santa Barbara.

He thought he had been a failure. He didn't know that it is better to fail trying to do what he was trying to do than to succeed at anything else.

But that was the only thing he didn't know. He knew the difference between right and wrong – no cheerful thing to know. He knew that life (including his own) is demoralizing. But I never knew him to duck – except once, when I was ducking too. One day I told him he ought to take a year off. "And do what?" "Think." "If I ever started to think, I'd have to think about why I'm not a socialist, a pacifist, and a Christian. I'd rather not."

Clark Kerr called him the last of the giants. He was certainly one of the great men of the age, and just as certainly as good a man as a great man can be. He was a paragon of clarity. He was exquisitely witty in our sense of sassy and in the Greek sense of apt. He was a marvelous (and most unlikely) combination of bravery and bravado.

I shan't miss him. I have all of his life and some of his letters at my disposal. Here are some of his letters to me (in full): "I am a great admirer of your work. Are you doing any?" "Dear (in the sense of expensive) Sir: Stop bothering me." "Have you written any good books lately?" "How about getting me some of those pipe cleaners. Think how I saved you from Hearst."

In a lucky life like mine there are one or two people you don't miss when they're gone; living or dead they're looking over your shoulder. Anyway, I'm an optimist, and I abide serene in the starry confidence that we or our latest descendants shall see his likes again.

:   :   :   *God's Panhandler*   :   :   :

Among the mitred of the Earth, few since Richelieu have had
the clout of the late Francis Cardinal Spellman – "Was his
middle name Cardinal, Pop?" – of New York. A friend of the
poor and the rich, he found a place in the order of things for
both breeds and left them in their separate places. Silver and
gold had he none, but he ran an archdiocese that was rolling
in it. And to keep it rolling he refused a forty-hour week
to the Church's cemetery workers. The workers walked off
the finger-freezing job in January 1949, and became the most
widely celebrated grave-diggers since *Hamlet.*

Calvary Cemetery belonged to St. Patrick's Cathedral, so
the office of burying the dead was Cardinal Spellman's. His
administrator of that office was Bishop James Francis McIn-
tyre (who would one day also get his middle name changed to
Cardinal). Between these two gigantic bananas of Christen-
dom the agitation was enough to unstring the grave-diggers of
New York, but the grave-diggers remained strung.

The Cardinal called the strike an "anti-American, anti-
Christian evil," "a strike against the Church." But Dorothy
Day in her penny-an-issue *Catholic Worker* told the strikers
that their strike was Christian and that they themselves were
the Church.

Thus brandished Dorothy Day the Cross. She did not ask
the Cardinal's permission or petition him. She bypassed the
Prince of the Church and went right to the top – to Christ the
King – and got the green light. The strikebreaking Cardinal
led a hundred seminarian scabs through the Catholic picket
line and dug the graves. But the grave-diggers of St. Pat stood
pat and won the strike.

It had been a long, long time since anybody had gainsaid

From *The Progressive*, February 1981.

His Eminence – any hierarch or lowerarch, or layman (or lay-woman out of the Bowery, even one who, in her ecclesiastically appropriate mantilla, would one day receive the Eucharist from the hands of the Pope). Nor did Dorothy Day gainsay him now; she ignored him, since his authority, by extension from Rome, extended only to faith and morals and his stricture against the "immoral strike" was patently bogus.

Dorothy Day's papers were in order; nobody, and no Cardinal, could catch her out, devotionally, liturgically, or sacramentally. (You can bet your breviary that Spellman tried.) She was the most conservative of Catholics in her "indiscriminate and uncompromising love of the Mystical Body," in her holy obedience to the Holy See and her holy adherence to the canons of the Roman Catholic Church.

And this the Cardinal Archbishop knew. He knew that all his clout was helpless against Dorothy Day and her cloutless Catholic Worker movement. Again and again he let it be known – oh, he had his means of letting it be known – that he was thinking of rebuking her. And his rebuke could have been his order to close down her forty merciful Houses of Hospitality and communal farms all over the country and suspend the *Catholic Worker*, which preached absolute pacifism – refusing to support the "Christian" fascists in the Spanish Civil War! – and absolute poverty: "It is only when we embrace voluntary poverty for ourselves that we can expect God to provide for us."

And if the Cardinal had ever ordered her to give up her work, would she obey? "Gladly," she said, and added, with her rich, unjaded smile, "There are many ways, you know, to handle a Cardinal."

There are many ways to handle a Cardinal.

And the Cardinal knew it, and knew that hers was the surest way of all: the indiscriminate and uncompromising love of God uncluttered by clout, uncluttered by cant, uncluttered by cassock, uncluttered by cathedral.

In her youth she had been an anarchist atheist, saying, "Do what you will," and doing what she would among her fellow-hellers in the Hell-Hole, a literary saloon in Greenwich Village. A college socialist, she wrote for the socialist and communist papers and had long since reached the settled conviction that organized religion, "the Church," was a flim-flam – all tip and no iceberg. And then she was transformed and became more Catholic than the Catholics: a mountain moved by faith. She found herself an anarchist Christian saying, "Love God, and do as you will."

She wasn't interested in the form or reform of the State or the "just" war to preserve it or the just revolution to overturn it. Like Peter Maurin, the French roustabout philosopher of "utopian communist communalism," with whom she established the first House of Hospitality, she was interested only in the person, always in the person, the person who would be restored by personalism and would one day make a society "in which it is easier for people to be good."

:

So His Eminence Francis Cardinal Spellman was compelled, when she came out in the vanguard of the grave-diggers, to pretend she wasn't there – perhaps to grind his teeth of nights, perhaps to pray for her in his closet, but never to say a mumbling word in public by way of anathema, rebuke, or even inquiry. Her holy mischievousness finessed him, and all the rest of his life (and hers) she continued to egg on the grave-digging malcontents of his archdiocese.

"He was afraid," said Jim O'Gara of the Catholic *Commonweal*, "that he just might be dealing with a saint."

A saint?

All she ever did was shelter the homeless and feed the hungry and clothe the naked and never ask questions of them, without ever believing that she could do more than that – or disbelieving that to God all things are possible. "He that believeth on me," said Jesus Christ, "the things that I do he shall do likewise." All she had done was the least of the things he had done – and the most of the things he had enjoined upon her (and upon you, and upon me, and upon His Eminence) in Matthew 5, 6, and 7.

She was the Martha of "many things" *and* the Mary of "the better part," first and last a believer. She believed that there was no salvation without those three chapters of Matthew and no salvation against them. Jesus Christ enjoined the works of mercy as the criteria of salvation – ministry to the down and the out, to the lovelorn of a loveless society (and a loveless Church?). Dorothy Day was not bucking for sainthood – "I don't want to be dismissed so easily" – but for mere salvation.

The church moves glacially, with all that real estate on its back, and the Cross besides. But in one transformed woman's lifetime of eighty-three years it moved torrentially in the direction of the preachment her practice preached. When she and Peter Maurin began their work in the Bowery forty-seven years ago with the first of their hospices for the dispossessed, she was one of the weirdos of a rabidly reactionary American Catholic Church given over to Cardinal Spellman's anti-communist crusade. (The striking grave-diggers of 1949 felt constrained to take an oath "as Catholic gentlemen" that they were anti-communist.) But her indiscriminate and uncompromising love was fiercely infectious, and over the indiscriminate and uncompromising decades her apostolate influenced some of the very best young Catholics in the land, with names like Merton, Harrington, Berrigan, Cogley, and thus was the American Catholic Church transformed torrentially.

In 1972 she went to jail for the eighth time – she was seventy-five years old – for picketing with the United Farm Workers in California. And in that same 1972 President Theodore Hesburgh of Notre Dame presented her with the University's highest honor, the Laetare Medal, for having "comforted the afflicted and afflicted the comfortable." It wasn't Dorothy Day who had become respectable; it was the Church, called to respectability by John XXIII.

In 1977 she was eighty, and another mitred porkchopper was asked if he could name "a good or great" American Catholic. He could name one – could Archbishop Jean Jadot, the Apostolic Delegate to the United States: Dorothy Day. When she is 180, or 280, or 380, the Tribunal of the Congregation of Rites of the Roman Catholic Church may have finished its glacial examination of her "case" and concluded that while she was here she was doing what came supernaturally. Canonization asks for proof of miracles (usually two); of Thomas Aquinas someone said, "His whole life was a miracle."

Let us, this once, steal a phrase from e.e. cummings and assert that Dorothy Day never up-grew or down-forgot. She was one tough, lusty Christian, full of brightness and beans to the last. God's panhandler, she asked and she asked and she asked. She once, near the end, asked for something for herself: a Bible with large print. "I read so much, and my eyes tire."

:

No more.

She died in her room, one room, at Maryhouse on the Lower East Side, leaving us all behind, the young of many riches, the old of many more riches. The *Worker* costs a penny a monthly copy; I have thought of sending in a million-dollar subscription, which would bring me the paper for 8,333,333 years (and three-and-a-third months). Maybe I could get Dorothy to give me an assist, without having to sell what I have and give it to the poor.

Not likely. She was a sharp sinner; she will be a sharp saint. I see myself outside the Pearly Gate, a South Side Jewish boy from Chicago, disguised as a Quaker. "Well, young man," says the Pearly Gatekeeper, a little superciliously, as well he might, "and what do you think you're doing here?" "I want in," I say, "I'm a friend of Dorothy's." "That," says the Gatekeeper, "is what they all say *now.*"

: : : *A Long, Long Talk* : : :

You begin at the beginning and finish at the end. At the beginning, forty years ago, we were young; very young, as it seems now. He was the editor of a little butcher-paper tabloid in Madison, Wisconsin, the LaFollette *Progressive*, and I was blacklisted by the slicks because I was anti-war and had knocked the American Jews who wanted to be just like the Gentiles. "I'll give you five bucks a week," he said, ever afterward insisting that he started me at ten – "but I'll print your stuff."

I'll print your stuff.

Nobody else would.

It was a deal. It still is.

He was one hell of an editor. But he was one hell of an editor because he was one hell of a man. A perpendicular man whose backbone, as Thoreau says, you couldn't pass your hand through. One who would rather go broke working for himself than get rich working for somebody else. There were the jobs he turned down in New York when *The Progressive* was busted. There was the philanthropist he turned down who, when *The Progressive* was busted, wanted 51 percent of "the stock" in exchange for a mess of pottage.

Independent as a hog on ice, out there in America somewhere, out there where the prairie radicalism of LaFollette and Norris and Borah and Altgeld, Wheeler, Tom Walsh, the Wallaces came from. That little mom-and-pop rag out there in America – Mary Sheridan Rubin was Managing Editor, Book Editor, Copy Editor, Production Manager, Proof Reader. That ferociously independent little mom-and-pop rag published in a low-rent storefront out there in America, and everywhere read in Washington and the ministries of Europe

From *The Progressive*, October 1980.

by people who wanted to know not what New York was like, but America.

In the slick world beyond the prairie the nonslicks were all subsidized by New York angels. (And New York angels have been known to have heavy, heavy wings.) One after another the nonslicks folded when their angels fluttered away – *Scribner's, The Mercury, The Century, The Forum,* no end of them. The uniquely unangeled *Progressive* in Madison survived on its mom-and-pop budget and the piddling contents of the hat it passed each year among its twenty, thirty, forty thousand cherubim. Twenty, thirty years ago *The New Republic*'s monthly rent was a year of *The Progressive*'s, and *The Reporter* was throwing thousand-dollar bills at writers. "Why," said Jack Fischer of *Harper's,* "did you give Morry Rubin that piece on 'Bed' for fifty dollars? I could have got you five hundred for it."

If you were writing from hunger, like me, and you said Yes to Morry Rubin, you didn't eat. If you were a biggie like Stuart Chase, Charles A. Beard, Norman Thomas, William O. Douglas, Roger Baldwin, or Richard Hofstadter, and you said No to Morry, you didn't sleep. So the biggies wrote for five bucks or ten, and turned it back to Morry, for the same reason that the subscribers, when *The Progressive* was busted, kicked in with five bucks or ten, or fifty cents – because they, too, were writing (and reading) from hunger, the hunger for a stand-up paper edited by a stand-up man. When Young Bob LaFollette was attacked in the Senate – this was 1942 – because *The Progressive* published a front-page piece called "We've Got to Lick Churchill, Too," and Young Bob (*The Progressive*'s publisher) asked Morry (*The Progressive*'s editor) if he thought he should go on publishing the author – I was the author – Morry said, "Why not?"

My agent, Ivan von Auw, once told me that I'd never write books as long as I went on writing for *The Progressive:* "I know it's only a few days a month, but it drains your creative energy." What Ivan didn't know was that I got my creative energy from Morry Rubin.

One hell of a little magazine – does anybody know of one hell of a big magazine? – produced not by a company, or a corporation, or a conglomerate, but by an editor. Fifteen years ago a man who is now editor of one of the world's two or three (or one) great newspapers, then stationed abroad, asked me if I would sound out Morry about taking him on as his successor. Morry wasn't looking for a successor. But seven years ago, his health failing, he asked Erwin Knoll to kick the big time and come to Madison to succeed him, and Erwin of course said Yes; and Morry lived to hear him say, when the Government tried to keep him from publishing the H-bomb "secret" last year, that it wasn't important that *The Progressive* survive, but that it fight.

We loved each other, Morry and I, the way people love each other (if they love each other at all) after forty years of marriage: love ripened into friendship, adoration ripened into admiration, jabber ripened into silence. The things that people pretend not to know about one another Morry and I knew; and so we were able to be of use to one another on a couple of tight occasions – once or twice afloat, fighting a pike into a rowboat on the Chippewa Flowage, once or twice ashore when the pike one was trying to land was oneself.

You begin at the beginning and finish at the end, is what you do.

But there isn't any end. There's that long, long talk he and I repeatedly promised each other we really had to have some one of these days, somewhere. That interminable talk. We still have to have it some one of these days, somewhere interminable.